ESSENTIALS OF INVENTORY MANAGEMENT

ESSENTIALS OF INVENTORY MANAGEMENT

R. Bhargava

CYBER TECH PUBLICATIONS
4264/3, Ansari Road, Daryaganj, New Delhi-110002 (India)
Ph.: 011-23244078, 011-43559448 Fax: 011-23280028
E-Mail: cyberpublicationsdelhi@yahoo.com
Website: www.cybertechpublications.com

ESSENTIALS OF INVENTORY MANAGEMENT

R. Bhargava

First Edition 2011

Published by :

G.S. Rawat for **Cyber Tech Publications**
4264/3, Ansari Road, Daryaganj, New Delhi-110002 (India)
Ph.: 011-23244078, 011-43559448 Fax: 011-23280028
E-Mail: cyberpublicationsdelhi@yahoo.com
Website: www.cybertechpublications.com

CONTENTS

Preface

As a vital function of an organization's operational structure, effective inventory management is key to improving a company's customer service, cash flow, and ultimately, its profitability margin. While it may sound simple, it is, in fact, far more complex than most managers perceive, requiring very specific knowledge and understanding. It is based upon a framework of unique tools and techniques essential to achieving complete success. Best Practice in Inventory Management gives you these essentials, with in-depth coverage of the latest practices in the field. The book delivers a wealth of solid solutions for lowering inventory overhead, bettering customer relations, and increasing productivity and performance. The techniques are placed within the context of stores operations, which can be applied in a variety of situations, from manufacturing and distribution to warehousing, consumable stores, and spares and service.

Best Practice in Inventory Management follows a logical progression, beginning with targets and moving forward through inventory structuring, individual item control, and coordination. In the process, it probes cutting-edge strategies, including Pareto analysis, Just in Time (JIT), and Material Requirements Planning (MRP), and offers a rational approach to the risks of stockouts. Aided by a host of new applications, practical methods, and real-world examples, you'll learn to implement a variety of processes vital to inventory structure and control. From effective stock monitoring to forecasting, setting, and assessing stock level guidelines, this book outlines the crucial steps in having suitable product available at an acceptable price and within a reasonable timescale.

— Author

1

Introduction

The objective of this chapter is to provide you with a basic un-derstanding of the nature of inventory as both a tangible, physi-cal item actually kept within the facility ("real life" or "shelf count") and as an intangible item existing within the company's records ("paper life" or "record count"). Since you frequently make purchasing, sales, customer service, production planning, and other decisions based on whether or not an item is shown as being in-house *as per your records*, an item's paper life can be just as important as its real life.

Inventory—Who Needs It?

All organizations keep inventory. "Inventory" includes a com-pany's raw materials, work in process, supplies used in opera-tions, and finished goods. Inventory can be something as simple as a bottle of glass cleaner used as part of a building's custodial program or some-thing complex such as a mix of raw materials and subassemblies used as part of a manufacturing process.

Inventory Costs

Inventory brings with it a number of costs. These costs can in-clude:

- Dollars
- Space
- Labor to receive, check quality, put away, retrieve, select, pack, ship, and account for
- Deterioration, damage, and obsolescence
- Theft.

Inventory costs generally fall into ordering costs and holding costs. Ordering, or acquisition, costs come about regardless of the actual value of the goods. These costs include the salaries of those purchasing the product, costs of expediting the inventory, and so on.

Holding costs include the cost of capital tied up in inventory (the opportunity cost of money[1]); storage costs such as rent; and costs of handling the product such as equipment, warehouse and stockkeeping staff, stock losses/wastage, taxes, and so on.

Acquisition/ordering costs come about regardless of the actual value of the goods. These costs include the salaries of those purchasing the product, costs of expe-diting the inventory, and so on.

THE PURPOSE OF INVENTORY

So why do you need inventory? As discussed in a just-in-time manufacturing environment, inventory is considered waste. However, in environments where an organization suffers from poor cash flow or lacks strong control over (i) electronic infor-mation transfer among all departments and all significant sup-pliers, (ii) lead times, and (iii) quality of materials received, inventory plays important roles. Some of the more important reasons for obtaining and holding inventory are:

- *Predictability:* In order to engage in capacity planning and production scheduling, you need to control how much raw ma-terial, parts, and subassemblies you process at a given time. In-ventory buffers what you need from what you process.
- *Fluctuations in demand:* A supply of inventory on hand is protection: You don't always know how much you are likely to need at any given time, but you still need to satisfy customer or production demand on time. If you can see how customers are acting in the supply chain, surprises in fluctuations in demand are held to a minimum.
- *Unreliability of supply:* Inventory protects you from unre-liable suppliers or when an item is scarce and it is difficult to en-sure a steady supply. *Whenever possible* unreliable suppliers should be rehabilitated through discussions or they should be replaced. Rehabilitation can be accomplished through master purchase orders with timed product releases, price or term pen-alties for nonperformance, better verbal and electronic commu-nications between the parties, etc. This will result in a lowering of your on-hand inventory needs.

- *Price protection:* Buying quantities of inventory at appro-priate times helps avoid the impact of cost inflation. Note that contracting to assure a price does not require actually taking de-livery at the time of purchase. Many suppliers prefer to deliver periodically rather than to ship an entire year's supply of a par-ticular stockkeeping unit (SKU) at one time. (Note: The acronym "SKU," standing for "stockkeeping unit," is a common term in the inventory world. It generally stands for a specific identifying numeric or alpha-numeric identifier for a specific item.)
- *Quantity discounts:* Often bulk discounts are available if you buy in large rather than in small quantities.
- *Lower ordering costs:* If you buy a larger quantity of an item less frequently, the ordering costs are less than buying smaller quantities over and over again. (The costs of holding the item for a longer period of time, however, will be greater.) See Chapter 5, Planning and Replenishment Concepts. In order to hold down ordering costs and to lock in favorable pricing, many organizations issue blanket purchase orders coupled with peri-odic release and receiving dates of the SKUs called for.

Types of Stock

Inventory basically falls into the overall categories of raw mate-rials, finished goods, and work-in-process. Remember:

- *Raw materials:* Used to produce partial products or com-pleted goods.
- *Finished product:* This is product ready for current cus-tomer sales. It can also be used to buffer manufacturing from predictable or unpredictable market demand. In other words, a manufacturing company can make up a supply of toys during the year for predictably higher sales during the holiday season.
- *Work-in-process (WIP):* Items are considered to be WIP during the time raw material is being converted into partial product, subassemblies, and finished product. WIP should be kept to a minimum. WIP occurs from such things as work de-lays, long movement times between operations, and queuing bottlenecks.

Other categories of inventory should be considered from a functional standpoint:

- *Consumables:* Light bulbs, hand towels, computer and photocopying paper, brochures, tape, envelopes, cleaning mate-rials, lubricants, fertilizer, paint, dunnage (packing materials), and so on are used in many operations. These are often treated like raw materials.
- *Service, repair, replacement, and spare items (S&R Items):* These are after-market items used to "keep things going." As long as a machine or device of some type is being used (in the market) and will need service and repair in the future, it will never be obsolete. S&R Items should not be treated like finished goods for purposes of forecasting the quantity level of your nor-mal stock.

Quantity levels of S&R Items will be based on considera-tions such as preventive maintenance schedules, predicted fail-ure rates, and dates of various items of equipment. For example, if an organization replaced its fluorescent tubes on an as-needed, on-failure basis, it would need a larger supply of these lights on hand at all times. However, if the same company re-lamped all of its ballasts once per year, it would buy a large quantity of tubes at one time and only keep a small supply on hand on an ongoing basis.

Since S&R Items are never "obsolete" or "dead" until the equipment or device they are to be used for is no longer in serv-ice, these items should not be included in calculating dead stock levels.

- *Buffer/safety inventory:* This type of inventory can serve various purposes, such as:
  - — compensating for demand and supply uncertainties.
  - — holding it to "decouple" and separate different parts of your operation so that they can function independently from one another.
- *Anticipation Stock:* This is inventory produced in antici-pation of an upcoming season such as fancy chocolates made up in advance of Mother's Day or Valentine's Day. Failure to sell in the anticipated period could be disas-trous because you may be left with considerable amounts of stock past its perceived shelf life.

- *Transit Inventory:* This is inventory en route from one place to another. It could be argued that product moving within a facility is transit inventory; however, the com-mon meaning of the concept concerns items moving within the distribution channel toward you and also out-side of your facility or en route from your facility to the customer.

Transit stock highlights the need to understand not only how inventory physically moves through your system, but also how and when it shows up in your records. If, for example, 500 widgets appeared as part of existing stock while they were still en route to you, your record count would include them while your shelf count would be 500 widgets short.

TRACKING THE PAPER LIFE

In order for you to gain an understanding of the relationship be-tween an item's real life and its paper life within your own sys-tem, you should follow a single item on its path through that system. In other words, track an item's physical movement through your facility while noting what is happening to its pa-per life during that same time period. You will be able to dis-cover when one of these lives moves ahead of the other and when there are system errors such as an item is moved but there is no paperwork authorizing that action. Exhibit 1-2 provides an example of what could happen if an item's paper life and real life begin to leapfrog ahead or be-hind one another without the stockkeeper understanding the process.

Electronic Data Interchange

Stockkeepers who do not understand how and when an item's paper life is first created within a system become even more con-fused if there is no hard paper copy audit trail they can follow. How could:

- an order be placed?
- an order be accepted?
- confirmation of the order be given?
- shipping instructions be given?
- notice of shipping arrangements be given?
- a paper life be created for an item in advance of it enter-ing the facility?

- All occur without there being any hard paper copies of these transactions existing. All of these events and more can occur in a paperless environment through electronic data interchange.

Electronic data interchange (EDI) is where routine business transactions are sent over standard communication lines (such as telephone lines) between computers within a company or be-tween your computer and that of a vendor.

An example of EDI within a company is at the time of order entry, information about that order is electronically transmitted to shipping or operations for order selection and shipping, to ac-counting for billing purposes, to sales for order verification, and so on.

An example of EDI with a vendor is you electronically place an order directly from your computer into the vendor's com-puter. The vendor's computer then electronically confirms the order and transmits information about the order to the vendor's shipping and accounting departments. The vendor's computer also electronically notifies a carrier of the upcoming shipment. The carrier's computer electronically confirms the pickup and provides the vendor with pickup and delivery information. The vendor's computer then notifies your computer of the date, time, etc. of the upcoming delivery. All of this would be accom-plished without any human intervention other than the original placement of the order.

For EDI to work, all of the system participants must agree to strict rules regarding message content, format, and structure.

"VPC

The objective of this chapter was to point out that inventory exists within your system as both a physical item and as an item existing within your records.

There are many reasons for obtaining and holding inven-tory, and inventory can play a variety of roles within the life of any organization.

In order to control and manage the items coming into, through, and out of your facility, it is important to understand not only where an item is physically located at any given time, but also how that existence is being acknowledged within the system.

2

A New Inventory Paradigm

CONCEPTUAL BASIS AND SURVEY RESULTS

Overview

This chapter introduces and tests a new paradigm of the rôle of inventories in the operation of business enterprises. It starts out from the fundamental research results of the 1950s, and analyzes the traditional paradigm formulated in this period, called the golden age of inventory research. However, changes in the economic and business environment led to the emergence of the need of a different approach. The proposed new paradigm is introduced and its relation to the traditional one is outlined. Two surveys were conducted among Hungarian managers to test the validity of the new paradigm—one survey among manufacturing managers and another among logis-tics managers. The results are supportive, showing that managers' thinking mostly corresponds to the logic of the new paradigm. There are a lot of further research opportunities stemming from the paradigm proposition.

Introduction

History of researching inventories shows a very interesting pattern. There are peaks and drops both in time and by functional areas, and one can meet extreme stand-points about their importance in the economy and in business. This chapter puts down the foundations of a new paradigm for researching inven-tories. We have enough information about the turn of the century changes in enter-prise management to put business inventories in a new perspective, getting them out of the passive role assigned to them for decades and including them as an active part of company strategy. The increasing interest in practical inventory management (measured for example by the number of downloads of inventory-related items on the Internet) and in inventory research (see the growing number of participants at inventory conferences and sessions) clearly express the importance of a revival of the best traditions when some of the best minds of economics and management research focused at least part of their interest on inventories.

Our starting point is the golden age of inventory research in the 1950s. We will discuss the paradigm that served as a foundation of research in this era. This tra-ditional paradigm was based on the characteristics of economic and managerial thinking of the time, and served its function very well for decades. However, as the economic and business environment changed, the need for a new paradigm has emerged. This chapter describes the changes in the environment and introduces the elements of a proposed new paradigm.

A NEW INVENTORY PARADIGM

It is explicitly stated in the exposition of the new paradigm that it has to be validated in practice. Managers' views are tested in two surveys, results of which are summarized in the second part of the chapter. One of the surveys was com-pleted among manufacturing managers, the other one among logistics managers. The survey results support the new paradigm, but further research is necessary for its full elaboration.

The traditional Paradigm of Inventory Research

I think everyone agrees that the golden age of inventory research was in the 1950s. This was the time when both conceptual and mathematical models of inventories were first formulated, following the sometimes interesting but basically very simple approach of earlier decades (Sprague 2000). Whitin (1957) had a truly classic con-ceptualization of inventory management, but even operations research (OR) hard-liners contributed to conceptual clarifcation (the article most referred to is probably Ackoff [1956]). The fact that some of the best minds in economics and OR joined inventory researchers helped both conceptualization and mathematical formula-tion of the inventory problem, with the most important contributions coming from Stanford University (Arrow, Karlin, and Scarf 1958; Scarf, Gilford, and Shelley 1963). A summary and analysis of this age is in Girlich and

Chikán (2001). A rich collection and analysis of the classical models can be found in Chikán (1990). The most quoted book on managerial applications is Silver and Peterson (1979 and fur-ther editions).

It is interesting that economists contributed to development of models that we would now call OR models; very little attention to inventories is attributed to main-stream economics. Perhaps there are understandable reasons for this continuing negligence of inventories in economic research. However, attempting discovery of these reasons is beyond the scope of this chapter. Here I concentrate only on business-level approaches, with reference to some cross-effects between the two study fields.

The traditional paradigm of inventory research is based on three pillars:

1. Inventories can be handled and optimized independently of other mana-gerial circumstances (such as logistics, operations, or financial resources). This assumption made it possible to treat inventories as a single, controlled variable of a feedback control system, where demand is the diverting vari-able and the order placed is the regulating variable. All are within the inven-tory system and independent of other fields of company operation. Classical inventory models are mostly based on these control principles. It is worth mentioning that even though models were interpreted mostly on the SKU (stock-keeping unit, i.e., "item") level, this concept can be extended to the company level, handling total inventories of the company as an unstruc-tured volume.
2. The main role of inventories is to serve as a buffer to be used to
   a. smooth business processes, most of all production and sales; and
   b. maintain a fexible connection between the various organizational units (e.g., shops, factories, depots, etc.) of the company.

The first role is connected to the actual physical processes going on within the company, whereas the second role refers mainly to the managerial (control) processes. These two roles are obviously connected, but they can be clearly distinguished.

3. The performance measure of operation of the inventory system is the level of total cost associated with the sum of holding and replenishing inventories and to handling shortages. In this concept the independency paradigm is refected, based on the *ceteris paribus* principle. It is assumed that all other things being equal (which assumption can be valid in the case of the subsystems), inventory management can contribute to the increase of profit (the objective of the company as a whole) if it keeps its costs as low as possible. This approach is justifed by defning holding cost so that it includes the opportunity cost of inventory investment, for example, by calculating with the average (or, depending on company policy, the marginal) return-on-investment ratio of the company.

The traditional inventory paradigm was a consequence of some fundamental assumptions about the operation of the business enterprise. These assumptions came primarily from the economics literature. The most important ones are:

- The profit maximizing company, which made the cost-based decisions justifed and did not allow the use of noncost measures
- The economies of scale principle, which made use of the independency principle possible by considering inventory decisions as solely volume-dependent and not seeking economies of scope
- The conventional linear organization structure (the existence of functional silos), which again supported the independency principle by making coor-dination with other functional areas possible and necessary only at the highest level of the hierarchy

The traditional paradigm played a key role in inventory research of several decades after the 1950s. Some of the most important consequences of its application are:

- We learned a lot about item-level inventory systems; by the 1970s we knew practically all we know today about their operation, management, and decision problems.
- There were only few attempts to synthesize this knowledge. Two books of the 1960s must be mentioned: *Analysis of Inventory Systems* (Hadley and Whitin 1963) and *Inventory Systems* (Naddor

1966) are probably the most often cited works. Both are excellent books, but they deal with special classes of inventory models.

- The new management concepts of the period were very negative toward inventories; they handled them only as residua, that is, consequences of managerial decisions focusing on other issues like sales, production, or distribution. Both material requirements planning (MRP) and just-in-time (JIT)—in the extreme—led to the zero inventory illusion or at least to a business atmosphere where inventories were considered as a (not so) necessary evil.

The diffuse character of inventory research and the lack of synthesis are well refected in the survey made by the International Society for Inventory Research (ISIR; see Chikán [2002a, 2002b]), where respondents were asked to name the most infuential papers or books in their research area. There were fourteen items listed by the respondents to this question, and no work was mentioned twice.

A large number of mathematical models was published in this period, but dur-ing this time there were very few notable publications about actual managerial issues and business approaches. This led to a situation in the 1970s-1980s when there was a growing and gradually more deeply perceived gap between theory and practice.

Studies of the golden age of inventory research almost totally neglected inventory problems beyond item-level optimization. The ruling paradigm, and especially the assumption that inventory can be managed independently of other functions, did not make it necessary to examine cross-effects of item-level decisions and their relation-ship with other decisions regarding production, marketing, and so forth; it seemed to be enough to refer to the *ceteris paribus* principle. Classical works of the time did not even refer to the overall inventory problem of the company; adding the item-level optimums was considered to fulfll the job of company-level optimization. However, this common understanding was more or less implicit. The literature barely referred to the potential problems caused by cross-effects of inventories. (The logic used in the OR literature was analogous to the one used by economists who assumed that the model-company's behavior can be extended to the economy as a whole. This logic is refected in Carzo [1958]). Researchers accepted that item level models express com-pany behavior, however it has not been shown to be an optimal aggregate inventory management rule (Whybark 1994). It should be noted that the business framework for analyzing the role of inven-tories was also missing. In the 1970s there were few new results in the "theory of the frm," and even less in something that could be called the "theory of business." However, many of the classical works that we consider fundamental for understand-ing the general theoretical background of business were published in the period being discussed. Readers may refer to Putterman (1986) and Foss (1997) for a review.

In the same period, several new management concepts and methods were intro-duced. The most important ones were MRP and JIT, of which at least a side effect should have been reductions in inventories. However, studying inventory data of the period shows that although these methodologies proved successful in many individ-ual company cases, they did not reduce inventories at the level of national economies (Chikán 1994; Bivin 2006). This indirectly suggests that there had been processes going on in the economy since the 1980s-1990s that counterbalanced inventory reduction efforts. This can be considered as a sign of a need for a new business para-digm of inventories, which takes over the old cost-minimizing, inventory-reducing approach.

It necessarily took some time before the research community could have conceptu-alized these changes. There is a special relationship between business practice and research, which is not common in most areas of academic studies. The essence of this relationship is that new, innovative business practices mainly come from actual business life—they precede and not follow research results. The reason for this is that business is under so much pressure to innovate that practitioners are far faster in seeking and introducing new ways of doing things than any other segment of society. The common order of events is:

1. A company introduces a new approach, some innovation that corresponds to the requirement of the changing environment. The need to ft the envi-ronment is a fundamental thesis of organization theory (for the contin-gency approach, see Lawrence and Lorsch [1967]).
2. The new ideas spread rather fast; companies learn from one another in their everyday connections, at business conferences, and so forth. Companies jump on copying the innovations (frequently with the help of consultants, who are among the

first to notice new developments and trigger changes). Further developments may follow one of three ways, depending on the actual success of the new approach in practice:

a. After some time it may turn out that the new idea is a fad, not leading to serious results.

b. The overall results may be mixed: a new approach can result in good practice at some companies and may prove useless or even harmful at other companies. This is because very frequently the initial application of a new approach is not connected to a prudent analysis of the actual conditions under which a new approach can be successful.

c. The third case is when a new approach proves to be so successful in such a wide range of cases that business accepts it practically as part of common knowledge.

3. Academic research explains and generalizes empirical research: in case of a fad or a full success it explains why they happened; in case of mixed results it identifes the conditions of successful application.

This approach can be argued. Even though it is supported by long-term observa-tion of business developments, I am sure that there are a lot of exceptions. To illus-trate: From among innovations widely known by people dealing with inventories, I would consider BPR in the first, JIT in the second, and MRP in the third category (see a, b, and c above) calling attention again to possible exceptions.

In the aforementioned process, there is an accumulation of knowledge that indi-cates two things:

a) As the application of new approaches spreads over a given field of man-agement (like marketing, human resources [HR], and inventory manage-ment), after some phases, the new approaches may integrate into a new paradigm. A new paradigm for me means a fundamentally new way of thinking about the given management feld, which includes different actual principles and practices as well. (The classical reference to para-digm shifts is Kuhn [1996].)

b) Academics have a special role in the process. Compared to businesspeople, they are certainly slow-moving individuals. In business research, aca-demics are more followers than path breakers. However, academics still play a crucial role in business innovation in two respects:

- They actually explain the developments, help to find the answer to whether a given new idea is a fad or a really useful new idea, and whether the idea is generically beneficial or its usefulness is connected to some special conditions or circumstances.
- Academic research is indispensable in carrying out the integration of new knowledge into a new paradigm. It does the job of conceptual anal-ysis and generalization; and tests views via empirical studies. Without these two steps no meaningful statement about paradigm changes can be formulated.

EMERGENcE OF A NEW PARADIGM

As mentioned, the positive effect of the existence of the "old" paradigm was that for the end of the 1960s-beginning the 1970s we knew a lot about the nature and struc-ture of the item-level problems as negative feedback control systems; just in time to give way to a new era that was made necessary by the appearance of MRP systems, with explicit reference to the dependent demand inventories and company-level (or at least product-line-level) optimization. Of course, research on the item-level problems did not disappear, especially since MRP systems actually were in need of models to support lot-sizing decisions.

The appearance and success of MRP systems was mainly a result of the develop-ment of information technology and information systems (for the roots and devel-opment of MRP systems, see Chikán and Sprague [2008]). MRP was followed by MRP II and distribution requirements planning (DRP), making it even clearer that inventories do not just stand alone but are closely and complexly connected to other company functions. (This idea has already been analyzed by the duly famous Holt et al. book [1960], which was a forerunner of the new approach. A recent exposition of the interfaces between inventories and other functions is given in Stenger [2008].)

The emergence and spread of the JIT concept was a final nail in the coffin of the dominance of the item-level approach in management of inventories. Since JIT simply questioned the fundamental common understanding that inventories are valuable assets of the company, it became explicit that inventories are dependent on the organization of the company as a total entity, and that they can be reduced by the efficient organization of interaction of purchasing, logistics, production, and distribution—practically the whole "real sphere" or "material sphere" of the com-pany. It is common that some authors of that time (e.g., Babbar and Prasad [1998]) practically identified the inventory problem with JIT issues. This seemed to sup-port the practice-based view already known from earlier times that inventories are not managed at all; they are simply residuals of managerial decisions in other fields (mainly in sales and production). There is a lot of anecdotal evidence to support this view, which is 180 degrees different from the classical paradigm of inventory decisions. However, I could not find any research that should have proven that. Instead I believe that Sprague and Wacker (1994) and Whybark (1994) had it right: calling attention to the difference in hierarchy of those who make company-level strategic decisions and those who control actual inventories at a much lower hier-archical level This duality leads to the appearance of two different approaches: a rather definite inventory reduction approach at the executive level, and a more bal-anced view at the tactical control level. The former bases its approach mainly on financial return considerations and because inventories, at least at first glance, slow return on investments (since they mean inactive tying up of capital), it is a natural policy requirement to keep them low. However, the interest of low-level manag-ers is completely different. They do not care much about company-level financial return; they are concerned about service levels, production disruptions, shortages of supply, and so forth, and they are actually accountable for these. Therefore, their concept of "optimal" level of inventories is very different than that of their high-level bosses.

Of course there is a trade-off between the two approaches, which can be expressed by balancing the advantages and disadvantages of holding inventories at the two lev-els described—the strange thing is that there was little, if any, said about that in the inventory literature. Instead there appeared numerous articles and books on "zero inventory," which is a nonsense concept even if the authors in most cases do not mean it literally.

The above reasoning supports the need of a new inventory paradigm that takes into account the built-in duality of inventory management and makes it necessary to examine both levels and their interactions. There must be room in this new para-digm for both quantitative, mathematical models and approaches, and qualitative, organizations-oriented research.

The traditional paradigm provides a sound basis for the former; unfortunately, we have much less historical background for conducting organizational studies of inventory management.

Most companies cannot afford the talent of sophisticated inventory control sys-tems: neither the well-researched and -developed forecasting techniques, nor the performance measures, which would connect the company level and the tactical management level, are affordable at an average company. As Bonney (1994) puts it: "But successful inventory reduction appears likely to be limited to the relatively small number of organizations which can provide the commitment to improving their whole systems." Also, despite the development of information technology (IT) companies use unsophisticated inventory accounting, which prevents the meaningful connection between the physical and monetary approach to invento-ries. (I think this is an important component of the macroeconomic "mystery" that interest rates do not influence inventories; see Blinder and Maccini [1991].) Lean inventory management is a nice slogan. Unfortunately, this approach far too often loses sight of the fact that anybody can reduce inventories. The question is the price of this reduction, the often hidden costs of not having inventory on hand. As Sprague and Wacker (1994) put it: "firms do not want inventories 'per se' but want the benefits that inventories can bring." That is why I strongly agree with the practitioner's view: "smart, not lean inventory management will define leaders" (Lawton 2003). It is exactly this smart management that needs the support of a new inventory paradigm. Indeed there are more and more signs of the appear-ance of this need. This is expressed quite clearly by Miller and Deis (2007). They are consultants with extensive practitioner experience who conclude their paper on aggregate inventory management by saying: "Inventory can be systematically managed." Similarly, Barry (2007) starts his paper with the sentence: "Inventory management and forecasting are strategic issues." These practitioners and consul-tants clearly indicate the need of a new inventory paradigm. Indeed, the elements of this can be already found in their communication. What is needed is a system-atic, scholarly formulation of this paradigm. This is explicitly requested in Invatol (2008): "Despite the many changes that companies go through, the basic principles of Inventory Management and Inventory Control remain the same. Some of the new approaches and techniques are wrapped in new terminology but the underly-ing principles for accomplishing good inventory management and inventory activi-ties have not changed."

The new paradigm formulated in this chapter may put down the foundations of an appropriate approach. The interest of practitioners can be clearly seen by the huge number (sometimes thousands) of clicks on the inventory management sites of the Internet.

FUNDAMENTAL CHANGES IN THE GLOBAL ECONOMY

There is very rich literature on changes in the global economy over the past several decades; it is not the purpose of this chapter to discuss this in detail. I only sum-marize those dimensions of changes that, according to my view, have had the most important influence—directly or indirectly—on inventory management.

Today's Economy

The following characteristics of today's economy are useful for discussion of the new inventory paradigm:

Service economy: The requirements of today's customers are not simply to buy some products and services, but to obtain "solutions" to their prob-lems. This means that companies must offer a combination of products and services.

E-economy: By the use of up-to-date IT, a greater level of integration of the activities of various actors of the economy can be achieved. Also, IT increases the need and availability of speed of action and reaction by actors within the economy.

Network economy: Competition in the market goes on not only among individual actors but also between their networks. Thus, competition and cooperation go on not only in parallel but interlinked, making the whole operation of the economy more complex. Further, network elements and positions are changing constantly, making company relations less predict-able and more dynamic. At the same time, this leads to the establishment of long-term relations and strategic alliances as a reaction for safeguard-ing against impracticable changes.

Knowledge-based economy: Knowledge is now an increasingly important resource, a basis for obtaining competitive advantage. Companies need (and get) more and better-based information and use more sophisticated decision processes.

Responsible economy: Actors within the economy are forced to consider not only their own interests but also those of other stakeholders, including the human and natural environments.

Global economy: Decision makers must consider the whole world econ-omy when making investment, purchasing, or sales decisions, because potential competitors and partners can and will come from anywhere.

The emergence of these characteristics of the economy have led to important changes both in the characteristics of various actors within the economy and (directly or indirectly) in the role of inventories. Since this chapter is focused on the new role of inventories in business, let us now consider changes in business enterprises first and then turn to the new inventory paradigm.

NEW CHARACTERISTICS OF THE BUSINESS ENTERPRISE

Observations of real-life business and examination of the literature lead to the conclusion that the purpose and characteristics of the business enterprise have substantially changed in the past few decades. Both declared and actually followed goals seem to be moving beyond simple profit maximization.

Fierce competition has caused companies to raise their attention to customers' needs and to define the purpose of the business enterprise as "satisfying customer needs at profit." This does not mean a diminishing importance of profit, but does make life more complex for the enterprise: It has to consider customers' interests with at least the same intensity as its own interests. This means that the company is under a double pressure: It has to create value in one and the same processes for both customers and itself. I cannot go into full detail here regarding the new objectives and characteristics of the business enterprise. But to understand the new role of inventories, I list those characteristics that I consider most important for this current study. These new char-acteristics of the business enterprise are:

Focus on competitiveness, which results in an approach to creating and implementing strategy based on consideration of not what we can do well, but what we can do better than our competitors. This comparative view is essential in both strategic and operational decision making.

Functional integration, which leads to a different view of the connec-tion among functions (sales, logistics, innovation, production, etc.) of the enterprise. Cross-connections are considered not only in the results but right at the outset of processes. Integrated operation is ensured "in pro-cess" by coordination of the various functions at a much lower level of hierarchy than within traditional "silo" systems. This approach is often expressed in both formal and informal organizations, for example, in the form of operational cross-functional teams.

Process orientation, which means a focus on flows within the com-pany (and beyond its borders), considering complex connections among material, financial, and information flows. The main attention of man-agement is now turning to the process of value creation and all ele-ments of operation are judged by their contribution to this process. The value creation process (sometimes called the value chain; see Porter [1985]) crosses traditional functional boundaries, becoming the main carrier of functional integration.

Network (chain) view, which means that competition goes on in the global economy, not only between companies but among networks of them. Beyond that, the approach is that we talk about customer value creation as a set of a number of business activities comprising a network, within which organizational boundaries sometimes change rather rapidly (i.e., creation of a product requires given activities, which can be carried out in many different kinds of distribution of work, in different organizational and company forms). This approach reflects the fading boundaries of the firm, and provides a framework for understanding outsourcing and strate-gic alliances.

These four significant characteristics of today's business enterprise ensure its effective and flexible role in society. This is the main reason why (historically speak-ing) the ever-increasing needs of people are satisfied to an increasing extent, by busi-ness as opposed to self-support or governmental activity. Let us see now how we can determine the roles of inventories under the aforemen-tioned economic and business conditions.

NEW ROLES OF INVENTORIES: THE NEW PARADIGM

This section analyzes how the emergence of new economic characteristics has changed the role of inventories and how this role fits into the new enterprise. The new role leads to the need of a new research approach as well that considers the two levels of inventory decisions, and provides a framework for their joint integration into the new enterprise. The main idea is that the classical inventory paradigm must be enriched to ft the new situation: the new paradigm must reflect changes in the business and eco-nomic environment. It must be made clear that the new research paradigm for inventories should be nested in practice; it has to be validated against actual mana-gerial behavior.

The essence of the change is that we have to move our perception of inventories from a passive to an active role in company strategy. The new situation does not allow us to view inventories as residua; they have to be considered as an active con-tributor to a company's success. The definition of the active contributor is that, for this role, strategic decisions must be directly focused on inventories, and inventory policies must influence general strategy formulation and implementation throughout the firm. I believe (and will show some supporting trains of thought) that inventories can have this strategic role—not isolated, of course, but in a complex relationship with other strategic components.

A few remarks must be made before introducing the new paradigm:

1. The traditional paradigm should be made part of the new one since its validity and relevance to item-level decisions can be considered proven.
2. The new paradigm was not born all of a sudden. The path has been pre-pared by improvement processes within company operations, with the introduction of MRP, JIT, supply chain management (SCM), and so forth; that is, by the development of business activity.
3. The actual role of inventories that corresponds to the new paradigm can and will differ by company, depending on the character of its strategy. However, there is enough ground for generalization to permit fundamental research analyses.

Considering these, I hereby formulate a new inventory research paradigm that I believe corresponds with the current state of real-life economic and business developments. According to the new paradigm, inventories have strategic importance for compa-nies in three interconnected dimensions: value creation, flexibility, and control.

INVENTORIES AS CONTRIBUTORS TO VALUE CREATION

If we consider the new concepts of the changed economy, and the purpose and char-acteristics of the business enterprise, it becomes clear that the emergence of the ser-vice economy and, in connection with that, the emphasis on customer satisfaction in company operations lead to a basic question: Can inventories actively contribute to customer value creation? The answer is a definite yes, with reference to some evidence:

- Providing "solutions" to customer needs requires the offering of a mix of physical products and services in practically all business cases. This means a far more complex task than simply deciding on finished goods inventories. The decision on the composition of the "mixture" offered is a key strategic decision—for example, what kind of products and services should be provided by a gas station. There are a number of inventory considerations in such a decision that influence what sorts of customer needs will be met, how, at what level and probability, costs, and so forth.
- In the service economy, the main order-winning factor is often the service provided together with the product—guarantees, maintenance, develop-ment support, and so forth. The quality of these "solutions" can hardly be measured by cost parameters only, making some traditional inventory decision rules obsolete.
- In the network economy, a new kind of inventory emerges, which I call *relationship inventory*. This is an element of the total inventory of two com-panies, being in partnership and not only at arm's length with each other. The level and distribution of this inventory between the two companies depend on the actual relationship of the two companies, their individual and joint interests, strategies, and operational decisions. Characterizing factors of relationship inventories are, therefore, dependent on

the features of the partnership itself and not just of the individual companies.

Inventories as Means of Flexibility

It has been emphasized already in the traditional paradigm that inventories are buf-fers for meeting requirements of outside environments and inside organizations. Now this role has been greatly enriched, leading to its far greater importance. Inventories are not simply passive buffers sitting there waiting for usage, but are understood as living elements actively used in pursuing strategic objectives.

- Increased vertical integration and process orientation cause much stron-ger relationships between subsequent stages both within companies and with their partners. This leads to, for example, closer connections between inventories in various stages of fabrication: they become more dependent on one another and on the policies of customer service. Depending on at which level of fabrication policy-directed stocks are kept, lead times for meeting customer demand can be made shorter or longer.
- The locations of inventories in intercompany supply chains influence the smoothness of relations and can be used for optimizing joint profitability of supplier and vendor companies—for example, by utilizing differences in taxation of various countries or some local savings possibilities in shap-ing a complex distribution system.
- It is often said that in modern logistics systems, information is traveling instead of materials. However, there are many examples that show that the flexibility and speed of an electronic commerce system can be utilized only if it is supported by high-quality logistics systems, which include appropriately sized and located inventories (the prerequisites of flexible customer service).
- As economies of scope have become a strategic issue, the importance of the mix of inventory positions has increased, closely connected to the horizon-tal integration of intra- and intercompany activities. More market access decisions must rely on a comprehensive horizontal inventory policy.

INVENTORIES AS MEANS OF CONTROL

Inventories have been considered important indicators of macro- and microeconomic phenomena for a long time. They play a key role as business cycle indicators. Also—less often but importantly—the ratio of input and output inventories in manu-facturing is used as an indicator of the relation of overall demand and supply in the market (Chikán 1981; Kornai 1992). In countries or markets where this ratio is low (i.e., where companies generally tend to hold inventories on the output side), econo-mists talk about general oversupply, which goes together with a stronger economic position of buyers (customers). In the opposite case (where the input/output inventory ratio is high), it is easy to sell but hard to buy: high input inventories indicate the fear of not being able to buy goods when needed.

This indicator role of inventories and the possibility of controlling business pro-cesses by inventory decisions have been seldom used in the past. Recently we have seen examples under the new economic conditions that these can be expected to increase in number and scope. An interesting means of controlling processes in sup-ply chains are vendor managed inventories (VMIs).

A new feature of business is the growing importance of the CSR (corporate social responsibility) concept. As a part of this development, a new branch of company operation has emerged—reverse logistics, which typically includes keeping inven-tories of items waiting for remanufacturing, reparation, or recycling. Many mod-els show that reverse logistics activity can be controlled through inventory holding policies. In general we can summarize that—according to this new view and based on the aforementioned reasoning—inventories may be becoming a more active element of companies' strategic decisions and activities.

Managers' View of the New Paradigm Survey Results

To examine the existence of the new paradigm, two surveys were conducted among Hungarian managers.

Methodology

The first survey was carried out in the winter of 2005-2006 and used the follow-ing methodology:

- Nine questions were formulated directly oriented to the managers' per-ception and approach to inventories.
- These questions were connected to a questionnaire used for survey-ing manufacturing strategies and practices in the framework of IMSS (International Manufacturing Strategy Survey) and the GMRG (Global Manufacturing Research Group). Both surveys had been conducted sev-eral times in many parts of the world (including Hungary) and both con-tain a number of questions related to inventories.

As a result, there are nine questions directly related to our research focus and a set of complementary questions that could be used in the analysis and discussion.

The survey was originally sent to 245 companies. The companies were asked by phone if they were willing to contribute and in case of a positive answer, a student, appropriately prepared, provided the questionnaire to the companies and explained what was necessary. Fifty-one questionnaires were returned, representing a response rate of 21 percent. The research methodology was repeated with basically the same questions for the fourth time in Hungary, therefore there was no need for a pilot study.

The second survey followed exactly two years later in November and December of 2007. For the development of the questionnaire, the experiences of the survey reported in Chikán (2009) were used for a pilot study.

The questionnaire contained ffteen sets of questions: four on the characteristics of the respondent and his/her company, three on the inventory performance of the company, six on the principles and approaches actually applied in the company, and two on the trends infuencing their inventory behavior. The philosophy behind the composition of the questions was to ask the managers about their personal experi-ences and views, and not about general perceptions. I believe that this is the most reliable approach available in similar empirical surveys: generalization is the job of the researcher and should be based on the addition and integration of individual opinions.

The questionnaire was placed on the Web site of the Hungarian Association of Logistics, Purchasing and Inventory Management. A total of 138 responses were received in a roughly six-week period. The sample was random in the sense that we had not chosen any particular segments of the readers of the Web site. However, because the survey was based on the membership of a professional association, it can be expected that the respondents are more informed and at a higher professional level than the average managers in the country.

There was one common set of questions in the two surveys asking managers about their view on the role of inventories. There were the same eight questions in both questionnaires, which had to be answered using a 7-point Likert scale. From now on we shall refer to the first survey as "Manufacturing," and to the second as "Logistics," referring to the main functional orientations of the managers involved in the two phases.

For both manufacturing and logistics managers, the same two questions were on top: question B had the highest score, F the second highest. These are the crucial ques-tions regarding the new paradigm, which appears to be accepted by managers. The last place is occupied in both cases by the question most explicitly related to the old para-digm. The difference in the order of the other questions can be explained by the profes-sional orientation of the two sets of respondents. It is obvious that the buffering role (question C) does not disappear; it scores high in both groups. The explicit reference to the strategic role of inventories (question D) is better accepted by logistics managers. The analyses of the two samples show that respondents in the logistics group are higher in the organizational hierarchy than those in the manufacturing group.

A brief discussion of the two surveys follows. The logistics questionnaire focused on the managers' opinion on the environment leading to changes in the role of inventories, whereas the manufacturing survey went into details of the internal issues of the new paradigm.

The Logistics Questionnaire

We'll start with the logistics questionnaire, which deals more with the reasons for the emergence of the new paradigm.

Main Reasons behind Inventory Tendencies

Table above shows the results of a set of questions about the influencing factors of inven-tory efficiency, in the order of importance attributed by the respondents (respondents evaluated each option on a 7-point Likert scale).

A factor analysis provided practically the same results, connecting aspects a, b, g, h, and i into factor 1; d, j, and f into factor 2; and c and e into factor 3. The order of reasons surprisingly creates four groups of reasons, among which efficiency require-ments play the key role leading to higher profitability. Market orientation is in second place, while the two further groups serve as means to achieve efficiency and market goals. From the point of view of our analysis this means that the average company man-ager basically agrees with the approach to the influencing factors of inventory man-agement, which was advanced in the previous half of this chapter.

Business Trends Influencing Inventories

With the set of questions regarding business trends, it was desired to learn to what extent managers identify with the causes of the changing role of inventories—what they consider as the most important developments influencing inventories. Table 1.4 summarizes the results.

Business trends influencing inventories

Business Trend	Average Score
Focus on competitiveness	5.65
Pressure for complex customer service	5.31
Process view, value chain management	4.87
Internal integration of company functions	4.54
Globalization	4.28
Network economy	4.12
Knowledge economy	3.89
E-economy	3.85
Corporate social responsibility	3.51

If one compares the results with the main trends identified in Chikán (2009), then it can be seen that three of the four factors given there occupy the first three places in Table above. Only one (network economy) received a somewhat smaller average score. This shows a rather good correspondence between the theoretical considerations and the view of the managers.

Some Further Insights

We have examined the correlation between the choice of principles and the trend scores. Three methods were used and all of them supported a strong connection between the general "world view" of the managers and the inven-tory principles applied in their practice.

There was also an attempt to find connections between inventory principles and performance. This branch of analysis led to somewhat disappointing results: No significant correlation was found between the "modernity" of inventory principles and the effectively of managing inventories. This result may lead to speculation about the actual relevance of the new view on inventories. It may be that since our respondents were mostly top managers, their view may differ from those at the tactical level, which may divert the everyday practice from the principles suggested on top. To determine the real reasons of this feature, further research in the area will follow.

The Manufacturing Questionnaire

We would like to identify the charac-teristics of the respondents who gave different answers to the main inventory ques-tions. Simple correlation coefficients and cross-tables were used for the analysis.

First we describe some general conclusions drawn from the analysis, and then review the inventory questions one by one to see the characteristics of different respondents. Before starting the detailed analysis, it should be said that there is no significant connection between the respondents' manufacturing sectors and the answers; from this point of view our sample is homogeneous.

Characteristics of Respondents Choosing Different Roles of Inventories

We analyzed in detail the characteristics of the respondents with the eight different approaches to inventories. The following was obtained for the eight options:

A. *Inventory management is an independent company function.* When ana-lyzing the respondents' characteristics, we found that mainly those managers who gave a higher score to this question, where both external and internal cooperation focuses on the physical rather than the value substance of inventories. These managers attribute a significant role to collab-orative planning, consignment, or vendor managed inventory, as well as the physical integration with both the supplier and the buyer. Also, there is a significant correlation between the importance of price in the competi-tive strategy and giving a high score to A. There are several other answers of these managers that suggest that those who place a higher value on security of operation are more willing to give a higher score to A.

B. *Inventories can be efficiently managed as integrated components of the supply chain.* Not surprisingly, those who gave a higher score to this question are those companies that are actually closely integrated in their supply chain. This conclusion is drawn on the basis of several questions that clarify this relationship in the questionnaire. They feel more competitive than the average regarding their ROS and ROI, but not by their sales rev-enue and market share. Regarding their strategic development goals, they advance quality and reliability of their products, customization, and flexibility in changing quantity and assortment.

C. *Inventories serve as buffers among various functions and processes.* Giving a higher score to C is significantly correlated with several per-formance measures, which may mean that better-performing companies put more emphasis on smooth operation than the average companies. These companies, similarly to those in B, consider quality and reliability improvement very important (many of them do not perform well in qual-ity measures). There is a significant correlation also between advancing C and the speed of delivery plus high-quality customer service.

D. *Inventories are strategic tools.* Interestingly there are hardly any meaning-ful characteristics of the correlation between emphasizing D, the strategic role of inventories, and any other important questions of the questionnaire. It seems that those who consider D important form a very mixed group.

E. *Inventory performance is best measured by costs.* Cost is especially important for those who are competing on prices. These companies have a higher performance measure than the average (which, in fact, shows that the cost reduction approach to inventories is not at all obsolete). They do not put great emphasis on flexibility but want to improve unit production costs and productivity.

F. *Inventory performance is to be measured by contribution to competitiveness.* Interestingly, there is no significant correlation between the F percep-tion of inventories' role and the actual competitiveness of the company. The correlation is significant between emphasizing F and sales revenue and market share, but the connections with ROS and ROI are not significant. This can be interpreted to mean that these companies are more interested in growth than in improving intensive efficiency measures. The companies whose managers are in this group put emphasis on capacity utilization and automation, that is, the physical background of increasing manufacturing performance.

G. *Inventory considerations play a crucial role in forming product-line (assortment) policy.* This statement received the second lowest average score, which means that managers do not really rely on inventories in their "horizontal" policy. However, those who gave a high score to this question, showed the most consistent approach to other questions as well: they gave high scores to all product line (assortment) or economics of scale questions. They want to widen their product scale, increase customization, improve assortment flexibility, and improve product quality—they are all related to the main question.

H. *Inventories in vertically integrated manufacturing units.* This question was more or less customized to the sample of respondents, who were man-ufacturing managers. On the other hand, while statement G was about horizontal policy, it was logical to put this question about the vertical policy of the company. Interestingly there is a significant negative cor-relation between placing more emphasis on H and the companies' efficiency in material cost management; perhaps managers hope to improve cost efficiency by better inventory management in vertical integration. Otherwise the significant correlations were found mostly where they could be expected: with product quantity and assortment flexibility, with close connection to customers in following order fulfillment, customization, productivity improvement, and throughput time.

CONCLUSIONS

The new paradigm is based on the recognition that there is a gap between the interest of higher- and lower-level managers when handling inventories. The former is inter-ested in the contribution of inventories to the fulfillment of the purpose of the com-pany: meeting customers' needs at a profit. For the latter, inventories serve mostly the requirements for smooth operation and avoiding disturbances. This gap could be bridged under the circumstances of the first part of the last century, when optimiz-ing inventories independently of other company functions on the basis of the *ceteris paribus* principle was acceptable. However, in new developments of the economy and business made company operation far too complex for the traditional handling. This results in the need for a new paradigm.

The new paradigm is based on three components of the new role of inventories in business enterprises:

- Inventories are contributors to value creation.
- Inventories are a means of flexibility.
- Inventories are a means of control.

The validity of the new paradigm as a conceptual construct was tested in two sepa-rate surveys: one among manufacturing managers (mostly in middle levels of the hierarchy), and the other among logistics managers (mostly in high levels of the hierarchy). Results of both surveys supported the new paradigm; managers seem to think in accordance with it. The new paradigm looks promising after the tests. However, limitations in some specificities of the conceptual background and of the surveys make further work nec-essary on a more detailed and better-founded elaboration of the paradigm. It should be explained, for example, why no correlation could be found between efficiency and the views on inventories in either survey. More detailed questionnaires with a more sophisticated methodology should be applied. Also, other approaches, mainly case studies examining the relationship between inventory decisions at various levels of enterprises, may be useful in strengthening the foundations of the new paradigm.

3

Nonclassical Responses to Traditional Practice

OVERVIEW

Management of an organization's inventories would seem to be at (or at least near) the top of the agenda for a firm's financial managers. On the balance sheet, inventories are close to the top of the list of a company's assets and are often the largest number on the list. (Plant and equipment dominate primarily in capital-intensive industries.) For small- to medium-sized manufacturers (SMMs), inventory is too often a cause of bankruptcy, giving false claim to the notion of inventory as an "asset."

This work finds otherwise. Students of business are likely to receive only a cur-sory introduction to inventory management during their academic studies, and this most likely only at the microlevel. Examination of the most popular finance/financial management textbooks shows a surprising lack of coverage of inventory issues and concepts, particularly at the strategic level. Hope is expressed that the current empha-sis on supply chain management (with its surrounding issues) will help to remedy this dangerous gap in knowledge about a firm's structure and operation.

A "POLICY VARIABLE"

The firm's operations people are not in charge of any of the four pieces of required data: while the data may be readily available through the firm's ERP system, its actual sources lie elsewhere within the organization. The *c* is accounting's number for the combined materials/

labor/overhead cost incurred and which will be recog-nized when the item accounting transaction recognizes the transfer to the intended next inventory location. Of particular interest here is *i*—the cost, as a percentage of the item cost, of carrying an item in inventory.

Technically, the cost of carrying an item in inventory should be reasonably straight-forward: it's the sum of any taxes, insurance, storage fees, and so forth incurred when holding an item in stock anywhere in the inventory system. For example, all warehousing costs (including overheads) should be summed and then distributed in some sensible fashion across the entire inventory holding. This, as well as any inter-nal transportation costs, is typically judged to be approximately 5 to 7 percent of the cost of the item per year.

But this relatively low number may be missing the point. At a higher level within the organization, the question is to what other uses could this money have been allo-cated. In other words, what is the opportunity cost of having the cash tied up in inven-tory (hardly as "liquid" an asset)? Basically, the higher the percent that the operations people use, the lower will be the resulting inventory positions as the calculations are executed.

Table shows recommended values of this percentage over the years. As the source line suggests, these "inventory carrying cost" estimates are from the logis-tics folks, not the finance people. Typically, a selected percentage will be applied across the board for all inventories in the system, and so is often requested by the information systems group as part of bringing up, for example, a new ERP system. The source may be the "legacy" system or a representative of the operations group.

In operations management courses, we tell students that *i*—this "carrying charge percentage"—is a policy variable, which is a polite way of saying that the percent-age is made up to take into account the fact that "inventory is cash that is not flowing" and we need some easy way to help keep inventory positions down. Since even a medium-sized manufacturing company with a standard information system will calculate several thousand lot sizes every month or so, it is at least some help in keeping inventories low. The numbers shown in Table 2.1, which are in common use in manufacturing organizations, are certainly too high to be normally achievable "hurdle rates" for most companies. Hence, the phrase "policy variable" for these expressions of opportunity costs.

Reported estimates of inventory Carrying Charges

Year of Publication	Author	Charge as Percent of item Cost
1951	Melnitzky	25%
1955	Alford and Bangs	25%
1957	Whitin	25%
1958	Aljian	12%-34%
1962	Ammer	20%-25%
1962	Crook	25%
1973	Heskett et al.	28.70%
1974	Hall	20.40%
1984	Cavinato	25%
1986	Bowersox et al.	20%
1988	Coyle et al.	25%-27%
1990	Johnson and Wood	25%

Source: Lambert, D. M., and Stock, J. R. 1993. *Strategic Logistics Management,* 3rd ed., Homewood, IL: Irwin, p. 366.

The first known publication describing the EOQ and its derivation appeared in *Factory: The Magazine of Management* in February 1913. The author, Ford W. Harris, said: Carrying a large stock means a lot of money tied up and a heavy depreciation. It will here be assumed that a charge of ten percent on stock is fair to cover both interest and depreciation. It is probable that double this would be fairer in many instances. (1913/1990, 947)

Given that overall interest rates at the time were in the low single digits, Harris's recommendation of a 20 percent charge is consistent with the recommended policy variable numbers shown in Table 2.1.

AN ACCIDENTAL FINDING

While waiting in my coauthor's office while a phone call was in process, I (L. G. Sprague) picked up a copy of Brealey, Myers, and Marcus's *Fundamentals of Corporate Finance* and flipped through to the section on inventory manage-ment, finding the following paragraph in the introduction to the "Working Capital Management" chapter:

The second major short-term asset is inventory. To do business, firms need reserves of raw materials, work in progress, and finished goods. But these inventories can be expensive to store, and they tie up capital. Inventory management involves a trade-off between these costs and benefits. In manufacturing companies, the pro-duction manager is most likely to make this judgment without direct input from the financial manager. Therefore, we spend less time on this topic than on the management of the other components of working capital. (Brealey et al. 2007, 543; emphasis added) So much for our advice to students to "call fnance" to set this important value for all inventory decisions.

Pulling several other finance/financial management texts from the shelves revealed an oddity. Other standard finance/financial management texts have similar state-ments (exact copies for other texts with Brealey as an author). But at least Brealey's text has inventory in the index! From the sample of finance/financial management texts on the shelves, one could conclude that there is little interest in the study of inventories and their strategic management within business schools' curricula—at least within the required finance/financial management courses. This suggested the need for a small research project to see if our classical views on what's going on with respect to the strategic management of inventories within business schools' financial courses are correct.

Inventory: The Abandoned Asset?

The question was: Did our first simple sample of textbooks reflect the overall situ-ation within the academic community's handling of the topic of inventory with the next generations of business school graduates? If so, this could have an impact on where and how inventory and its management belongs in a business school curricu-lum. Alternatively, should inventory and its management be ignored as a topic for future business practitioners?

In the United States and the United Kingdom there are sources of education about inventories and their management outside the business schools. The American Production and Inventory Control Society (now known as APICS: The Association for Operations Management), and the Institute for Operations Management (IOM) in the United Kingdom both offer certification programs in inventory management through professional seminars and courses through universities and colleges. APICS supports education and testing for CPIM (Certifed in Production and Inventory Management) and CSCP (Certifed Supply Chain

Professional) programs. Education for these is provided through university-based courses, society-offered courses focused specifically on the examinations, and internet-based courses. These pro-grams tend to place more emphasis on inventory control (including information systems issues) than on the financial procedures and processes involved in corpo-rate-level decision making with respect to inventory.

If there is little consideration of how inventories are deployed and financed, and of their financial impact on the firm's overall performance, there will be a poor understanding of the firm's financial structure. Our suspicion is that inventory and its management have been largely ignored in the financial literature—most danger-ously in the business textbooks in common use. To investigate this possibility, we examined the situation by analyzing the contents of the best-selling finance/financial management textbooks.

Results

Our personal experiences with inventory and its management suggest that there is some truth to the idea that inventory and its management are left to the production managers of the world. This considerable "asset" is in fact controlled item by item and, therefore, lies below the radar screen of the firm's strategic decision makers. This can be described as an inventory control dominant scheme rather than an inven-tory management dominant system. The equivalent for cash management would be strict emphasis on the necessary minutiae of physical control of the bills and coins with little to no attention to the issues of medium- and long-term flows and locations of cash.

The good news on the horizon could be the rise of supply chain management as a topic being studied in business schools' programs, particularly in OM courses and occasionally in partnership with a marketing course or exercise. It is quickly obvious that when complex systems of inventories are being designed, developed, managed, and controlled, everyone needs to be on board—finance, operations, logistics, mar-keting, and information systems, to name only the most obvious players. Deployment of millions of dollars of assets in a global marketplace involves serious trade-offs that should not be made "without direct input from the financial manager" (Brealey et al. 2007, 543). Perhaps it is time for operations managers to be recognized as nec-essary participants in the strategic management of this important asset along with their colleagues in marketing and especially finance. There is a straightforward way to display the relationship between a firm's inven-tory management and control, and its overall financial health: the Dupont model (see, for example, Skousen et al. 1999, 3–10; Ross, Westerfeld, and Jordan 2006, 68–71). This model is more likely to appear in an accounting textbook than a finance/ financial management text.

CONCLUDING REMARKS

For most assets, firms attempt to maximize their holdings to achieve a reasonable balance among the set of assets. Cash balances, investments in marketable securi-ties, plant and equipment, and so forth are all assets whose holdings increase the firm's ability to respond more nimbly to changes in the economic environment. Inventory does not work the same way: it is best kept in motion, moving from sup-pliers to the firm and on to customers with value being added throughout its entire journey. Too little inventory and the firm may find dissatisfied customers improving the sales of their better-stocked competitors, or an expensive shutdown if manu-facturing goes from "lean" to "anorexic." Too much inventory and the firm could drown in a sea of red ink as an economic downturn squeezes the firm between rising payables and short-term debt, shrinking margins and collapsing inventory valuations.

Inventory control is well established as a business field, and education for the basics is generally available through business schools and professional associations. Between required accounting and operations management courses, business students are primarily provided with procedural and operational aspects of inventory control. Strategic management of inventories has not been an important feature in the most widely used finance/financial management textbooks. However, growing interest in supply chains, which inevitably require attention to serious consideration of "place" of product from raw materials through to retail shelves, is beginning to focus on issues that have apparently fallen between the cracks.

There is no need to wrest control of the strategic aspects of inventory management from the finance folks: they appear to have abandoned the field. For the future, we urge those in the expanding supply chain management business to add serious atten-tion to the balance sheet implications of inventory systems and their dynamics (see The Beer Game as an attractive and accessible example). Integrating materials from colleagues in systems dynamics should be encouraged.

There are few industrial marketing experts, but this is a field that could be devel-oped within operations management rather than a marketing department, which is typically focused on consumer behavior where the consumed good is not an indus-trial product. And those of us in operations management should widen our perspec-tive enough to encompass strategic inventory planning and management, perhaps creating links with our marketing and finance colleagues. Inventory—the abandoned asset—needs a new home.

4

Inventory Planning to Help the Environment

INTRODUCTION, CONTEXT, AND PROBLEM STATEMENT

Many people are concerned about the use of carbon-based energy sources, particu-larly oil, and how this is affecting the world. They are also concerned about popula-tion growth, people's lifestyles, and the use and frequent misuse of limited resources by organizations. Creating energy by burning oil, coal, or gas releases greenhouse gases that are thought by most scientists to be a major cause of global warming that, among other things, could melt the polar ice cap, raise sea levels, and increase fooding in many parts of the world. Disputes and wars arising from consequent shortages of land and water will probably increase.

Product design and packaging design are often environmentally poor. This can lead to excessive use of resources in manufacturing and might produce a product that uses too much packaging that ends up as landfill. Unsatisfactory production processes that produce waste and pollution are common.

In the light of energy shortages and the way that financial relationships are chang-ing around the world, most current industrial and business policies will need to be regularly reexamined from a financial, environmental, and human point of view. Given the vast scale of the problems of global warming, resource shortages, and pollution, it is often asked how individuals and organizations can do something that is environmentally useful. The more focused questions that are asked in this chapter are whether and how inventory policies can help alleviate environmental problems. Can we create usable inventory systems that provide a good service but that are envi-ronmentally better than current methods?

So far the effects of inventory planning on the environment have been little stud-ied. As a result, much of the content of the chapter is conjectural. The conjectures are based on examining the relationships between inventory and the environment. Then, how inventory planning could help to alleviate some of these environmental effects is considered. The proposals will be improved with experience in their use.

Context and Problem Statement

Inventory is synonymous with stock, which is normally something tangible that can be physically stored. Properly managed stocks can satisfy many needs. They can provide organizational flexibility; they can act as a buffer between different input and output rates; and they can help to overcome or alleviate many problems and situations.

Inventory is generally part of a multiechelon supply chain. The dynamic response of an inventory system to the demand for its stock items is determined by the inven-tory rules that are used together with the time that it takes to organize, manufac-ture and transport items so as to replenish the stock. The consequent fluctuations in stocks and their flows, particularly in a multiechelon system, can be surprisingly dif-ferent from what might be expected intuitively. However, although holding stock can have advantages, there are frequently disadvantages. Understandably, most inven-tory analyses aim to choose inventory ordering rules that balance these advantages and disadvantages. Cost is the metric that is most used to analyze inventory prob-lems, and traditional inventory analysis aims to minimize the total cost that arises from three sources: the cost of holding stock (surplus cost), the cost of ordering or getting ready to manufacture stock (ordering or setup cost), and the cost of running out of stock (shortage cost). It may be difficult to obtain realistic cost figures in many practical situations.

The potential environmental advantages and disadvantages associated with dif-ferent inventory policies are examined later in this chapter. Unfortunately, it is usually even more difficult to associate a realistic cost to environmental conse-quences than it is to assess the financial costs of inventory surpluses, ordering, and shortages that are used by the classical analysis. A realistic environmental analy-sis, therefore, requires environmental metrics that may be used to assess, analyze, and determine inventory actions.

The discussion focuses on selecting policies for managing inventory that will accord with the needs of a greener world. Important inventory decisions include choosing which items to store, choosing and applying appropriate ordering rules, deciding where to locate stores, and organizing and operating the stores over the logistics chain. Applying inventory control methods locally to individual stock items or individual stores is unlikely to make a major environmental contribution by itself. However, a much greater contribution is possible if environmentally responsible inventory management is applied to the supply and distribution chains of products. This is because the decisions then include the locations of manufacturing plants and stores, which affect transportation requirements. There is also a need for appropriate transportation and communications infrastructures. Potentially these have important environmental implications, especially when considered within the current context of industrialization and globalization.

Industrialization and globalization are important because they have changed manufacturing locations and increased the distances between where goods are produced and their markets. On the other hand, industrialization and globaliza-tion have developed largely on the basis of cost that depends, according to the product, on labor and material costs, the availability of skills, production organi-zation, and production technology. Locations have seldom been chosen because of environmental considerations, even though in many cases, globalization has led to more efficient production and to a redistribution of wealth between nations, both of which may be good. However, problems still arise that are similar to those that occurred during the Industrial Revolution. These problems include pollution and the exploitation of industrial workers. Therefore, the question is not whether globalization is good or bad, but under what conditions is globalization good and when is it less good. Taking account of environmental effects and factors, such as how individuals and communities will be affected, the questions that need asking include:

- What locations should be chosen for manufacturing and for storage?
- How should items be distributed?

- What rules or incentives should be applied to ensure that the production methods used are ethical and that the decisions that are being made are environmentally responsible?

However, even when there are convincing arguments for or against globaliza-tion and new specific locations for the stores and manufacturing plants have been proposed and accepted in principle, the changes will require investment and time to plan. Behavior will not change overnight.

Stocks are diverse and will be found in many fields, such as retailing, manu-facturing, medical, or military organizations. Within each group, many different products and demands will be found but, because different stocks have different advantages and costs and present different environmental hazards, it is unlikely that the same environmental strategies will be equally applicable to all items. For example, the financial and environmental costs of transporting heavy items are likely to be greater than for lighter items. For these reasons it is desirable to provide some general principles upon which to base environmentally responsible inventory strategies.

Some general problems have been outlined and it has been suggested that it is impor-tant to consider environmental factors when formulating inventory policies. The rest of this chapter examines whether inventory planning in the broadest sense (i.e., including locating stores and factories, controlling stocks in stores, con-trolling production levels, etc.) can be made more environmentally responsible.

A CONVENTIONAL INVENTORY CONTEXT

Reasons for Holding and Not Holding Inventory

A useful operational statement of the inventory problem is to decide when and how much of each stock item to order. The objective is usually to balance the advantages and the disadvantages of holding that stock. In most inventory situations, these *when* and *how much* decisions are embedded within a system that ensures that they are implemented and the system used. An inventory system thus includes procedures for record keeping, ordering, receiving, storing, issuing, and dispatching. The ordering decisions may be strongly linked to the manufacturing procedures, especially if the system emphasis is on making for stock as opposed to making to order. Inventory also has important financial implications. Inventory systems, therefore, need to link with the budgeting and financial control systems and how much stock should be held as raw material, in process, as finished products, and in transit. These ideas are now elaborated.

The main decisions associated with holding stock are to:

- Determine which items to stock
- Determine where the stock should be held
- Choose the inventory control systems
- Obtain and equip appropriate storage facilities
- Install the proposed inventory control system
- Implement and operate the inventory control systems that include proce-dures for obtaining and controlling the stock

Specific operational activities that exist within the chosen inventory control sys-tem are to:

- Record stock transactions
- Maintain appropriate records
- Review stock levels at appropriate times
- Order and receive the stock
- Store the stock securely in appropriate conditions (temperature, humidity, etc.)
- Dispose of the stock by using it, selling it, dispatching it, or scrapping it as appropriate
- Perform the necessary administrative activities such as paying suppliers, invoicing customers, stock checking, and so forth

The factors encouraging stock to be held are:

- Ordering: Placing an order incurs costs (including the administrative cost of ordering, the physical cost of receiving and accepting items, and possibly the cost of packing and transporting items). Ordering is often a fixed charge that may be spread over the quantity of items purchased. Thus, the order cost per unit purchased reduces as the quantity purchased increases.

Also, there may be discounts for buying items in larger quantities, further reducing the unit cost. Similarly, unit manufacturing costs are reduced if items are made in quantity and the setup cost per batch is spread over each unit of the complete batch. The unit cost of an item, therefore, usually reduces as the purchase or manufacturing quantity increases; this encour-ages buying in larger quantities and thus having higher average stock.

- Stock availability provides flexibility because items are available for immediate use rather than needing to wait for an order to be made and for a delivery to arrive. Hence, availability provides flexibility to a company, and reduces the occurrence of shortages and the consequential organi-zational problems. This is especially true for long-delivery-time items, because it may take a long time before additional items could become available. Stock may also be held to meet random fluctuations in demand, to smooth seasonal fluctuations in demand and supply, and to allow delivery and issue quantities to be different.

On the other hand, holding stock is discouraged because:

- Holding stock implies that more working capital will be needed.
- Having and operating a store requires renting or purchasing premises, pay-ing for insurance, staff, energy, equipment, racking, and so forth. Usually the more stock that is held, the higher the costs.
- Stored stock may suffer obsolescence, deterioration, damage, and pilferage.
- Having stock can mask problems that would otherwise be identified and possibly eliminated.

The last reason and other disadvantages, such as the possibility of stock being left over when demand falls, encourage the use of just-in-time (JIT) methods for items with certain demand characteristics. JIT aims to receive items just before they are needed rather than having the items available just in case. JIT is usually considered to be a demand pull system that emphasizes that inventory is waste and suggests that stock can mask problems such as long setup times, poor quality, unreliable equip-ment, and unreliable delivery.

If the inventory system operates in very uncertain conditions, the system needs to be designed accordingly. If the uncertainty arises because of poor quality sup-plies and uncertain timing of deliveries, the problems can be overcome progressively because they are repetitive organizational problems. This then changes the emphasis from holding stock to protect against the uncertainty to eliminating the problems. If that can be done, the need for stock is reduced and the result can become effective JIT; that is, a steady flow of items through the supply and distribution chain that arrive at the required location at the required time without accumulating items at intermediate locations. JIT descriptions frequently suggest the need to develop a net-work of suppliers that are located geographically close to the user so that deliveries can be made rapidly. Similarly, reducing long setup times allows items to be made economically in smaller quantities and so speeds up the organization's response. The quicker the response and the better the quality of the parts, the easier it becomes to base manufacturing quantities on real demand, and the closer the system comes to truly being a demand pull system. Nevertheless, JIT will be unsatisfactory in many situations, particularly where there is a lot of uncertainty, for example, with long lead-time items with irregular demand and where demand responds to visibility, as in retailing. Stocks will be necessary then, even if JIT is used in other parts of the logistics chain.

Uncertainty can arise in a particularly acute form in disaster situations, such as those posed by tsunamis and earthquakes; military conflict zones, particularly civil wars with associated refugee problems; new medical conditions, such as epi-demics; and so forth. All of these are inherently difficult to anticipate and stocks are needed so as to be able to quickly respond. However, because of so much uncertainty, JIT as described is inappropriate. Indeed, planning for disasters may require the use of entirely new inventory paradigms. These will not be discussed further here.

The discussion now considers the more common stock situations and examines the different stages in the logistics chain. These stages identify where stocks may exist. The discussion then considers some simple traditional inventory analysis.

The Logistics Chain

The logistics chain for stock items is taken to include material supply, manufacture, product storage, and product dispatch for customer use. Thus, within a logistics sys-tem the main stages for manufactured items include: mining the minerals (e.g., coal and iron ore); converting the mined material into raw material (e.g., steel); making piece parts;

assembling these parts into finished products (this may require con-structing several levels of intermediate subassemblies); testing the products; pack-aging the products; distributing the items to warehouses and other storage areas, wholesalers, and retailers; selling the goods; and sending them to the eventual users. From the environmental point of view, particular interests focus on how the product is produced; how it is used; and, after use, what actions are taken to ensure that the items are appropriately scrapped, reused, or recycled. Product design, pro-cess design, and manufacturing system design have an important influence on most of these steps. Additionally, there will be transportation between the different loca-tions within the chain, and there may be storage at the receiving and dispatch areas of any location. Emphasis on the total system is important from an environmental point of view.

In practical terms, the use of specific suppliers for some items may be, at least in the short term, almost inevitable because of material and skill availability. For example, the location of mines or specific manufacturing skills or overriding eco-nomic factors may mean that it is much cheaper and more effective to transport goods large distances than to produce them locally. An extreme example of this is the growth of crystals in space where quality conditions may justify additional cost. More prosaically, there have been some circumstances in recent years where it has been cheaper to buy completed products from China than to purchase the material to make the items elsewhere.

Some simple inventory rules that do not consider environmental factors will now be discussed. The simplest inventory control models consider inventory fows into and out of a single stock location. The inventory control rules respond to the demands for the item by eventually creating a replenishment order. However, if the replenishment or manufacturing lead time is longer than the available demand knowledge, it will become necessary to forecast the demand and to start manufacturing to meet the anticipated forecast demand.

In principle, stocks could be held before and after each stage and operation within the manufacturing cycle. Additionally, process stock may accumulate at each opera-tion and some of this may be transferred onto the next stage or operation. Thus stocks may be in transit between each operation. The same principle applies to the complete logistics chain for a product that could include many raw materials sup-pliers, multilevels of assembly, and products that are dispatched to many customers or warehouses. Probably the simplest inventory control model is the continuous review inventory control system; that is, the stock is reviewed after every transaction. If it is assumed that the demand is uniform, that there are no stockouts, and that the lead time *(L)* is fixed with delivery occurring just as the stock is about to run out, then it is clear that the system repeats itself and there are no shortages. In this case it is straightforward to derive the reorder level (ROL), *s*, and the reorder quantity (ROQ), *q*, that minimize the total cost of the operation.

A slightly more realistic situation occurs when the demand exhibits variability about a constant mean. The reorder levels and reorder quantities can be derived more or less as before, but now, because of the variability, each cycle of the system will be different and a safety stock is needed to provide protection against the random varia-tion of the demand. In this case the classical analysis balances the cost of satisfying a proportion of the demands (by holding safety stock) against the cost of shortages. The performance is a statistical measure that on average the system will aim to sat-isfy, say, 95 percent of individual demands.

Inventory problems are somewhat greater when there is more than one stage in the logistics chain, which of course is the usual situation. Interestingly, rules that appear sensible for a single stock location may amplify demand when applied to a process with two or more stages. Indeed, as a system becomes more complex, the dynamic system performance may start to exhibit unexpected characteristics. For example, in a simple two-stage process where each stage uses the simple EOQ model, the batch size representing the demand gets pro-gressively amplified.

It is common to combine inventory control rules with demand forecasting rules if it is considered likely that the mean demand will change with time. The rules for forecasting demand, for planning and controlling manufacture, and for planning and controlling inventory depend on the product and the nature of the market demand. If the demand changes rapidly, there is a need to identify trends, seasonality, and so forth, and build these into the forecasting system. A frequently used demand forecasting system that adjusts well to (not too rapid) demand changes with some randomness is the exponential smoothing system. Whatever rules are chosen, the rules, together with the lead times, respond differently to the demand that the system is trying to satisfy. In other words the dynamic performance of systems is affected by the use of different forecasting systems and different inventory control rules that determine when and how much to order. The response is also affected by data such as different lead times and different demands.

Many models have been analyzed (e.g., see Chikán [1990]). These models corre-spond to the consideration of many different factors and different statistical distribu-tions of demand. Each model is of course a simplification of reality and considers only a limited number of the possible variables that face an inventory control system designer. A fuller description of inventory control and its many rules will be found in standard texts, such as Silver et al. (1998).

DESIGNING AN INVENTORY CONTROL SYSTEM

An important problem is to decide what inventory control system should be chosen so as to respond appropriately when the system is subject to various types of demand.

In the context of this chapter we want to choose inventory control rules that are workable, have satisfactory dynamic performance, and also give good environmental performance. We want to provide good and consistent service and we want to ensure that holding stock is a good investment. Among other things, we need to determine the inventory parameters such as the reorder levels and reorder quantities, and the performance of the inventory control system over time. If we wish to make and maintain complex products such as automobiles and aircraft and their subsystems, it is essential to use systematic inventory planning. This is often achieved within a con-text that is based on material requirements planning (MRP) or enterprise resource planning (ERP).

Fluctuations in stock levels and in production levels can lead to shortages, rush orders, or surplus stock, each of which has economic and environmental implica-tions that need to be better understood.

Among the key questions that need to be answered about the inventory planning system include:

- Are products to be made to order or for stock? The answer to this is largely determined by the delivery lead time required by the market and the man-ufacturing lead time of the suppliers.

If the delivery lead time required by the market is less than the manufacturing lead time, then it will be necessary to hold stock. For example, if the manufacturing lead time is twelve weeks and the required customer lead time is four weeks, there is a need to start manufacturing in anticipation of future sales, and in this case to have eight weeks of stock in the pipeline. This obviously needs to be based on a forecast of customer demand and it implies that there will be stock held at various stages in the production sequence. Stocks held at different stages of the logistic chain allow appropriate service to be provided. If the forecast of what is a week's stock is incorrect or demand subsequently changes, there will be either a shortage or a surplus. For example, if the demand increases above the forecast then the consequence could be a decline in the planned service, whereas if the demand falls that could leave surplus stock.

- What rules should be used for controlling the stock? These will include any rules for forecasting, rules to determine when and how much to order, and rules for controlling production.
- Where should the stores and depots be located?
- Where should the items be made or bought?

To design a logistics planning and control system that has the desired least cost performance is difficult, but once the system is installed, observation and measure-ment can identify specific instances of the problems that could arise. However, to be more systematic, mathematical and simulation models of the possible inventory sys-tems could be constructed and used to evaluate the performance of a proposed system before the system is installed. Specifically, the response of the proposed system could be tested by putting both typical and unusual demands into the system model. Such tests could include checking the response to increased or reduced demand, checking the effect of occasional large orders, checking the effect of deliveries that arrive late or are of poor quality, and so on. Examining such instances encourages users to plan contingency responses to potential situations. This analysis should be extensive and may be quite time consuming for A and B items that would be chosen by using the well-known Pareto analysis (ABC analysis) i.e. high and medium usage-value.

Summary

The meth-ods could be chosen based on rules of thumb, mathematical analysis, and simulation possibly combined with local expertise that takes account of local conditions and the expertise and experience of the current operators. In other words, there are many advantages in combining mathematical analysis, simulation analysis, and practical studies together in a mutually supportive manner when examining the performance of traditional inventory systems.

As we shall see later, because of the need for agreed performance measures, and because the environmental timescale is unlikely to coincide with the operational activities of the inventory system, it is even more difficult to measure the environ-mental performance of an inventory system. Therefore, when designing the more complex environmental inventory systems, it is even more desirable to use a combi-nation of modeling techniques to investigate the outcomes.

AN ENVIRONMENTAL CONTEXT FOR INVENTORY

Inventory Systems Factors with Environmental Implications

The discussion now consid-ers individual logistic factors that potentially have positive or negative environmental implications and how they may interact with inventory decisions. The aim is to see whether this knowledge can help us design inventory systems that take account of environmental implications. Although it is environmentally very important to con-sider how a product (e.g., a car) is used, this is not considered here because it is not under the control of the inventory planner.

The discussion considers the operation of the logistics system and the steps involved in the lifecycle of the product including product production. Some of the factors that interrelate with inventory systems and that have environmental implica-tions are:

- Product design
- Process design
- Product manufacture
- Transport
- Alternative products
- Obsolescence

- Waste
- Packaging
- System induced effects
- Inventory storage.

Bonney et al. (2000) discussed the product introduction process, which was taken to include product design and process design, together with the manufacturing sys-tems design that is needed to control the production. The manufacturing systems design included plant layout and design, and facility design and evaluation. Bonney et al. suggested that an extended concurrent engineering (sometimes called a con-current enterprise) viewpoint could help to coordinate these different stages of the product life cycle. The listed inventory systems factors, including the product introduction steps in the product lifecycle, are now considered. After considering these individual fac-tors, the chapter proposes metrics to measure them and it then examines them to see whether they could form the basis for investigating the environmental effects of inventory and encouraging greener activities.

THE INVENTORY SYSTEM FACTORS

Product Design

Product design is probably the most important step in determining how resources will be used. Product design aims to create a product that will satisfy the market requirements in terms of function, quality, cost, and time. Product design—aided by appropriate tools such as value analysis, value engineering, standardization, and so forth—determines the materials used and the tolerances; in other words, how the product will be made and the product cost. Specifically, value analysis and value engineering may provide a helpful basis for simplifying the product, minimizing the number of parts in a product, and minimizing the environmental implications. It is advantageous to build all of the planned requirements into the product at the design stage rather than attempting to modify designs later. How design relates to manufac-ture is discussed next.

Process Design

Process design involves the use of standard parts (whenever possible), the choice of materials, the choice of machines and the processes used, jigs and fixtures, labor requirements, workplace design, and so forth. Designing for manufacture can be used to minimize the environmental impact of the production processes that are needed.

Product Manufacture

Product production is particularly important from the environmental point of view. A manufacturing organization aims to convert materials into products efficiently and then to distribute the products to customers and storage locations appropriately. The efficiency of the product production is largely determined by:

- The product design
- The process design
- The design of the manufacturing system that makes the product. This manufacturing system includes planning the material flow, choosing the planning and control methods including production and inventory control, quality control and financial control, the availability of appropriate stocks and resources to meet the demand, the organization used to achieve the con-version of materials into products, and the methods of operational control.

For products that are to be made for stock, the production/order requirements for products, assemblies, parts, and material will be determined by using demand forecasts, the current levels of stock, the inventory control rules, and the production planning rules.

For production that is made to order, inventory may rise as a result of changes to production quantities. In both situations stocks of materials and parts may be held for the reasons mentioned earlier and these may also be used to help to reduce delivery lead times.

Environmental effects result from: the planning process, changes in demand during manufacture particularly at the start and at the end of a product's life, the efficiency of the production processes, the scrap and waste that are created, and the pollution that occurs during production.

Changes in the physical quality and times achieved may lead to over- or underachievement of programs, quality targets, and so forth, and these may have environmental implications.

RELATIONSHIP BETWEEN INVENTORY AND TRANSPORT

In the early years of the Industrial Revolution, goods were usually produced close to the source of the essential resources such as iron and coal. The finished goods were then transported to the markets. However, spinning and weaving in the tex-tile industry in the United Kingdom were greatly influenced by climatic conditions; for example, damp conditions in Lancashire for spinning and drier conditions in Yorkshire for weaving. Later, materials such as coal and iron ore were brought to where the skills and the infrastructure of roads, canals, railways, and distribution systems were located.

Nowadays, the location chosen for production is more likely to be dependent on the perceived total cost of production, including labor costs, the availability or potential availability of skills and the education and training level of the workforce, and the available support infrastructure, which includes transport and communi-cation systems. Also important is the willingness of the community, government, and people of the area to accept the production facilities and associated infrastruc-ture, including possibly detrimental environmental consequences. Many developing countries will use potential employment opportunities as an excuse to develop their national infrastructure of roads, railways, and ports (sea and air).

Reasons for transporting goods include:

- Production efficiency—It may be more efficient to manufacture large quantities in one location and then transport the items to where they are required rather than transport the materials to near where they are required and then manufacture in smaller quantities locally.
- Skill—It may not be possible to obtain the required skills locally.
- Environmental—It may be better to refine things before sending rather than after because items will then be lighter and the transport volume and cost may be less. It may also be easier to reuse any waste such as off cuts and other scrap metal by reprocessing it at the source.
- Cost—Despite goods traveling greater distances, the sum of the travel and manufacturing costs may be lower because of

lower labor costs or lower material costs. However, sometimes the apparent lower costs may be based on using accounting methods that do not take into account the full cost of travel or the effect on local communities. This chapter specifically argues that the travel costs that are used should include environmental costs. Currently, for reasons already outlined, it is highly unlikely that the company concerned will take account of the environmental effects of the travel.

- Climatic—Sometimes processing may be easier in a warmer than in a colder climate and vice versa. Specifically, the climate also may affect the energy costs associated with production and storage.
- Quality—It may be possible to have fewer spinning faults in a damp cli-mate. Another example is that better quality fruit may be available for can-ning or freezing if the processing factory is close to the growing areas.

Holding stock at a specific place implies that there will be travel involved in taking items to and bringing items from that location. Different locations will have different associated financial and environmental costs, and, therefore, there is a need to choose appropriate stock locations and suppliers to minimize the total environmental (travel and infrastructure) costs. With this as an objective, there may be an advantage to restrict sales from a particular source to specifically defined geographical areas. This may become a rigid company policy or one that is encouraged by appropriate pricing so that environmental and organizational costs are minimized. For example, reducing travel would be encouraged by companies having a green tariff that charges reduced rates for local deliveries by being part of a regular schedule, and charges premium rates for longer distances, urgent deliveries, and environmentally damaging travel.

With retailing, there will be less customer travel if the shop is close to the com-munity that it serves. On the other hand, large out-of-town supermarkets necessarily generate travel, and current supermarket locations are frequently based on where large sites are available, the cost of land/rent, and so forth. When shops are located in city centers, much inconvenience arises from congestion, parking, and so on. With distribution centers there is the need to choose the location and also decide whether to have multiple distribution centers or a single center. Internet and mail-order retail-ing and the method of delivery that is used also affect the environmental costs of collecting and delivery.

Analogously, if local production is encouraged, the amount of travel that is required is reduced. With perishable items such as food, there may be additional advantages such as improved quality. Marketing now likes to highlight when some-thing has been locally sourced as this plays on local loyalties and implied quality. On the other hand, reduced dependence on local sources and local manufacture by using sources that are farther away implies greater transportation of goods and, in general, longer delivery times.

Specific situations to be avoided include when similar products are sent in similar quantities between different areas or countries, for example, bottled water between different countries. Except in times of humanitarian disaster, bottled water almost universally is considered environmentally bad because of its production methods, its packaging, and its transport. However, a major deterrent to reducing this trade is the very clever marketing that means that many people now perceive bottled water to be of better quality than tap water. Also, selling bottled water is highly profitable. This raises the question whether rules designed to encourage environmentally good actions would be considered to be an infringement of individual freedom or a con-straint of trade placed on restaurateurs.

Alternative Products

Alternative products are available in many consumer and industrial situations. Some of these items may have a much lower environmental cost than others but are of similar functionality. Their use should be encouraged and information about such situations should be available so that designers and users can make informed judg-ments. However, with food products, in addition to the local sourcing issue discussed earlier, there are also many products whose withdrawal could have positive health benefits. It can be seen that if this information was formalized into environmen-tal rules, then this would overspill into actions that would affect commercial deci-sions and personal choices and achieve little except resistance to the idea of external involvement. Again there is the potential to affect freedom of choice, and care needs to be taken in such situations.

RELATIONSHIP BETWEEN INVENTORY AND OBSOLESCENCE

Obsolescence is a stage in the product life cycle when, for whatever reason, the end of the product life is about to arrive. The time when this occurs depends on the perishability of the product, fashion, the dynamics of the market, external influences such as technological changes (design methods, rapid prototyping, etc.) and material changes (such as the availability of different colors, textures, and strengths of new materials), health and safety requirements, environmental influences creating change, and the economic trade-off between reusing or throwing away items.

A difficult problem is to decide whether an item should be scrapped rather than refur-bished, particularly when the performance of a refurbished machine may be poorer in terms of productivity, environmental effects, and so forth. A new machine could have lower energy consumption, more precise operations, and produce less waste.

Obsolescent stock is the set of items that is still usable but exists unused at the stockists at the end of the product life cycle. The disposal of this remaining stock may itself have an environmental cost. The stock levels at the time when a product model changes need to be planned and controlled so that they are appropriate to the costs and risks that their shortage or surplus incur.

It may be also possible to use some excess stock for spare parts, but ideally spare parts provisioning should be planned as part of the transition procedures. Generally, the sales potential of obsolescent stock declines rapidly as a new model becomes accepted, particularly if there has been a major technological improvement or fashion change. Influences on obsolescence include:

- In general, the longer that stocks are held, the more difficult will it become to sell the items.
- Imbalance in the stocks that are held; for example, if there are more right-handed than left-handed items available and the items are normally sold in matched pairs, it is likely that stocks will be leftover and some items will need to be scrapped.
- Technological improvements
- Fashion changes

Potential obsolescence is a major reason why retailers have sales, particularly of seasonal or fashion items such as clothing; a reason why car producers sometimes produce special edition models that include more extras than normal; and so forth. In situations where items cannot be sold, often because of a complete change in the fashion or technology, then the leftover products may need to be scrapped and become part of waste (see the next section).

RELATIONSHIP BETWEEN INVENTORY AND WASTE

Waste is somewhat more general than obsolescence and is affected by the perish ability of the product. Waste can arise from incorrect ordering, items that have been damaged in store, or items that have corroded or perished because of poor storage or packaging. Waste also occurs when, to a specific user, the effort to recycle or use for another purpose is perceived to be uneconomic. Examples of this arise with builders whose wood scraps or small quantities of items are leftover from the immediate job in hand. Much food is wasted because of being left unused for too long. At the end of a day, cooked food in restaurants is often scrapped for health and safety reasons.

In many circumstances waste can be reduced by creating appropriate storage con-ditions, for example, by controlling temperature and humidity. This might include refrigerating or freezing items to extend their life. Such improved storage can allow items such as fruit to be available year round. Influences that increase waste include:

- Items becoming damaged
- Deterioration of the items
- Obsolescence of the stock held
- Poor organization either by the supplier or the potential user

RELATIONSHIP BETWEEN INVENTORY AND PACKAGING

Packaging is often required to protect or handle a product and so it is linked to product design. Packaging is commonly required to reduce damage in transit or pro-vide security against theft. Eventually, this packaging usually becomes waste. For this reason, there have been attempts to make packaging recyclable and to place the responsibility for the cost of its disposal on to the producer of the goods who chooses to use the packaging; the additional cost should encourage designers to make more effort with their packaging design. Another example is the use of plastic bags for convenience of carrying or for marketing. A recent consumer-led initiative to reduce the use of plastic bags (some UK supermarkets probably encouraged the initiative for environmental and cost reasons) provided incentives for customers to use their own bags or to recycle the old. Another approach that has been adopted by some organi-zations is to charge for the use of bags.

Ways to reduce packaging requirements include:

- Design products to minimize packaging
- Build some of the packaging function into the product
- Design the packaging so as to minimize environmental impact, for exam-ple, by using recyclable or biodegradable packaging
- Use multifunction packaging so that it becomes part of the labeling and product selling function, for example, on the cans of drinks
- Design packaging that can be reused or used for other purposes

Relationship between Inventory Systems and System-induced Effects

It was commented earlier in the chapter that system-induced fluctuations in stock levels can result from applying the inventory control rules. This section outlines how this occurs.

There is a great deal of knowledge about how to analyze the performance of control systems, particularly those based on electrical, electronic, and mechanical components. Without this knowledge, the performance of automobiles, aircraft, and much military equipment (including radar systems and missiles) would be poorer. The basic principle of a control system (also known as a servomechanism or as an error-actuated feedback device) is that the difference between the desired and actual performance of the system at any time is used as a signal to change appropriately whatever is being controlled. Simple examples of control systems are the tempera-ture of a room being controlled by a thermostat, the distance from a target or the angle off from the target being used to control the path and response of a missile, or the depression of a spring that may, among other things, help to stabilize the suspen-sion of a car. The behavior of a physical control system is frequently represented by means of differential equations.

Analysis of the system representation can show the dynamic performance of the system including the transients, overshoots, and steady-state solutions. Many management control systems use the same principle of having a performance target (e.g., the desired quality in a quality control system, a standard cost in a budgetary control system, the planned inventory in an inventory control system, or the required production quantity in a production control system) against which achievements are monitored and used to adjust actions.

The major differences between management control systems and hardware sys-tems are that management control systems may be less predictable because some of the system components are people who may have motivations that are not necessar-ily in complete accord with the system designers; indeed, these people are likely to display intelligence and variability and they may be motivated by information pro-vided by the system. Another difference is that the controllers of management sys-tems are usually progressively trying to improve the system performance. However, despite this, control system ideas have been used by many investigators to analyze and design management systems so that they will have the desired performance. Tools that have been used include Laplace transform methods, z-transform methods, modern control theory, and, of course, simulation.

Work of interest in this area includes Forrester's (1961) work on what he calls industrial dynamics. Meadows et al. (2004) examined what would happen to the world's resources if the then-current policies continued. Work relevant to production and inventory control include Laplace and z-transform methods. Work that uses con-trol theoretic models applied to the logistics area includes Towill's (1982) continuous models, particularly of inventory and logistics systems; Grubbström and Molinder's (1996) analysis of matrix representations of material requirements planning (MRP) models using Laplace transform methods; and Popplewell and Bonney's (1987) analysis of production, inventory, and forecasting systems using z-transform discrete models to represent systems that are planned on a periodic basis. More recently Dejonckheere et al. (2003) used the approach to study the bullwhip effect.

Many of these studies show that different rules used for controlling inventory and production levels in a logistics chain can lead to fluctuation in the material held and in the production levels, and that this can lead to potential waste. However, good design can reduce the amount of variability and create stable systems that have "appropriate" performance.

Inventory and its Storage

This is largely an architectural problem. There is a need to produce a functional building that is well insulated, easily accessible, matches the road infrastructure so that any extra traffic generated by operators and deliveries is appropriate for the loca-tion, and so forth. It is desirable that the building is designed to minimize the amount of power and resource involved in constructing and operating the stores, and the size is influenced by the levels of stock required. Delivery frequency affects the traffic volume, and, as discussed separately, the relative locations of the different parts of the logistics chain can change the amount of transportation required.

MAJOR RISKS FACING THE INVENTORY PLANNING SYSTEM

Major risks associated with inventory items arise in the following situations:

- At start-up, because lack of knowledge makes it difficult to forecast cus-tomer demand. As a result there can be too much or too little stock and too much or insufficient capacity to manufacture the items.
- When major changes are needed to the product, for example, for market-ing, technological, or safety reasons. The effect could be that an organiza-tion is left with a lot of obsolescent stock.
- The dynamic effects of the inventory system can create surpluses and shortages. Shortages may require taking rush remedial action, for exam-ple, a priority delivery that may need an additional journey that uses extra energy.
- Close down procedures may leave too much or too little stock, again with the danger of leaving obsolescent stock or needing rush remedial actions.
- Major changes in the demand characteristics such as trends or steps in demand.
- Data uncertainty, particularly with costs, environmental metrics, and lead-time data. Manufacture and material-supply lead times

are not necessarily constant and this may lead to surpluses or shortage of stock and require the kind of remedial actions already mentioned.

Other risks (and opportunities) arise from noninventory events. For example, natu-ral occurrences such as foods and adverse weather conditions could affect transport availability. External technological changes, including computing and communica-tion changes and improved quality of data, might improve the functioning of the operational inventory control system. The inventory system will need to respond to any changes.

Assessing the Environment

To understand the relationship between inventory and the environment better, there is a need to be able to measure the environmental performance of the total system. In other words, system performance should be expressed in terms of an environmen-tal cost, which includes the effects of producing, storing, transporting, using, and scrapping the product considered over the complete product life cycle and the whole logistics chain. This could be described as life-cycle environmental costing.

Much work is needed to develop appropriate metrics. To date most organizations have made very little assessment of the environmental impact of holding inventory because, other than broad measures like the carbon footprint, there is little agree-ment about environmental performance metrics. On the other hand, if metrics (here-after called the environmental cost) that estimate the environmental impact could be produced and agreed upon, then almost certainly models similar to the classic inven-tory models could be developed and used. Indeed, whenever there are trade-offs and appropriate information can be obtained, it should be possible to rework the standard inventory analyses to minimize the metric representing the environmental costs. To measure system performance, simulation models could consider the effects, say, of different levels of energy use or of transport use.

Some suggested approaches related to potential problems are listed in a sequence that roughly relates to progressively improved environmental understanding:

- Problem avoidance and problem measurement

- Comparative analysis
- Consequential analysis
- Adverse effects analysis
- Modeling

Each is briefly discussed next.

PROBLEM AVOIDANCE AND PROBLEM MEASUREMENT

Problem avoidance and problem measurement assumes that, other things being equal, it is sensible to reduce activities that potentially have adverse environmental effects. Thus, specific aims of the proposed changes could be to:

- Reduce the use of resources, for example, of minerals and energy.
- Reduce the production of effluent, for example, by using different pro-cesses, better faltering, better work procedures, and so forth.
- Avoid the use of toxic materials. If toxic materials are found to be present, then as soon as is practicable, use procedures to alert their presence with possible recall. If necessary, these procedures should be international and any cover-up must be avoided.
- Choose manufacturing and stores locations that help to minimize travel.
- As far as possible, reduce the environmental implications of transporting goods from the known stores' locations (e.g., use routing and scheduling activities to reduce the distance traveled, choose appropriate modes of transportation, etc.).
- Produce products in a way that will minimize environmental penalties in production, when used, or when modified or scrapped at the end of their life. This may require planning for refurbishment and disassembly, minimizing unnecessary processing and waste of all kinds, and producing products using efficient methods that work well and produce goods of quality.
- Treat items appropriately so that they are not damaged in the stores.

- Avoid spills.
- Avoid dumping.

Many of these items could be monitored or fully recorded, and this could later become the basis for more detailed actions. For example, moving through the afore-mentioned list, one could measure the energy expended by metering, one could check the quality of effluent, and the number of journeys undertaken could be recorded, as could the fuel consumed. Some of these points are developed further later.

Comparative Analysis

The data from the previous section shows what the system is doing and whether it is improving. With comparative analysis, the aim is to take this further.

Comparative analysis compares the effects of varying the main factors for the pro-posals under consideration (such as the locations of manufacture, travel method, plan-ning methods, etc.) on the full logistics chain. Possible performance measures could include the consequences such as cost, quality, travel distances, the time that it will take to transport, uncertainties, and so forth. These performance measures would then provide a factual basis for making intuitive decisions, even though, because of differ-ent weightings, not everyone will necessarily come to the same conclusion. The more knowledge that is obtained then the closer the analysis comes to being a simulation.

Consequential Analysis

This approach uses modeling to better understand the consequences that would arise from hunches. The more detailed that this becomes, then the closer the approach moves toward formal modeling. Where factors are found to have a dramatic effect on inventory parameters, this suggests that it may be worth investigating the relation-ships more thoroughly.

Adverse Effect Analysis (modeling)

If, in given types of situation, it is possible to make a realistic assessment of the environmental consequences of an inventory decision, then it should be possible to analyze specific instances of the problem avoidance list. Many of the initial actions could be classified as good housekeeping and are probably worth doing in their own right. Specific instances of this would be to examine production methods or to exam-ine design methods. These would almost certainly pay for themselves even before any environmental analysis was performed. However, with environmental analysis, the effect on resource usage (indeed the effect on most of the problem avoidance measures) would be a routine consequence of the analysis. The consequence of each analysis provides data relating to another situation equivalent to another case study. Gradually, these would lead to a progressive increase in understanding. This in turn would help to formulate the procedures to be adopted. This data could eventually become the basis for modeling.

Modeling

It might have been inferred from the thrust of the argument that modeling may become more possible as knowledge improves. The author thinks that this is a desir-able objective that would improve understanding progressively. Modeling is a practi-cal possibility in many situations. Based on sensitivity analysis, it may be possible to identify some factors as second-order effects and then to eliminate these from further immediate study. The effect of combinations of factors and a variety of mea-sures can be modeled for subsequent analysis and discussion. Hopefully, this would lead to obtaining agreed upon composite measures. Modeling, once based on the use of these agreed upon composite measures, can be used again.

Another use of modeling is to evaluate conjectures in sufficient detail to see whether the consequences of the conjecture are substantial. An example of this is whether a measure such as an entropy cost could be used to partially represent the cost of maintaining control of systems, for example, to avoid system quality prob-lems (Jaber et al., 2008). The aim is initially to check whether some representation, if reasonable, will have important effects, and then to provide guidance on what is needed for further investigation.

It is assumed that modeling can eventually be used to derive a realistic assess-ment of environmental effects in many types of situations. This would allow specific models to be created that may be used to minimize the error in the estimate of that composite measure, which was earlier called the environmental cost.

Metrics

Most of the actions associated with the aforementioned aspirations may be recorded and the simple consequences monitored, for example, the use of resources, the amount of effluent, the use of toxic materials, the travel consequences of changing the locations of manufacturing and stores, and so on.

The metrics mentioned so far have been somewhat simplistic. They provide a factual basis for auditing and for action, but they do not provide a sufficiently good environmental measure to rank activities or to provide an environmental cost or a decision algorithm. Indeed, it is probably not realistic to rank different actions expressed in terms of an agreed upon single environmental metric. However, the measures can be the basis for interpreting situations and improving the quality of environmental decisions. These ideas are now developed further.

AMALGAMATING INVENTORY AND ENVIRONMENTAL CONSIDERATIONS

Potential environmental savings are most likely to occur where inventory and envi-ronmental considerations interact. Bonney and Jaber (2008) considered the main categories of players who influence inventory use and control. The paper suggested that there are five categories of players related to inventory and the environment: international organizations, nation states, local governments, companies and other organizations and, finally, people. The categories are outlined in Section 3.4.2. There is a need for systematic and easily usable methods of environmental inven-tory modeling, as this would allow us to assess environmental consequences and hence give environmental considerations high priority. Specifically, these methods need to recognize that the timescale over which environmental problems manifest themselves is often much greater than the normal timescale of management decisions. (Of course timescales could also be shorter, but in that case the environmental problems would usually be identified and eliminated during product testing.) Equally important are to be able to make good commercial decisions that do not have adverse environmental consequences, and to make good environmental decisions despite possible short-term adverse commercial consequences. In short, decisions need to be profitable but we also need to leave a world that is ft for future generations. When there is a trade-off between commercially and environmentally based decisions, then environmen-tally good activities need to be encouraged. To achieve this in practice will probably require a combination of education, commitment, incentives, and penalties.

If it is possible to represent environmental considerations approximately, sim-ply by changing the costs, then one would expect the inventory analysis and conse-quent derived rules to have basically the same structure as traditional analyses. If, on the other hand, more complex formulations are needed to represent environmental implications fairly realistically, then the model structures and the ordering rules that are derived may need to completely change.

After considering metrics in greater detail, environmental inventory models are investigated. First, however, the players and their responsibilities for activities that potentially affect the environment are discussed.

Categories of Players Involved

Environmental effects and resource usage do not necessarily have geographic bound-aries. Polluted air and water may travel many miles from their source. Shortages of resources can affect everyone with changes to resources' availability and prices. The effects could trigger disputes and, in extreme cases, could require international agreement to reconcile the differences. For these reasons it is important to identify who has responsibility for specific activities and to create frameworks within which all the parties (players) can work. The following is an attempt to structure the rela-tionships between the players.

In their brief examination of the environmental needs for inventory systems, Bonney and Jaber (2008) considered five (hierarchical) categories of players who have an influence on the environmental implications of inventory. The five players and their roles were suggested to be:

- International organizations, which should set frameworks within which nations, by agreement, will work.
- Nation states, which should first identify and balance international needs with the needs of their own nationals and enterprises; and, second, should provide rules and legislation that set the context within which players at the lower levels of the hierarchy would operate.

- Local governments, which should interpret and implement the national rules (for example, those related to building regulations, possibly adjusted in the light of local conditions), and guide local enterprises and individu-als toward better environmental solutions.
- Companies and other organizations, which should be "as green as possi-ble" consistent with their other organizational requirements such as need-ing to work within the law, make a profit, and provide a good working environment for their employees.
- People, who need to act responsibly within the frameworks set by the other players, but who should also aim to influence decisions within orga-nizations with which they have contact as employees, members of profes-sional bodies, customers, etc.

Of the five players, the first three set the rules or frameworks within which the others work, but it is the companies and individuals that specifically make the deci-sions that choose and use inventory items. For these reasons this chapter focuses on providing guidance specifically at the company level.

PRINCIPLES WHICH TO BASE RESPONSIBLE INVENTORY DECISIONS

The environmental consequences of some actions are potentially so great that there is a need for organizations to develop formal procedures to sign off new proposals for systems, workplaces, and products. The procedures need to be systematic but expeditious. They should not be used to slow developments, as there will be an ongo-ing need to introduce new solutions quickly as better knowledge is obtained. Ideally, the procedures should be internal to the organization but open to inspection from the time of certification.

In other words, it is suggested that an inventory planning system that was designed to take account of views on all of the factors that were dis-cussed should be approved using agreed procedures that retain some flexibility. They should be more like agreeing quality systems, health and safety systems, or auditing procedures, rather than systems such as the Swedish system for workplace design, planning procedures for local authorities, or, even more exacting and costly, drug approval in medicine. A tentative list of principles upon which decisions could be made include:

- Identifying who is responsible for what. This needs translating into who in the management function is specifically responsible for designing the system, who will be operating the system, and who is administratively responsible for checking that the system is operating effectively. Problems that arise need to be quickly rectified to the satisfaction of local operational require-ments and the wider environmental requirements.
- Ensuring that decisions are economically and environmentally good. If and when there are doubts, then these should be noted. If the consequences are potentially great, further research should be carried out.
- Avoiding environmentally bad decisions.

Possible ways to check these conditions are to:

- Simulate the proposed system as indicated in the previous section.
- Pilot any radical or controversial proposals before installing.
- Monitor performance after installation.
- Regularly audit the procedures and their performance; identify any reme-dial actions that are required and have procedures in place to ensure that they are implemented.

It is the responsibility of management to ensure that appropriate procedures are in place so that good actions are performed and bad actions are reduced or eliminated. This section asks whether incentives could be used to encourage environmentally good activities and penalties used to discourage environmentally bad actions.

The decision making is straightforward if a good environmental solution is also financially better for the user. The problem then becomes one of justifying the investment that is required, and then agreeing upon actions such as training staff in the new procedures, investing in the required technology, implementing change, and ensuring that the new procedures are then followed. The problem is then one of investment appraisal. It would be acceptable to use standard investment appraisal methods in this case. The decision making is less straightforward, however, if the solution was not financially better but the environmental arguments were strong. How does one assess the investment in this situation? First, it would help if incentives were provided to encour-age the good actions, and possibly sanctions to discourage the not-as-good actions; but for this to be practical the actions would need to be based on generic measures such as energy expended, distance traveled, and so on. These would need to be part of some wider agreement so that it is not to become an open invitation to bring in protectionism by the back door. Possible actions could range from setting appropri-ate trade tariffs, introducing subsidies that ensure that the financial or performance penalties were not too great, or introducing legislation. As we are interested in getting good results over a very wide range of items, successful outcomes would require the enthusiastic involvement of many of the population. In turn, this would require that the purpose of the activities would need to be clearly explained, and that the reasons for the proposed restraints, incentives, or penalties on the activities made clear.

First, we need to be able to identify the actions that are environmentally "good" and those that are environmentally "bad." To encourage good actions and discour-age bad actions will require agreement on what is good and bad and some sort of measurement to know what is happening. The history of voluntary actions is not very encouraging and so, almost certainly, most actions will need to be backed by encouragement through personal commitment/involvement or through incentives or taxation. As an example related to a slightly different area, lower taxation on energy efficient cars may encourage people to use smaller cars. Corresponding disincentives such as high tax and petrol duty on gas-guzzling cars could be used to penalize high fuel usage. This is an example of a green tax that makes it less expensive to carry out good rather than bad actions.

However, there will always be people who can afford to ignore incentives. Therefore, encouraging green actions (e.g., recycling waste) may need to be backed by appropriate laws supported by sanctions, or possibly by using community publicity to shame antisocial actions. Unfortunately, the potential unpopularity of some green taxes, such as an increased tax on fuel, might make it difficult for politi-cians to implement such measures. Even though indexing tax on fuel for cars had been agreed on in the United Kingdom, when that coincided with a rapidly increas-ing price of (crude and) refined petrol, it led in early 2008 to protests by truck drivers and motorists, and an unwillingness by politicians to face the growing opposition. In addition to such green taxes, the only other experience so far is limited to carbon trading programs that have been criticized by some for being used as schemes that allow groups to avoid environmentally appropriate behavior.

To manage most situations in a sensible and justifiable way, we need metrics to inform us about the implications of actions that have been taken, and eventually those that will be taken. Ideally the measures should relate directly to the action being mea-sured; for example, fuel consumption is likely to be a good candidate for assessing the impact of car use and the data is available for individual car models. However, in general, great care must be used when setting up metrics and developing approaches that are intended to encourage environmentally good behavior, particularly if the measures are indirect. So far performance measurement systems seldom obtain the expected results and they often introduce the law of unforeseen consequences. Therefore, metrics will need time to be piloted, to settle down, and also to develop over time. They also need to be accompanied by appropriate educational support.

The following analyses indicate some investigations that could be undertaken to study the interrelations between inventory and the environment, and to obtain insights about the importance of the factors:

- Produce a preliminary list of possible factors and actions.
- From that list produce a possible ranking.
- Carry out ad hoc actions including good housekeeping (e.g., of product design and process design). Also use quantitative common sense (e.g., if something is wasteful, then study how to reduce it).
- Produce simple ad hoc models (e.g., travel and layout models).
- Produce simple overall models.

The procedures for producing the list and its evaluation should become more for-malized as experience is gained. However, the following is a suggested investigation procedure. Each of these steps is now discussed. A second set would be obtained by systematically stepping through the stages in the product life cycle. A third would be to step system-atically through the geography of the logistics chain. Additionally, any other focus that the managers, who have local knowledge, consider important or appropriate to the organization should be considered. This will produce a tentative priority listing applicable to that company.

Before a detailed investigation of possible actions starts, it is important that an organi-zation should attempt to rank these factors. Ideally a possible ranking would be obtained by producing a Pareto assessment of their potential environmental importance. If this is not possible, local knowledge and intuition could reduce the list of possible contenders.

Good housekeeping will almost certainly pay for itself even without environmen-tal improvement; for example, simplifying designs and the design procedures would reduce the number of stock items; reducing set up times will speed up production and increase flexibility; and improving material flow and insulating stores would all have beneficial effects.

An example of the use of algorithms to reduce travel distance when the stores' locations are known should make it possible to measure the expected effect of mak-ing certain specific actions, and subsequently to measure the actual distance traveled and the modes of transport that are and could be used.

The development of simple overall models probably needs to be deferred for more detailed examination. Implications: where do we go from here?

General Discussion

It is probable that the human race is on an unsustainable environmental path that is caused by its activities. The consequences are thought to include global warm-ing and overuse of resources. Any solution will need major policy changes by governments and companies, and also changes in the behavior of the majority of the people on the planet. The longer we take to respond to the situation, the greater is the likelihood that we will move toward catastrophe. The three major environmental problems facing the world are probably: the creation of greenhouse gases, the overuse of resources (including minerals, water, land, and the living environment where discernable effects on fish, forests, and biodiversity are occur-ring), and pollution.

Specific problems arise because in most developing countries, but particularly China and India, environmental considerations have usually and understandably come second to economic pressures. In particular, energy has been produced largely from coal, currently a relatively dirty fuel. Against this, the "developed countries," particularly the United States, have been unwilling or unable to reduce their rather profligate use of energy. For example, the United States generates roughly 25 per-cent of carbon emissions although it has only 5 percent of the world's population. Countries that currently have the benefits of using energy do not want to reduce their consumption. On the other hand, countries that have not had the benefits of bountiful energy in the past now aspire to catch up. It is interesting that the model of growth throughout the world is so pervasive that it is hard to describe the situation without using words like *benefits* and *catch up*. However, finite resources do not allow the current model to continue. It would appear that not only is it going to be difficult to obtain agreement on unified actions, even the terminology will need to change. Sustainability is a minimum requirement.

To reduce unnecessary environmental damage will require a major change in the balance of activities. We need to do more good things, such as produce more renew-able energy, reduce energy usage by insulating, reduce waste, produce items more efficiently by improving the efficiency of the processes, improve the efficiency of systems, use things better, design better, and reduce packaging, while avoiding bad things such as using energy unnecessarily. There is a need to save nonrenewable energy by reducing the use of nonrenewable energy sources (such as coal, oil, and gas) and reducing pollution. However, it is unlikely that doing these things will be sufficient. There is almost certainly a need for a more radical rethinking of priori-ties, which will provide additional factors to take account of, even for action that is primarily focused on inventory in a general sense.

Although many companies are trying to do something, unfortunately, there have been many instances of companies superficially greening their product image as a marketing tool to encourage customer purchases rather than as a commitment to adopting policies that will help the world to become a greener place. Nevertheless, the continuing focus on environmental needs appears to be transferring into real efforts in some instances. It is to be anticipated that this will continue and deepen, but whether it will be done soon enough is difficult to ascertain.

The market is progressively becoming more environmentally aware with pressure coming from many sources including:

- The United Nations, European Commission, government, and states
- Specific groups of consumers
- Pressure groups
- The media including radio, television, newspaper, and magazine reports
- Individuals

Governments are beginning to set more realistic targets, but, in general, they have been unable so far to match their achievements to their planned timescale.

Perhaps the aim should be to focus the rethinking that is currently taking place as a result of the financial crisis to find and fund ways of overcoming the even more worrisome environmental situation. Financial cooperation could be used so that countries will work together to help the planet. Specifically, the source of energy and other resources is an important part of the environmental cost. Major investment is needed. Perhaps, taxation should be levied on carbon-based energy sources, with these funds used specifically to invest in renewable energy production methods.

However, much of this is rather pious and wide ranging compared with the task that was set for this chapter; namely, to focus more tightly on inventory and its asso-ciated problems over the logistics chain.

Questions to ask About Inventory

It is important to understand the implications—the opportunities and risks that arise from different inventory actions. Among the questions that could be asked are:

- Could it be environmentally advantageous to change the logistics control system including the amount and the location of stocks and the manufac-turing plants?
- How would the total system performance change if appropriate inven-tory control policies were used? Specifically, what would

be the gains and losses obtained by using different types of systems?

Specific inventory questions are:

- How do we determine the best locations to manufacture specific goods?
- How do we determine the best place to hold stock? Can we relocate stocks so that total travel is reduced?
- Could holding appropriate stock allow the amount of transportation to be reduced (e.g., by using bulk deliveries or using more environmentally friendly but slower modes of transport such as rail or road rather than air freight)?
- Do reduced stock levels increase the need for urgent deliveries?
- Can one obtain the environmental and cost advantages from bulk deliver-ies by delivering a range of items together while retaining low levels of stock?
- What are the environmental consequences of different distribution systems?
- What are the effects of home delivery systems?
- What are the effects of Internet shopping?
- How do we prioritize the suggested actions when answers to these and other questions are obtained?

We need to obtain answers to these and many other questions about inventory if we are going to ensure that inventory planning can play its full part in creating a sustainable environment.

SUMMARY AND CONCLUSIONS

How inventory planning relates to the environment has been the main theme of the chapter. The points that were made included:

There are many environmental problems and human activities are contributing to these problems. The problems include:

- the increase of greenhouse gases in the atmosphere, largely caused by the use of hydrocarbon based energy, will lead to global warming and cata-strophic consequences for the world;
- our excessive use of other resources means that current actions are not sustainable;

- pollution is affecting water and air quality, bio-diversity and the quality of living in many localities.

The scale of the problems is so severe that urgent, preferably coordinated action is needed to reduce everyone's contribution. However, even working to the most opti-mistic time scale for implementing changes, the expected environmental implications are very disturbing. They include climate change, temperature rises, water shortages, and flooding that will adversely affect everyone. It is essential that actions are taken as soon as possible by as many players as possible using every means possible.

Actions can be of the following kinds: use less energy and other resources, produce less pollution, increase the availability of renewable energy sources, perform activi-ties more efficiently, produce better designs, insulate better, recycle more, produce less waste, etc. Also, in general, improve as many as possible of the current activities that have an adverse effect. Several ways were suggested earlier in the chapter by which better inventory planning could help the environment.

Unfortunately, appropriate environmental cost data are seldom available or easy to obtain. Therefore, at the present time it may not be possible to determine optimal solutions. Despite that, many positive actions can be undertaken and the results can be closely monitored. The aim is to do something positive while at the same time gather-ing data and improving our knowledge of the effectiveness of the actions. We need to learn; we need to learn quickly and then we need to use that knowledge as soon as possible to improve our performance, at least nationally but preferably worldwide.

Five groups of players had an interest in inventory decisions, namely: international organizations, nation states, local governments, companies and other organizations, and people. It was suggested that companies and individuals within these companies were in charge of the main inventory decisions and that these decisions need to be made within the context provided by the first three players.

Every means possible should be used to encourage desirable actions in the time scale involved. Comments were made about incentives, taxes and legislation. In par-ticular, financial incentives should be used to encourage environmentally positive actions and taxes used to discourage less good activities. In addition, an extensive information campaign will be needed to encourage appropriate actions. The infor-mation will need to be of two kinds; first there is a need for general information so that everyone is aware of the problems and of the need to find solutions and secondly, there is a need for specific information about ways that environmental performance can be improved. This information will not appear spontaneously; persons will need to be responsible for the provision and other persons for the use of such informa-tion. Information provision could arise from industry wide advisory groups perhaps supported nationally. Implementation will need to be guided by people within the companies with appropriate authority and enthusiasm to ensure that action is taken. Legislation may be needed to encourage less enthusiastic implementers to take the necessary actions.

In the short run there are going to be some situations where what is the most desirable action is inconclusive because of a lack of clear facts within companies. However, all is not lost. Before we get precise answers, we can make do with rough and ready solutions but, additionally and in parallel, procedures will be needed that will steadily improve the measures and the company data that will be available upon which to make decisions in the future. We need to measure the results. In short, the suggestion is that the companies should do the obvious, find out more and then refine the data and the solutions that arise from the chosen actions.

Even with the use of analytic methods and even with attempts to assess environ-mental costs, the results will be strongly influenced by the numbers that are selected to represent the costs. Obtaining the figures raises two issues. The first is conceptual and requires deciding how exactly one is going to represent the environmental cost. The second is a practical one that in addition to obtaining the basic data, the data also needs to be interpreted to ensure that like is compared with like particularly if competitors are ignoring long term environmental effects to obtain a cost advantage. Inventory decisions and all other decisions will be very difficult if the environmental costs are not known. To take account of environmental factors, it is likely that further technical developments in modeling are going to be needed and if these investigations are to be taken seri-ously then the problems to be solved need to be far more focused. Different kinds of inventory will require different priorities and investigations may need to be related to particular industrial sectors. Now is the time to move away from generalities to the detailed hard work that will be required to determine the needs for many companies backed by appropriate incentives and legislative framework.

The chapter has briefly outlined some of the points that need considering if inven-tory planning is going to play its part in moving towards a sustainable planet. There is much to learn and the lessons need to be applied quickly. An overriding principle is that progress will have been made if things are environmentally better after deci-sions are implemented than they were previously. However, because of assessment problems is should be recognized that there will always remain difficult decisions even when managers of projects are really trying to do their environmental best. This is not an excuse to allow the less conscientious decision makers to wriggle out of their responsibilities, it needs to be recognized that decisions will need to be tem-pered by humanity, economics, and the possibility of a sustainable environment as well as satisfying non-commercial human needs of community, open spaces, etc. A range of potential problems is likely to arise but they must not be allowed to inhibit actions. Among them are that analysis may point to solutions that are apparently in conflict with competition or an open doors policy and any enforcement will need to be based on comparing like with like. Another difficulty is that the time scale over which environmental effects may manifest themselves is different from the planning horizon of normal economic business decisions. If so, a business decision could, knowingly or unknowingly, select a profitable but less good environmental decision

Unfortunately, as was indicated earlier, current decision making has been deter-mined using non-environmental arguments. Furthermore, in many cases artificial costs, taxes, import duties and subsidies have further distorted current decision mak-ing. For example, there is little consistency in taxation levels between countries or between different modes of transport e.g. travel by air does not pay the same fuel tax as car travel. In general, taxes are used by countries primarily as revenue earners although sometimes there may be an attempt to influence behavior by putting higher taxes on less favored activities such as alcohol and tobacco. However, taxes also influence behavior and so they should be part of the armory used to obtain better environ-mental behavior. Possibly, when desirable changes are identified associated legislation will be needed so as to bring costs in line initially with expenditure and then, eventu-ally, with expenditure plus associated environmental costs. Complexity is a danger.

Finally, inventory even defined as broadly as in this chapter, is only one small part of a company's operations. If the world is serious about protecting its environment, a similar approach will need to be applied by each organization to each functional area including construction, estates, office work, sales teams, etc. Nothing less than a rethink with different priorities is likely to match the scale of the problems facing us. Those that do it well will contribute to the well being of the world and will also have started to face the problems that are likely to grow progressively in importance.

5

Energy and Inventories

OVERVIEW

The progressive consumption of the nonrenewable energy stocks is determining wide fluctuations in the cost of energy (primarily gas and oil), influencing both absolute values and volatility, and leading to attention on the strategic role and function that these resources play in the economy and life in general. It is well known that the debate has quickly spread to encompass other issues, such as the availability of alter-native resources, including nuclear power generation; the scarcity of the "classic" sources, such as fossil fuels; and the impact on the environment (e.g., Rout et al. 2008). Similarly, there has been growing interest for a more rational and respon-sible consumption of energy in the industrial processes and services, this being not only a fundamental issue for sustainable production, but also a strategic leverage for competitiveness, due to the increased contribution of energy to the final cost per unit produced. Inevitably, these issues will exert, and are already exerting, an increasing and noticeable influence on the management of supplies and inventories, thus open-ing new horizons and opportunities for research in this field.

This chapter focuses on these issues starting with several situations, already discussed in literature, in which inventory features (such as levels and quantities) are notably influenced (and frequently determined) by the energy content of the inventory itself, and by the cost of the energy source. This is the case with dams (water reservoirs), gas/oil stocks and, more recently, warm/cool storage. These cases will allow the reader to perceive and understand how, why, and in which ways stocks may be linked to energy. The subsequent sections will concentrate on those other relevant aspects that cannot be neglected when the relationships between stock features and energy are considered. As a reference, the cases of the biomass supply chain (and, more generally, biofuels) and the "cold" supply of goods will be discussed. These examples will introduce the final comments, which will remind the reader that, when energy is employed, environmental aspects (e.g., emissions) are also to be taken into account. Therefore, several topics will be addressed to illustrate how, when the relationships between energy and inventory are considered, traditional economic analysis should be backed by an accurate appreciation of the environmental costs.

INTRODUCTION

Inventory is also defined as "the stock of any item or resource used in an organization" (Chase and Aquilano 1995). Basically, types and forms of the resources used, and their consequent inventory, vary according to the area investigated, including raw materials, finished and semifnished parts, subassemblies, and supplies. In many sectors, energy is a fundamental raw material necessary for both production and ser-vices, even in its different forms, such as electricity, heat and steam, and mechanical energy. In other sectors (e.g., power stations), energy is the last product to be supplied to final or intermediate customers. Frequently, these systems convert energy from one type to another, thus behaving as the more conventional productive systems, that is, adopting stock-keeping policies, and ordering and accumulating the resources nec-essary to meet demand. The description given and the growing attention to energy policies underline the importance of incorporating energy-related issues to inventory principles and vice versa. (Incidentally, it is interesting to note how, as in Hudson and Badiru [2008], energy is classified into two basic types: kinetic and potential, where potential energy represents stored energy, as well as energy of position.) As far as early literature on the economic features of energy storage is concerned, the contri-bution by Grubbström and Hultman (1989) is to be mentioned, with particular refer-ence to the proposed model for energy storage of a system subject to heat transfer.

As an introductory comment, it is convenient to keep in mind one of the basic principles of inventory economics, which is based on the provisioning costs (e.g., setup and purchasing) and the costs related to stock creation and maintenance (e.g., see Winston 1994). The latter cost is generally given per unit of inventory and per time unit and it may be connected both to the opportunity costs (capital tied up to the inventory) and to the pure components of the holding activities (e.g., risks and costs of obsolescence, taxes on inventory, damages and spoilage, stockout probabili-ties, insurance, buildings, operating costs, etc.). In addition, purchasing costs may include, in the case of production, variable costs, labor, raw materials, and, as in the case of the present contribution, energy.

Of course, the activities related to stock energy or substances to be used for energy generation must also comply with these inventory laws and principles.

However, in the case of energy-related raw materials and energy itself, the price paid for the raw material or the pure energy (i.e., oil, gas, carbon, and, as derived energy sources, electricity and process residuals such as hot water and air) cannot be neglected either. In fact, this component may be estimated by opportunity cost and, above all, it may fuctuate widely within narrow time windows because of speculation or demand -offer mechanisms. This aspect signifcantly impacts model-ing; it implies that the purchase price cannot be assumed as constant over time, nor can the holding cost be considered as a given and consolidated value. These two principles may be considered connected thanks to the opportunity cost mechanism. In addition, this reasoning suggests that the variable holding cost deserves further analysis, in accordance with the needs implicit in inventory-related energy issues.

A PRELIMINARY SCHEME

In a general framework, the scheme proposed in the European Commission (EU) reference document (2008) may be suitable for the present case. Energy inputs into a process with a given productive capacity (e.g., tons per week) may differ in type: steam, electricity, and fuels. Once the resource requirements have been adjusted by their conversion efficiency (e.g., 35-55 percent for electricity and 85-95 percent for steam generation), it is possible to appreciate the gross requirement of energy for the production capacity. The concept may be extended to include energy recovery and different flows of products in the process. As the productive system may provide both products and services, the different forms of net exported energy ($Æ_{i?on}$) may represent system outputs, too. These are the cases of energy amounts used in other process units, but, as a function of the bound-aries considered, it is also the case of industries recovering their warm residuals for district heating. In such situations, $E_{i,out}$ terms represent recovered resources. Of course, the production of product type 1 may also generate byproducts (as in various chemical processes; i.e., P_2, ... P_k, ... P_M), as well as wastes (in terms of residuals) which, in turn, could require energy ($E_{W,\ in}$) to be disposed of (e.g., incineration), eventually generating an energy export ($E_{W,\ rec}$). Finally, technical solutions may allow the recovery of a part of energy ($E_{i,\ rec}$) within the process itself. Other energy efficiency indicators may be formulated, according to investigation needs, such as definition of the system boundaries, appreciation of system-oriented or product-ori-ented energy requirements, multi-product environments and technical comparison of different processes.

However, the conclusive remark is that the whole set of energy contributions described is transferred into the final products; in other words, each product contains an energy contribution that also depends on the process and the type of energy used, thus making a substantial difference in terms of equivalent emissions into the envi-ronment, too. Finally, it should be noted that two types of energy contributions exist: the first is a fixed one (everything needed to support production, regardless of the quantities produced, such as lighting, maintaining vessel pressures, minimal flows in pipes, and furnace temperatures), and the second is a variable contribution (e.g., the energy spent for cutting and heating raw materials).

More extensively, it is quite interesting to note how, according to a modern view, goods are no longer evaluated mainly on the basis of their economic value or asso-ciated monetary flows, but also according to their energy requirement and content. For example, this concept is applied to buildings (Yohanis and Norton 2006), where energy is categorized into embodied and operational energy, and to photovoltaic facilities (Muneer et al. 2006). The former case suggests an interesting dualism between setup (embodied energy) and holding costs (operational energy), while the latter example gives outstanding evidence of how the two approaches (economic and energetic) may lead to controversial conclusions (the payback of the energy embod-ied in the facility is about eight years, while the monetary payback is estimated around ninety-five years). From a wider point of view, it can be stated that energy is a commodity encompassing each object, which, on its turn, requires (or releases) energy during its life and up to its end.

Stocking Energy Vectors

The fluctuations in the availability of energy-related raw materials, together with the volatility of their processing, have led companies and national states to organize their own network of reservoirs, buying and stocking these materials during positive periods (low prices, common availability) and consuming them during negative ones. Such an approach may also be determined by seasonal needs, as in the case of stocking fuels during the warmer period to be sufficiently protected during the winter.

This is the case of strategic gas stocking and also of any traditional household that collects wood and biomass during the harvesting period to be protected for the cold season. These simple examples show how stocking materials with energy-related purposes is very similar to the classic role of inventories, which are used as flying wheels to smooth the imbalance between demand and offer, covering peaks and buffering during troughs. Energy-related stocks also play an important strategic role, preventing national trau-mas during seasons of political disruption (oil shocks, interrupted gas provisions).

Historically, literature has paid greatest attention to the study of oil stock, prob-ably because of its political relevance, raw material versatility (oil is used in heating, power generation, and propulsion) and transportability, and geographical distribu-tion (in this respect, all the other energy sources—carbon, gas, and biomass—differ significantly). However, the technological changes and infrastructure development set the basis for new opportunities for energy-related means, as in the case of gas.

Gas is generally transported by pipelines from the extraction sites to the final des-tination. Such a solution presents both advantages and disadvantages, as the simple comparison with traditional manufacturing might show:

1. Pipelines are "rigid" transport systems, connecting specific points of a given network: a given supplier is connected to a specific

set of customers and vice versa, even if, thanks to the pipeline grid, different nodes may be reached.

2. However, supplying consists of a continuous flow, which may be preferred to discrete provisioning, where levels vary according to steps in input and continuously in output.
3. The pipeline may be critical, as sudden breakdowns (or shutdowns) of critical points may interrupt a relevant part of the flow, or even the entire flow.
4. The gas in the pipeline is a sort of work-in-progress stock, increasing its cost while moving through the pipe itself, because of the energy required to move it and the part of the infrastructure used.

From this point of view, liquid natural gas (LNG) and regassifers represent an inter-esting alternative (Energy Information Administration [EIA] 2003), giving flexibility to the system. The first plant of LNG started in Arzew, Algeria, in 1964. Since then the growth has been impressive, supported by technological changes and cost reduc-tions at the different phases of the chain (Greaker and Lund Sagen 2008). Regassifers require gas stocking in harbors or, in general, close to the coasts. The natural resource is stocked and shipped by cooling the gas itself at extremely low temperature, thereby incurring an energy cost for the pumping at relevant pressure and for keeping tem-peratures at low levels (transportation takes place at -160°C). The same applies at the final destination, where ships fill stocking vessels with the transported LNG low temperatures until the gas is released into the pipeline distribution. Such a system is of great interest for its modeling and potential implications (Holz et al. 2008):

- It opens up the gas market to new suppliers who are not necessarily con-nected by pipelines to the final customers (several natural gas fields are far from major markets).
- Such a distribution system makes the natural gas supply chain more flexible, for example, in the choice of provisioning harbors, routing, and deliv-ery stock points (the impact of the infrastructure is reduced, too).
- From this point of view, greater competition is stimulated and the oppor-tunities for natural gas exploitation widened. (At present, this fuel is com-monly used in power generation and

is an interesting propulsion fuel, too, although its potential is limited by the scarcity of distribution points.)

However, the distribution of costs varies when compared to the traditional pipe-line: a higher cost is paid for stocking (cooling and stock pressure) as an initial setup cost, while the cost of energy (distributed along the pipeline due to gas pumping) is counterbalanced by temperature preserving costs. Even if, from the 1980s, both liquefaction and regassifcation costs decreased significantly, it should be considered that the LNG chain is also energy intensive. About 15-20 percent of the raw mate-rial is claimed to be consumed for the entire processes (liquefaction, transport, and regassifcation).

Gas storage facilities are used to accumulate gas during the year and to regulate gas production, making it more stable. This approach covers strategic, economic, and technical issues (see, e.g., EIA 2006). Storage may be completed underground in exploited gas fields, aquifers, and caverns, although artificial tanks and pipelines themselves may play an integrating role balancing pressure and demand. This leads to competition over prices and contemporary smoothing of peaks in demand. For example, in Italy, demand is extremely seasonal: in winter it is roughly twice the summer figure, thus favoring the hypothesis of stockpiling during the summer and null stock at the end of the winter season. Extracted gas may be transported and stocked closer to the final user, the alternative being to avoid extraction and keeping the natural reservoir untouched. In such cases, a difference (immediately apparent to inventory researchers) emerges in the inventory holding. When gas is kept in its natural field, the holding cost is null, but if the gas is extracted and stocked prior to its final usage, the holding cost emerges as a consequence of stock maintaining (in a simple approach, the marginal cost), plus capital tied to extraction and transport. As a consequence, storage capacity is the most relevant constraint and the strategic function of gas for civil and industrial purposes suggesting the growing importance of this factor. When dealing with gas storage, a large stock capacity also prevents the need for overdimensioning pipelines and extraction sites. It also exerts a mod-erating action on the market during critical periods, reducing price fluctuations. An interesting and complete model may be found in Amundsen (1991). A careful— and inventory-based—evaluation of the true convenience of gas stocking is made complex by the number and variety of parameters specifically involved. Above all, taxation emerges as a critical parameter (together with price caps), being a typical leverage used with political aims to address the strategic storage aspect of gas reser-voirs. These aspects are quite complex to model, including their unpredictable effect on demand and, consequently, on the inventory needed. By way of example, the price to access storage in Italy, which is still almost monopolistic (Holz et al. 2008), also includes fees for space, injection, withdrawal, movement, and strategic storage (Italian Authority for Electric Energy and Gas 2006). It is evident that the common or independent movement of any of these figures will affect the interest in gas stock-ing, together with any expected fluctuations in price and demand.

In conclusion, the issue of gas storage is an emerging research area, deserving of particular attention because of its inventory-related features. Of course, even greater attention has been paid in the past to a similar case, namely, petroleum reserves (e.g., see Meyer et al. 1979; Oren and Hong Wan 1986). This is the main reason why, in the present contribution, it has been preferred to discuss energy resources and vec-tors other than oil, which can be regarded as a well-consolidated issue. However, the great attention paid to oil, due to its strategic role and to the shocks of the 1970s (e.g., the embargo in 1973 and the Iranian crisis in 1979), is similar to the recent attention to natural gas. Of course, differences in demand, taxation, and technical solutions (related to the physical properties of the two substances) make the two cases very different. Furthermore, the problems posed by natural gas present some conceptual similarities to hydrogen concerns, even if the two orders of scale are completely dif-ferent. For example, as in Kreith and West (2004):

- Liquefaction of hydrogen requires a large amount of energy.
- Storage occurs at very high pressures, with a considerable energy input.
- Its transport still presents daunting obstacles.

Nevertheless, the conceptual similarities mentioned add interest to the develop-ment of models for the optimization of the chains of these energy vectors, includ-ing the amount of energy at the generation phase, the energy requirements, and the infrastructure investments for subsequent transport and stocking. A second category of stocks related to energy is represented by water reservoirs, generally accumulated by dams. Where it was an option, the generation of elec-tricity by means of hydropower has always been competitive because of its costs, and it continues to be so now because of environmental awareness and attention to power generation with low CO_2 emissions. In fact, hydropower is one of the most consolidated and time-proven ways to produce energy by renewable resources, and its technological development reached a mature standard some decades ago. The management of water resources exploited in dam-based plants has already been dealt with in the literature. As in Prabhu (1980), water reservoirs allow interesting applica-tions of continuous time inventory models, being a storage process with random input and output of finite capacity. His bibliography shows how P.A.P Moran formulated his theory on dams in 1959 and the first works date back to the 1950s (H. E. Hurst, J. Little, Tjalling C. Koopmans, J. Gani and R. Pyke), mentioning how demand may be originated both by electric energy and water to be supplied. The elegant approach adopted, based on the queuing theory, is worthy of application to the economics of inventories, considering the holding cost of water storage. In a modern view, such a cost should include:

- The cost of the structure, together with its maintenance and updating
- The costs related to the environmental impact, comprising not only the local changes (effect of dams and water storage on the site, such as soil assessment, changes in humidity and temperature, reflectivity of the artificial lake surface), but also the entire flow of the original intercepted streams
- Hidden costs related to the missed opportunities for water utilization, such as agriculture and fish farming; in particular, it should be noted that extremely dry seasons may oblige the managers to lower dam levels, i.e., spillage, to prevent irreparable damage to agriculture, industry, and other activities, thus determining an additional holding cost that should not be overlooked

In conclusion, the need for accurate models of stock management, visibly quantified by the water level, emerges as particularly relevant. Such models should help in smoothing irregular provisioning of the inflows, taking into account the risks related to future incomes (stock usage may determine a deficit due to dry seasons or a loss in capacity accumulation during a wet period and already high stock levels). The issue of water resource utilization and, more specifically, its optimization is comprehensively discussed by Loganathan (2008) and the authors wish to acknowl-edge his contribution.

When the specific issue of energy is taken into account, various technical solu-tions to its generation (e.g., fossil fuels, nuclear, hydro, etc.) present their own specific features (Couto de Oliveira et al. 2002), which are differently, though significantly, influenced by the management policies in the stock of the energy generation source. For example, operating costs are mainly determined by fuels in fossil-based power stations, while equipment construction and environmental impact mainly affect hydro and nuclear power plants. In particular, water reservoirs, when freed to be turbined for electricity generation (outflow), might become the reservoir of the subsequent power station (inflow), like serial inventories. In addition, the decision to produce "clean" energy by water saves the larger operating costs of the alternative fossil-fuel power sta-tions, but reduces the stock of water in the reservoir, too; that is, the production capac-ity for the future is reduced in favor of a present use. Of course, the problem of the relative influence of immediate cost functions on future ones is perceived differently, according to the sensitivity of the system to the scarcity of water, as in small capacity hydro networks and extreme water fluctuations from season to season.

The appropriate modeling for these systems may vary (e.g., stochastic dual dynamic programming proposed by Pereira and Pinto [1991] and Read and George [1990], or simulation-based as in Read and George [1990]), since decisions and the consequent optimization depend on the forecast in inflows.

Finally, underground thermal energy storage (UTES) technology should be men-tioned. Such a technology implies the storage of energy wastes and, typically, solar thermal energy in reservoirs for future use (Sanner et al. 2003). The convenience of such a technique depends on the technical solution adopted (aquifers, boreholes and pipes, and cavern storage), which offers different equipment flexibility and invest-ments (setup cost). Furthermore, holding costs are related to the cost of the deprecia-tion of the dedicated buildings, plus the decay in the energy content, so the energy level of the stock held must be maintained to prevent its value per unit of time from decreasing over time, also depending on the demand profile, which determines when the stocked energy will be used. Variable costs are determined by the energy used to move fluids from and to the reservoirs. In fact, thermal storage may occur on different time horizons, from short-term utilization up to seasonal.

The UTES tech-nical solution and the underlying problems leave plenty of room for optimization, which could be carried out according to inventory principles, especially because of the developing research and market interest in high temperature (>50°C) heat stor-age. Nevertheless, underground storage goes beyond the case of thermal energy. For example, excess energy may be stored by compressing air and pumping it into salt caverns, abandoned mines, and depleted gas fields or buried pipes.

An alterative, as in hydro plants, is pumping water into higher basins for subsequent turbining (Patel 2006). The high storage capacity of the compressed air solution is also associ-ated with relevant investments; for example, due to the problem of cooling the com-pressed air, the cost of the power system varies between $1000–$1500 per kilowatt). However, storage capacity may be a strategic element of choice when positioning new wind farms, enabling energy to be stored when wind power exceeds electricity demand.

In fact, the development of renewable sources, such as wind and solar gen-eration, focuses attention on the intermittency implicit in these types of resources. As penetration levels increase, finding a balance between fluctuating renewable gen-eration and fluctuating demand becomes more difficult and more expensive to man-age (Moutoux and Barnes 2007). Solutions to mitigating the intermittency of wind generation by storage are, in addition to the cases already mentioned, conventional batteries, flywheels, ultracapacitors, flow batteries, and superconducting magnetic energy storage. A complex case is described in Denholm (2006), where a completely renewable generation system combines wind energy, compressed air energy storage (CAES), and biomass gasification. Baseload wind systems using CAES may require combustion of natural gas and the development of long distance transmission, thus decreasing the environmental and social compatibility of the system. However, the use of biofuel might reduce the net carbon emissions of the system, increasing its renewable features. CAES systems are also mentioned as an emerging technique (EU 2008), because of their ability in managing peaks of demand and offering opportuni-ties for efficiency improvement (Najjar and Jubeh 2006).

UTES is generally intended as energy stocking for the colder period; however, stocking for warmer periods may also be practiced. The basic question is that demand for cooling buildings has significantly increased in recent years due to sev-eral factors, such as population and rising comfort standards and, not least, global warming. The most common equipment for building cooling is electrically driven devices. A significantly less energy-consuming alternative is to stock "winter cold" in the form of snow and ice for subsequent utilization during the summer. This ancient technique is feasible in large areas of the world. A large-scale application is the snow cooling plant at the hospital in Sundsvall, Sweden, operating since 2000 (Skogsberg and Nordell 2001). Snow is stored in a shallow pit (140 × 60 m) of watertight asphalt, with a capacity for 60,000 m^3 (40,000 tons) of snow. Meltwater from snow storage is cleaned and pumped to the hospital and, after the cooling usage, the heated meltwater is recirculated into the snow storage. The average cool-ing energy required by the hospital during the summer amounts to approximately 700 MWh, with a maximum cooling power of 1.4 MW; 93 percent of the cooling demand was attained by 19,000 m^3 of snow and the rest by a cooling machine. Most of the snow (75 percent) was natural, integrated as needed by snowguns. Without thermal insulation and cold extraction, a 30,000 m^3 snow pile in Sundsvall would be gone by mid-June. A 0.2 m cover of wood chips reduces melting considerably; in this case, 75 percent of the snow is preserved and may be utilized for the energy saving described, which, in conclusion, is characterized by an extremely cheap cost of energy (average close to 60 €/MWh) and a long life expectancy (40 years). Moreover, snow/ice cooling plants have a great potential in industry, agriculture, and comfort cooling; artificial cooling media are often inflammable, poisonous, and environmentally hazardous.

In conclusion, the problem of energy stocking is strategic and is gaining increased importance with renewable energies (e.g., stocking solar heat during the day for night usage or the presence of wind during a period of no demand). The issue is also addressed by the EU reference document on energy efficiency techniques (2008). As forms of energy are very different, some of them are more difficult or impossible to store. Mechanical and thermal energy cannot be easily stored (e.g., dams and hot water tanks). However, the most important case is electricity. Potentially, electric-ity is stored in batteries, which is a form of chemical storage, just like fuels. This probably represents the most successful form of energy storage in terms of trans-portability, energy density, and duration. In conclusion, the advantages of storage technologies are obvious, but they also offer strategic potential to improve both eco-nomics and the environmental performance of renewable energy sources; external fuels are no longer necessary and excess generation by renewables may be efficiently used (Gross et al. 2003).

Holding Costs and Energy

Variable holding cost is a research issue that has attracted attention for years. Works may be found in the literature in 1980 (Muhlemann and Valtis-Spanopoulos 1980) and 1982 (Weiss 1982), while a comprehensive review on perishable good inven-tories may be found in Nahmias (1982). There are further excellent investigations dating from the 1990s (Goh 1994; Giri and Chaudhuri 1998) and more recently by Alfares (2007) and Ferguson et al. (2007). The contribution by Goh (1994) is partic-ularly valuable because of the two types of holding cost functions discussed: (1) the nonlinear function of the period spent in inventory by the item, and (2) the nonlinear function related to the amount of on-hand inventory. As far as the link between vari-able holding cost and this chapter topic is concerned, it is worth noting that variable holding costs may depend on the variability of the economic value of the item and on the energy required to preserve it. This is the case of food, where the energy and the relevant technical equipment required to preserve it is largely influenced by external conditions (temperature, humidity, etc.), thus depending on season and geographic stocking of the products, as in the case of the different levels of energy needed to preserve food in winter and summer.

Just to mention a couple of familiar examples, freezers and refrigerators are com-monly used, together with the consequent problem of energy bills and the decision whether to keep things fresh in the refrigerator or pretreat and freeze them. Energy is necessary to preserve food and other products such as drugs, but also blood; the greater the energy used (frozen food vs. fresh), the longer the life of the product. Another case of increased holding costs is related to the heating power; a biomass subjected to compression (pellet and briquettes production) increases its energy con-tent per unit of weight, thus increasing its commercial value and, therefore, its holding cost. The holding cost of biomass deriva-tives increases as a consequence of the manufacturing process added value and the cost of storage away from moisture. In other words, the relative values of the holding costs introduce the dilemma about the timing and the opportunity of transforming the biomass into its derivatives. However, the value of the item stored may also decrease over time, for example, because of its energy content decay or because of the energy spent to preserve the stock itself. The former is the case of batteries, the charge of which decreases over time, and the second is the case of regassifers and UTES.

The work by Alfares (2007) introduces a holding cost variable according to a step function, this being an interesting model for value increase of biomass because of pellet or briquette manufacturing or, in general, for products for which longer storage periods require extra care. The same contribution (Alfares, 2007) emphasizes how the model proposed problems, where an item is stored in different places with differ-ent holding costs (e.g., perishable items, for which the longer the time to be spent in storage, the more sophisticated the services and facilities needed and, consequently, the higher the holding costs). Also Giri and Chaudhuri (1994) remark on how vari-able holding costs are related to supermarket management of fresh food: increasing costs are determined by improved storage facilities to prevent spoilage and maintain freshness. Of course, integrating policies other than preservation may be put into action, such as markdowns or removal of spoiled products. (See also Ferguson et al. [2007] for a real-life application of variable holding cost models.)

However, as technological and strategic issues drastically influence the matter in question, it is not possible to neglect the impact of alternatives in the supply chain management. An example is offered by Bendiksen and Dreyer (2003) referring to fish processing in Norway. Even if the focus of the study is on plant locations (of a specific region and product) and the relative value, the impact of the technological change related to the supply chain of the product considered is evident, as it may bring into question the strategic geographic position of the plant itself. The possibil-ity of storing fish on board immediately after the open-sea capture without quality loss might change the structure of the chain and the consequent distribution of inven-tories. Time for open-sea fishing is extended by onboard storing. The most relevant technological change exists on new vessels, where the catch is frozen on board, thus changing the supply to processing plants from fresh to frozen raw material. Such a change determines the need for new storing plants for frozen fish (twelve new plants in five–six years, according to the Norwegian case) and processing cycles. In addi-tion, the technological change modifies the approach to the strategic location of fish processing plants, together with the role of the supply-chain actors. Closeness to customer areas or fast transport stations becomes more remunerative than closeness to rich fishing areas. What is relevant to our purpose is that such a case also shows an example of a different distribution of inventories obtained by putting a larger energy content at the preliminary stage (cooler fish storage conditions for longer periods). This is not a new approach in the food sector; for example, cheese and meat may be seasoned or smoked for longer conservation, but such a practice requires longer times and energy contributions (smoking, drying buildings, ventilation, temperature and humidity control). When compared to fresher products and regardless of the taste, the difference lies in higher prices and longer shelf lives. Nevertheless, the emerging concept is that at the preliminary stages, the product acquires higher val-ues because of the contribution of energy (frozen stage and storage). Fluctuations in market demand may be covered thanks to a larger inventory level and a longer prod-uct life (frozen). The case discussed introduces the topic of "cold logistic chains," which are significantly affected by energy-related issues.

"Cold" and "fresh" Supply Chains

Heating and freezing are some of the oldest physical processes for food conserva-tion, and the contribution of energy to the processes themselves is evident. Certainly, heating was formerly used because it was easy to heat by fire; however producing cold temperatures, excluding places where ice naturally forms, turned out to be a compli-cated task for centuries. In the nineteenth century, Norway conducted a flourishing trade in ice and transported it as far as the tropics. The first cold-storage premises were opened in Chicago in 1878, almost contemporarily to the first consignments of frozen meat from South America and Australia to Europe. The first household refrig-erators appeared on the market in 1910. In 1925, trade in frozen goods for the home began in the United States. Refrigerators became widespread from 1950 onward and freezers from 1960 (Geiges 1996). Nowadays, chilled and frozen foods are moved worldwide. The different transport chains, together with their technical features, are described in James et al. (2006). Along these supply chains, energy plays a strategic role, being necessary to guarantee quality-based processes, influencing the economic performance, too. For example, supermarket refrigeration systems consume about 20 percent of the total energy of the store. This figure must be corrected to also take into account the auxiliary equipment consumption (14 percent) and the energy used for the building air-conditioning (17 percent; Getu and Basal 2007).

However, cold supply chain management implies a rather peculiar approach. An interesting introduction to the problem may be found in Bogataj et al. (2005). The emerging factor in cold supply chains is the visibility and the control, in par-ticular of the temperature at each step of the chain, which is necessary to pre-serve food and guarantee its quality to final customers (these issues easily extend to perishables). Of course, the progress in technologies and logistics has boosted the cold chains, thanks to monitoring, efficient transportation, and communica-tion information technologies. It should be noted that temperature control is a critical issue; temperatures higher than the set values may definitely compromise the product, while lower ones may compromise the quality. According to Bogataj et al. (2005), this issue is also emerging thanks to regulations such as EN92/1CEE on temperature recording in transportation, stocking, and selling points, giving us the modern concept of "cold traceability." In their contribution, starting from Grubbstrom's (1967, 1998) approach to net present value (NPV) and MRP, Bogataj et al. (2005) argue that the analysis in frequency space may be more effective than the traditional time-based one, offering the opportunity to model perturba-tions in temperature and the necessary prompt reactions to them. The variations in temperature (disturbances) are introduced as delays determining an impact on product deterioration, therefore adding an additional cost due to planned cooling. The NPV analysis allows the appreciation of the impact of energy-related costs in the inventories distributed over the supply chain and the entire time horizon. Such an approach may allow the understanding of the basic difference between the fresh product chain (shorter product lives, fast transportation, lower energy contribution) and the frozen product chain (longer product lives, slower transportation, higher energy contribution). The two chains may be compared, remembering that mixed situations may be found in practice (e.g., freezing–defrosting–cooking–freezing or fresh delivery–freezing). The study of food supply chains is of challenging interest to inventory and produc-tion researchers. In fact, the fresh food chain is affected by peculiarities close to typi-cal production issues, but worth investigating (e.g., Akkerman and Van Donk 2007):

1. Frequently, setup times are sequence dependent (think about cleaning, equipment regulation, and selection of packages) both in time and costs.
2. Storage should be limited for fresh food, not only because of perishability and shelf life, but also because of dedicated equipment and space, which could be additionally limited when product mixing is to be avoided.
3. Processing should be fast, by means of traced and high-quality systems.

ENERGY-RELATED PRACTICES: IMPLICATIONS ON INVENTORY MANAGEMENT

It has been shown how the contribution of energy to productive costs may be par-ticularly relevant. However, it could even be overwhelming in specific industrial sectors, such as the production of silica bars, steel, and primary aluminum. This has led practitioners to focus on technical solutions allowing the reduction of energy consumption per unit produced and energy waste, so as to gain competi-tive advantages. Frequently, such technical solutions impact inventory features, stocked quantities, and their management. The following section will illustrate some of these cases to clarify the problem and note its impact on inventory management.

The Aluminum Case

Aluminum is widely recognized as the "green metal," because of its ease of recy-cling, durability, and properties, such as lightness and resistance to corrosion. The productive cycle of aluminum and its alloys is based on minerals (primary indus-try, using bauxite) or recycled scraps (secondary industry), the latter process being several times less energy intensive. Recycling processes, as in the case of steel and copper, significantly contribute to the sustainable development of society; metals are continuously reused at the end of product lifetimes. However, the energy spent on melting and refining the material is definitely lost because of metal solidification in ingots. Therefore, an approximately identical quantity of energy is to be spent if the material is subsequently reused for casting or die-casting processes, gener-ally leading to cost and pollution inefficiencies from a chain perspective. This has generated interest in alternative structures of supply chains, as described in Diana et al. (2007). The traditional aluminum supply chain is also described and studied in Khoo et al. (2001), where a conventional supply of solid ingots is considered. An alternative practice was initially observed in Germany and is spreading in Italy. It is linked to the supply of the molten metal, transported by adequately equipped trucks carrying coated and insulated ladles. Of course, this supply method enables the final user, when properly equipped with cranes, to save the remelting energy and reduce the storage costs (as fewer ingots are stored in warehouses). The refiner gets some advantages, too: the productive cycle of furnaces may be optimized to reduce energy consumption and storage costs are also reduced. Of course, there are some disadvan-tages, especially from the managerial point of view:

- The necessary closer cooperation between the user and the supplier is not always perceived as a competitive advantage, particularly on the buyer's side.
- Both melting (supplier) and production (buyer) cycles have to be synchro-nized to prevent dead times in the buyer's production. This may occur when trucks are late or when production is delayed even though the molten metal, contained in the transported ladle, may be kept in the liquid phase for a given time with limited energy contributions. Such a requirement makes the system more rigid from the managerial point of view.
- The limitation is particularly apparent with uncertain delivery times, con-sidering the truck-based transport system is more prone to delays.

- The quantity of material transported by the truck is less in the case of liquid metal than in the case of solid ingots because of the ladle shape and weight.
- Investment in new equipment (ladles, cranes, fixtures) is needed.

These considerations represent a Pareto efficient frontier, which can be identified by analytical models (Diana et al. 2007). Such an efficient frontier is of particular interest when environmental concerns are considered, too, as emissions saved at the remelting phase are partially lost by the reduced transport capacity. In addition, a mix of different types of supplies (i.e., sometimes metal ingots and other times mol-ten metal ladles) may be a strategic leverage to mitigate the impact on the productive system flexibility. From the inventory point of view, this practice leads to a decrease in the final product stocks at the supplier, which induces a reduction in stocked raw material at the buyer. These aspects are highlighted by certain cost components, such as:

- Aluminum ingot solidification costs, which cover the time for which a chosen machine (and the related space) is dedicated to containing the mol-ten metal during the transition from liquid to solid phase, plus the time needed to cool the solid ingot before safe handling.
- Yearly depreciation of the specialist equipment (e.g., portable ladles to carry out transportation and overhead cranes with related fixtures).
- Ingot holding costs, which include the space required as well as the inven-tory equipment, plus management and financial costs (capital tied up and opportunity costs).
- Costs due for ingot melting at the buyer's site.
- Warm-up costs of the liquid aluminum from the transported ladle tem-perature to the furnace temperature and for maintaining the temperature at the ladle before use.

The case described presents some similarities with steel and iron production.

THE IRON AND STEEL CASE

The iron and steel industry is one of the most strategic and consolidated, but it is also one of the most energy intensive processes, accounting for the 19 percent of the European industrial energy use in 2004. A common plant type consists of an electric arc furnace (EAF) feeding a continuous casting line, the final products of which are square-section billets. Given the high temperature of the process (about 1500°C), billet cooling requires time before delivery to the final customer. Such a productive phase takes time and so it is susceptible to optimization, especially because of holding costs for the "warm inventory," which are directly proportional to the time interval during which a billet remains in the warehouse, even if it is simply cooling (Zanoni and Zavanella 2005; Ferretti et al. 2006). A survey on steel plant management (Tang et al. 2001) emphasized that the optimization may refer to the whole system or to only a part of it, as typical stages of steel production are steel making (SM), continuous casting (CC), and hot rolling (HR). In this case, when the billets are produced for a subsequent rolling phase, the loss of energy related to their cooling is evident. In fact, such a situation implies that billets are cooled, warmed, again, and then rolled. Cooling requires time and space, while warming needs a dedicated furnace and the related energy contribution. Alternative technologies, such as compact strip production (CSP), present a higher energy performance and a simplification in the process stages. Basically, slab continuous casting is coupled with continuous strip rolling, thus implying the on-time utilization of cast material, shortly after its exit from the EAF. A limiting process is represented by endless strip production (ESP), which will allow producing strips directly from liquid-core steel. Savings in holding costs (space, cooling, and stocking times) and the reduction of the work in process (WIP) are evident. These savings are to be added to the lower capital tied up with slabs, and the lower emission levels connected with suppressing the reheating process.

The viability of using the energy content transferred to the billet during the SM phase, immediately after the CC, has also been exploited by transporting billets in special sarcophagi made by refractory. It is reasonable to assume that the same con-siderations made for the aluminum case still apply: the two production systems (SM plus CC and HR) must be synchronized, additional equipment is required, and, in the case of truck transport, capacity per delivery is reduced.

It is worth noting that such a practice is recommended in the EU (2001) best avail-able technologies (BATs). In particular, the reduction of heat loss is recommended for intermediate products, thus impacting WIP storage, logistics, and product fows. Minimizing storage time and insulating the slabs/blooms (e.g., by heat conservation boxes or thermal covers) is suggested. Furthermore, changes in logistics and intermedi-ate storage lead to the maximization of hot charging, up to direct charging or rolling.

Both of the cases described show how inventories may give up one of their tra-ditional roles—the function of decoupling (acting as reservoirs or buffers) two pro-ductive stages or subsequent levels of supply chains. Such a change is dictated by energy-related issues, which, in their turn, impact on convenience (cost compres-sion), sustainability (emission reductions), technological changes, and management principles (scheduling, WIP, and lead-times evaluation).

BIOMASS AND ITS DERIVATIVES

Recent years have seen a renewed interest in biomass, together with a growth in its transformation processes and the use of its derivates used as fuels. Such an interest is linked both to environmental concerns (neutral cycle of biomasses, which act as CO_2 traps during their lives, releasing it because of usage or decomposition) and the cost increase of traditional materials for energy generation (e.g., oil and gas). Basically, biomass can be regarded as sun energy stored to be further extracted by different processes, such as wood burning. Biomass represents the first type of fuel used by mankind, but its prospective in supply and storage are quite new, given the pecu-liar aspects of its more recent applications. This fact is probably twofold. First, new biomass processes are flourishing and becoming competitive. Second, biomass has usually been considered as a local resource, even though the demand and the avail-able sources are not homogeneously spread all over the world. Some countries have excess biomass for their own energy economy, while in other countries, biomass availability is limited due to population density and industrial activity (Forsberg 2000). Furthermore, the increasing use of bioenergy in Europe has already created a new market for the supply of this resource, which can be satisfied (in the short term) also by an increase in the access to biomass over a larger geographical area, thus increasing the interest for the relevant supply chains, particularly processes, storage, and transportation. In other terms, using an appropriate logistic system, access to biomass can be improved over a large geographical area (even though some coun-tries, such as Italy, explicitly encourage "short" [70 km] biomass supply chains). Both the studies by Forsberg (2000) and Hamelinck et al. (2005), using life cycle inventory (LCI), confirm that long-range transportation may also allow an efficient exploitation of biomass, without losing its environmental benefits.

However, as the authors suggest, the optimization of the chain should consider the processes occurring at the different levels of the chain itself. In fact, technological evolution enables biomass transformation to facilitate its storage and transport along the chain up to its final use (examples of derivatives are biofuels, pellets, briquettes, and chips). These transformations require energy utilization, which basically deter-mines the increase of the specific heat (i.e., kilojoules per kilogram or kilojoules per cubic meter) and the density of the biomass, opening interesting frontiers to research applied to the optimization of the biomass supply chain and its inventories. For exam-ple, Gigler et al. (1999) discuss the configuration of biomass supply (willows) to energy plants. Basically, wood may be supplied to plants differing in power size and material utilization (combustion or gasification), but alternatives characterize the chain steps. Wood may be stocked as chips, dried (forced cycles), and finally delivered after a given time span (the typical horizon is from a few months to one year). Alternatively, willows may be simply cut (chunks or stems), transported, and centrally chipped. According to Gigler et al., the former alternative is more economically attractive for deliveries within six months, while the latter applies to longer-term deliveries. A significant impact is exerted by drying, which can be energy based (forced drying) or natural, thus determining an impact on costs, emissions, and energy requirement by the cycle. A further interesting finding is that supply chains for gasification plants are more expensive than conventional combustion ones if the cost evaluation is expressed

in euro per ton dry matter (DM), but the cost is lower when expressed as euro per kilowatt hour, due to the higher efficiency of the technological cycle. This shows the appropriateness of a nontraditional analysis, which does not take into account solely conventional costs (e.g., euros per ton or euros per year), but also engineering-oriented measures such as euros per kilowatt hour or euros per kgCO_2 to consider emission costs. For example, Figure 4.3 shows the trend of the lower heating value (LHV), measured on field, of wood residuals (chips) in the sawmill department of an Italian company. As time flows, natural drying lets LHV increase, thus resulting in an increased chip value as fuel. However, holding costs mitigate this positive effect, leading to a lower net value, which depends on the stocking equipment.

The distribution of pellets represents a very interesting reference, too. According to Vinterback (2004), distribution may represent 30 percent of the cost for a resi-dential pellet consumer, and inventory may be greater than 50 percent. Sensitivity to moisture by the pellet fuel makes storage a rather critical activity. Improving pel-let distribution and, in particular, inventory management at the distributors might point users toward this heating alternative, appropriately considered as environmen-tally friendly. Technological innovation has considered storage at the final customer by the producer—even if demand profile and productive capacity generally make inventory a necessary solution—and room control during pellet storing, even at the transportation phase. The ordering mechanism is a rather interesting situation for inventory modeling; there exists a reordering point, a maximum storage capacity, and the need for a safety stock and uncertain demand.

It is worth noting that wood supply chains are complicated by the profiles of demand and raw material availability, the latter being related to the seasonality of forest management. This case is frequent in the pulp industry (Carlsson and Ronnqvist 2005): the availability of raw material naturally increases in the forest up to midsummer, while harvesting builds up the stock between autumn and early spring, depending on both cultivating traditions and regulations. In the case of pulp, demand from mills is considered stable while, in the case of biomass fuels, demand is affected by high seasonality, so that the need for balancing raw material availabil-ity, production capacity, and fnal demand reflects on a series of inventories distrib-uted over the supply chain.

In general, the design of a biomass supply chain is particularly interesting because of the transformations of the producto (which substantially change their techni-cal parameters) and the impact of transportation on optimal choices (Hamelinck et al. 2005; Gronalt and Rauch 2007). It is also accepted that, within the renew-able resources framework, biomasses present a complicated scenario, because of the variety of feedstocks, conversion technologies, and final usage (e.g., domestic or industrial, electricity- and heat-oriented ones). Therefore, a key issue is to secure sus-tainable supplies of relatively low cost fuels (Gross et al. 2003). However, their benefits are evident, being largely available, flexible (as described), and environmentally friendly. As shown in Hamelinck et al. 2005, Gronalt and Rauch 2007, and Gross et al. 2003, biomass presents interesting features for its alternatives in supply chains and the related inventories. For example, demand is affected by seasonal fluctuations to be added to "regular consumption (the latter component being significantly deter-mined by the paper and furniture industries and/or the combined heat and power plants, producing both heat and electricity)." As far as transportation is concerned, biomass in loose form is competitive within a short range (50 km) and wood chipping is effective in intermediate ranges (up to 100 km), while longer distances require biomass transformation into derivatives (e.g., pellets, biofuels). Safety stocks must be kept at terminals and plants (expressed in millions of loose cubic meters), guaran-teeing a set service level in a variable lead time context, limited stock capacity, and seasonal availability of raw material. Harvesting windows are limited, according to regulations and selected species, and the energetic properties of the raw materials are also highly variable, as in the case of wet springs and snowy winters and vice versa, thus explaining why pretreatments are frequently hoped for. Furthermore, harvest-ing methods may differ and transformation processes, even by mobile equipment, may take place at different levels/steps of the chain, altering biomass features and introducing energy contributions.

These observations lead to attention on conversion processes, which differ in tech-nology cost and environmental impact (e.g., see Hamelinck et al. 2005), but also offer to assimilate, from the distribution point of view, biofuels (such as refined ones) to fossil fuels. Basically, bioenergy may be transported in different forms (chips, pellets, charcoal, ethanol, etc., and, of course, electricity). Such bioenergy chains, includ-ing their different products and densification processes—aimed at improving prod-uct technical features and reducing transport movements and volumes occupied at the storage stages—differ in external energy input and energy density of the out-put. Furthermore, they also differ in vulnerability to, for example, moisture (drying may be natural or artificial, but ineffective storage may thwart the process), bacte-ria, accidents (such as material losses for storage activities; about 15 percent), and self-ignition. It is interesting to note that biomass deterioration is mainly dependent on the material properties, such as moisture content, available nutrients, and chemical structure. It also depends on the type of storage (Jirjis 1995): for example, the low-moisture content of pellets limits the growth of microorganisms (Lehtikangas 2000). Inventory models encompass these aspects in the concept of holding costs, includ-ing obsolescence and perishability. In addition, changes in heating value suggest opportune modeling of these parameters familiar to inventory researchers and prac-titioners. According to Hamelinck et al. (2005), storing in open-air costs 1.1 €/(m^{3}y), while pellets and dried chips must be bunkered at 87 €/(m^{3}y), up to liquid storage costs at 310 €/(m^{3}y). However, it should be emphasized that biomass inventories (and, more generally, energy-related ones) should be optimized not only according to cost func-tion, but also according to CO_2 balance calculations, this being a rather critical aspect to sustainability. Although the environmental savings with respect to fossil fuels are evident (electricity produced by pellets is in the 7–32 kg_{CO2}/MWh range against the 370–1200 kg_{CO2}/MWh range of gas or coal), some renewable technologies should still increase their competitiveness with fossil fuels, thanks to environmental external ele-ments. To this end, it is opportune to point out that technology changes may modify the perspective, as in the case of carbon storage in soil and litter. Furthermore, both environmental and economic balances should take into account that biomass may generate "coupled products" (e.g., glycerine from the production of rape methyl ester), thus providing additional usefulness to these natural resources (Kaltschmitt et al. 1997). Finally, CO_2 emissions and energy required in biomass supply chains severely influence the chain sustainability. The ratio between the primary energy and the delivered energy is around 1.25 for European crop pellets (the ratio rises to 1.87–1.93 for methanol chains), that is, extra energy inputs to the chain (mainly derived by fossil fuels) and material losses represent more than one-quarter of the final energy pro-duced (the pellet chain loses about 15 percent of the initial energy). Similarly, Cocco (2007) compares three bioenergy chains, offering evidence particularly favorable to electrical power generation from biomass (miscanthus and poplar) both in terms of net balances and ratio between output and input energy. Within the framework of the assumptions made (e.g., average yield per hectare and irrigation requirement), it is interesting to observe how energy inputs flow through the chain.

CONCLUDING REMARKS

Energy belongs to and surrounds everyone's life and, probably, both increased con-sciousness and repeated shocks have increased the awareness of this. Inventory theory, thanks to its principles and rationale, may substantially help the understand-ing and the efficient use of this resource. To this end, the present chapter aimed to show how energy is related to stocks and how it may influence them. Industrial cases and examples from supply chains were presented to let the relevant aspects of the inventories, which are related to energy, emerge. The environmental topic was also addressed, this being directly linked to energy in terms of emissions and environ-mental accounting. The whole set of issues proposed shows how the energy-related issues are still to be investigated in the view of inventory theory, opening wide oppor-tunities to researchers and practitioners, with a consequent benefit to the society.

6

Healthcare Supply Chain Management

INTRODUCTION

A recent visit to a local emergency room (ER) motivated one of the coauthors to liter-ally investigate the crucial element of supply chain management (SCM) within the healthcare system. After experiencing eight hours of delays in the ER waiting room and witnessing incredible lags in the medication dispensing process and even further impediments to the delivery of treatment modalities, the researcher became outraged with the thought of a high-performing healthcare system's lack of better supply chain management and service delivery. As a healthcare consumer, this scenario is likely to happen to all of us.

One might contemplate, how does an industry based on customer service fall short in the arena of inventory, patient, and materials management? According to business researcher Vicki Smith-Daniels (2006), in a field where precision is literally a matter of life and death, it seems strange that a crucial supportive function like inventory control and purchasing is often a hit-or-miss process. Healthcare, unlike other indus-tries, has not given supply chain management the detailed attention that it so rightly deserves and needs to ensure patient safety and reduce overall healthcare costs.

Inventory management in the healthcare industry presents several interesting challenges both from a managerial and operational perspective. The stakeholder relationships, product considerations, and managerial and regulatory policies typi-cally seen in healthcare are unique and worth investigation. Before delving into specific inventory control issues or demand characteristics that make healthcare SCM particularly difficult, it is important to recognize the magnitude of this industry.

According to statistics published by the Centers for Medicare and Medicaid Services, healthcare spending topped $2 trillion or 16 percent of the gross domestic product (GDP) in the United States in 2005 (Centers for Medicare and Medicaid Services 2007). In addition, this percentage is projected to increase to 18.7 percent in ten years (Heffer et al. 2005; Catlin et al. 2007) state that healthcare expenditures increase at an annual rate of 6.9 percent. In addition, there has been a shift from public to private healthcare financing in the United States, as well as other countries around the world. Most of these efforts are an attempt to continuously find new ways of both controlling healthcare expenditures and paying for prescribed treatments and pharmaceuticals.

Especially given the current economic crisis, a growing amount of attention is being given to the rising costs of healthcare and specifically pharmaceuticals. Healthcare providers, insurance companies, government agencies, and consum-ers alike are forced to address this issue and to explore alternative methods of cost reduction or cost containment (Culyer 1990; Jönsson and Musgrove 1997; Marmor and Okma 1998). To gain a better understanding of the significance of this issue, it is prudent to first identify the magnitude of healthcare expenditures. According to the Plunkett Research Group (2008), "The health care market in the U.S. in 2007 was made up of hospital care (about $697.5 billion), physician and clinical services ($474.2 billion), prescription drugs ($229.5 billion), nursing home and home health ($190 billion), and other items totaling $668.8 billion."

As shown, the financial aspect of the healthcare and pharmaceutical industries is quite staggering. Much of the research in this field has focused on the relevant costs of healthcare (Organization for Economic Co-operation and Development [OECD] 1994, 1995, 1996; Comas-Herrera 1999; Castles 2004); however, Rothgang et al. (2005) examined data reported by the OECD from 1970 to 2002 to investigate trends in the level of governmental involvement with healthcare systems. Although some shifting has occurred over the years, convergence toward a mixed system of both public and private healthcare seems apparent.

A significant area of healthcare costs is the pharmaceutical area, which represented approximately 10 percent of annual healthcare expenditures in the United States and about $550 billion globally in 2007 (Plunkett Research Group 2008). Despite the size and importance of this industry around the world, especially in developed countries, the area of healthcare SCM and inventory management has been given relatively little attention. Several researchers have estimated that inventory investments in healthcare range between 10 percent and 18 percent of total revenues (Holmgren and Wentz 1982; Jarrett 1998). Any measures taken to control expenditures in this area can have substantial impacts on the overall efficiency of the organization and its supply net-work and, as a result, the profitability of healthcare providers.

In 2003, Guillen and Cabiedes examined the pharmaceutical policies of European Union (EU) countries from the mid-1980s through the 1990s. As explained in their research, the costs of pharmaceuticals continue to increase while countries struggle to find financing to support these drugs. They noted that much of the healthcare services are shaped by the pharmaceutical policies, and they also identified three reasons justifying a focus on pharmaceuticals when examining healthcare supply chains: the reliance of modern medicine on drugs to both prevent and cure sickness, the significance of pharmaceutical expenditures around the world, and the charac-teristics of the pharmaceutical industry (i.e., use of technology, innovation, etc.). Almarsdottir and Traulsen (2005) also identified a number of reasons why pharma-ceuticals deserve extraordinary consideration in controlling inventory. These specific characteristics make the pharmaceutical industry a very powerful force in its own right. As with any industry, the range of products can vary tremendously depending on the market, customer demand, the scope of services, and other managerial decisions. For the purposes of this chapter and the specific research cases we present, our focus is mainly on the supply chain of pharmaceuticals. The stakeholders and their interrelationships, the product characteristics, and the policies employed all have some impact on healthcare SCM and inventory control. We explain some specific conditions and terminology used in healthcare in more detail in the following.

STAKEHOLDERS

Here we summarize some unique factors influencing how healthcare stakeholders interact, how they are controlled, and how they manage operations. A detailed analy-sis is provided in the next section.

Doctors are the primary caregivers in the healthcare system; however, it is impor-tant to recognize that physicians, in many cases, are contracted service providers. They are not actual employees of hospitals in which they work. Although this enables hospitals to expand their service capacities and offer better customer service, they must also relinquish some measure of control to these doctors. Autonomy, as it relates specifically to customer care, is valued above all else by doctors. Patients trust that physicians are prescribing treatments and medicines that will address their individual medical needs. Attempts to restrict the choices or influence the conditions of medical treatment are met with a great deal of resistance.

Another consideration is that, unlike many industries of this size, *hospital admin-istrators* and pharmacy managers have to manage very complicated distribution net-works and inventory control problems without the proper training or educational backgrounds to do so efficiently. This in no way implies that these individuals lack the intelligence to perform these tasks. Most hospital administrators and pharmacy directors are themselves doctors, which means they are highly skilled and educated in medicine; however, they are not the engineers or supply chain professionals who are commonly employed to manage similar systems in other industries.

The hospitals order the majority of their supplies from a selected *group purchas-ing organization (GPO)* that purchases directly from the production companies.

Products

Product formulary is the term used to identify the variety of drugs offered by the hospital pharmacy and is a source of both conflict and cost for the hospital. This formulary is comprised of specific medicines each designed to address a particu-lar medical need, but physicians' opinions may vary on the most effective drugs for satisfying patient requirements. Providing prescription options for the doctors is important, both to the doctors and hospital; however, this increases the number of drugs that must be carried by the hospital pharmacy for patient treatment if it desires to maintain such a high level of customer service. In addition, the product formulary changes quite frequently as physicians' prescribing behavior reacts to advancements in medical research and technology.

It is also important to recognize that pharmaceuticals have a number of other requirements. They must be handled by trained personnel and experts in this field. Extraordinary resources are committed to developing these items, to manufacturing them, and to controlling their distribution and usage. All of these aspects are highly regulated by governments and other regulatory agencies, and they may require addi-tional documentation. Finally, unlike other areas, customers have a limited role in the product selection process. As patients become more aware of alternative treat-ments, they may influence doctors as they prescribe medications; however, more times than not these choices are made for them.

Many of these items are also *perishable* and must be destroyed if not used. Perishable items have a limited shelf life and in many cases have special transpor-tation and storage requirements. Part of the concern with pharmaceuticals is that outdated or expired items may be overlooked and dispensed to patients, which could have potentially disastrous effects both in patient care and public relations. The per-ishable item inventory control problem is a difficult one and has been studied many times using a periodic review approach (see Fries 1975; Nahmias 1975, 1982), with less attention being given to continuous review systems; however, there have been a number of works in this area in recent years (see Weiss 1980; Schmidt and Nahmias 1985; Chiu 1995; Liu and Lian 1999; Lian and Liu 2001). Although these studies provide valuable insight into the management of such products, none of these models have been tested in pharmaceutical inventory control. Given the combination of high costs and perishability of prescription drugs, it seems that more study is warranted as pharmacy managers look for help in setting optimal order policies.

Policies

Substantial efforts are made to regulate the healthcare industry. Government involve-ment is high, as it can provide both oversight of caregivers and funding for care recipients. Previously, healthcare systems have paid little attention to the manage-ment of inventories. However, with the implementation of *diagnosis-related groups (DRGs)* in 1983 by the United States government, these systems have turned their attention to cost containment as a means of increased profitability. The original objective of DRGs was to develop a patient classification system that related types of patients treated to the resources they consumed. Hospital cases are segmented into 1 of approximately 500 groups expected to have similar hospital resource use. DRGs are used to determine how much Medicare pays the hospital, since patients within each category are similar clinically and are expected to use the same level of hospital resources.

Interestingly, public and managerial policies targeted at cost control have failed in many cases to produce the necessary changes in stakeholder behaviors to achieve such outcomes. Efforts to control pharmaceutical prices have provided little relief as drug manufacturers attempt to recover the resources spent research-ing and developing these products. These companies also target physicians and patients with advertising campaigns as they attempt to influence prescribing behavior. Another reason policy has been somewhat ineffective at cost restraint is the conflicting stakeholder goals that appear throughout the supply chain. Doctors and hospital administration are often at odds as they try to balance the issues of prescribing autonomy and product variety. While the doctors want a large variety of brand-name drugs, the hospital management strives to minimize costs in the overall system by seeking generic drugs as substitutes for medicines preferred by physicians. Hospitals and GPOs have different objectives. Hospitals focus on nego-tiating the best prices for a wider selection of drugs from different pharmaceutical companies, while the GPOs are interested in larger orders from only a few phar-maceutical production companies.

Inventory control variables are called *par levels* in healthcare inventory man-agement. The min par level is equivalent to the reorder point: if the inventory level decreases to or below this level, an order is triggered. The max par level is equivalent to the order up level (or base stock).

This chapter focuses specifically on SCM issues from the perspective of the hos-pital. We recognize the importance of other members of the supply network in this industry; however, the subject is simply too voluminous to cover adequately in this setting without restricting the scope somewhat. As such, the authors have selected to focus on supply chain problems as they are viewed by hospitals, which is appropriate given their significance in the supply chain and the costs they incur. In the following sections we identify critical managerial areas that distinguish the healthcare environ-ment from other industries that have received attention in the past. Pharmacy directors are turning their attention to controlling costs in the areas of SCM and pharmaceutical inventory control.

Supply and purchased services account for the second largest cost component for a hospital, and it is clearly recognized that SCM is one of the principal areas for improvement in organiza-tional performance. Supply chain management in hospital systems all over the world shows great variability both in performance and in focus. Such a variabil-ity combined with the growing cost of care and pharmaceuticals determines rel-evant differences in health service efficiency and unacceptable annual increases in healthcare costs.

The remainder of this chapter will serve to address several key areas of healthcare SCM and pharmaceutical inventory management. A review of the relevant manage-rial and quantitative modeling literature is provided. Here attention will be given to both the overall study of healthcare SCM and the quantitative approaches to inventory optimization. The practice of pharmacy operations will be described with specific attention given to the movement and distribution of prescribed medications within a hospital. Solutions focused on addressing SCM challenges will be presented and a specific case of a local hospital will be discussed in more details. Gaps in healthcare SCM and inventory research will be listed and recommendations for SCM research and best inventory control practices are suggested.

MANAGERIAL RESEARCH IN HEALTHCARE SCM

Traditionally researchers have taken two approaches to studying healthcare SCM: analyzing the managerial concerns and evaluating various quantitative models. First, the managerial aspects of such supply chain systems are discussed. The stakehold-ers in the healthcare supply chain and value chain are examined along with the conflicting goals in the system. Thereafter, the most common managerial approaches in healthcare SCM are summarized, including outsourcing and vendor managed inventory (VMI). In existing research, the focal point has primarily been on descrip-tion of the system rather than developing innovative models or performing quantita-tive analyses. However, these descriptive studies are important to documenting the actual healthcare supply practices.

Stakeholders and relationships

The financial aspects of the healthcare industry are significant, but it is also an industry very important to all members of society as it involves a wide range of stakeholders. Burns et al. (2002) examined the healthcare industry for three years in order to investigate its value chain, to uncover significant industry trends, and to identify the major stakeholder groups involved with healthcare services. Evidence showed that both vertical and horizontal integration were present in healthcare. Vertical integration was illustrated by hospitals teaming with insur-ance agencies or ambulatory services to combine various portions of this delivery network. Noticeable horizontal integration manifested in the form of hospitals purchasing other hospitals or in the formation of groups purchasing organiza-tions. A significant result of this research was the identification of the following groups as stakeholders in this industry: (1) payers, (2) fiscal intermediaries, (3) providers, (4) purchasers, and (5) producers. Each of these groups is explained in more detail in the following.

Any person or organization responsible for supplying the funds to pay for medical expenses is identified as a payer. Based on this definition, examples of payers would include government, employers, individuals, and employer coalitions. Insurance agencies, health maintenance organizations (HMOs), and pharmacy benefit manag-ers fall under the category of financial intermediaries. Any group supplying health-care screening, treatment, or any other healthcare-related provisions are considered to be providers. Such entities would be physician offices, hospitals (or hospital sys-tems), surgical centers, alternative and satellite facilities, ambulatory services, and pharmacies. Individuals or groups procuring any of these services are viewed as pur-chasers; however, it is important to note that this category extends beyond the basic consumers of healthcare services.

This group also includes a wide variety of product resellers, independent distributors, pharmaceutical wholesalers, and so forth. The final group is the producers whose responsibility is the manufacturing of healthcare products, equipment, and technology. This includes pharmaceuticals, surgical equip-ment, information technology services, medical devices, and other capital equip-ment found throughout the healthcare system.

Tarabusi and Vickery (1998a, 1998b) stated that attitudes and habits of local phar-macists and physicians must be known for good access to markets. This research identified the importance of cost-containment programs in the pharmaceutical industry by comparing the approaches employed by the United States and countries of the European Union. Globalization and international partnerships have grown as pharmaceutical companies strive to control the research and development costs associated with these drugs.

Value Chains

The notion of value in the healthcare service value chain can be described by the interrelations of relevant stakeholders. Value chains were first introduced by Porter (1985) and are significant marketing tools because they afford managers the oppor-tunity to assess the specific value added by each member of the supply network. Supply chains provide a mechanism for delivering that value to consumers. The original view of a value chain focused on a company's internal activities specifically designed to create value for customers; however, this concept has been extended to include the entire product and service delivery system (Bower and Garda 1985; Evans and Berman 2001).

Pitta and Laric (2004) provided a model of the healthcare value chain and supply chains, as they exist in many practical situations. Figure 5.1 illustrates that this sup-ply chain is not linear or sequential in nature but closely follows the flow of informa-tion through the system. The success of the system or value created are linked to the transfer of quality information as the medical care received by patients relies heavily on information processing.

The first two groups interacting in this network are the patients and physicians. This stage of the process is generally initiated by the patient and provides valuable information necessary to adequately address whatever needs they might have. This research showed that individuals are much more likely to share very personal infor-mation with their healthcare providers when they believe this information is needed for medical purposes and when they trust the confdential nature of the patient– doctor relationship. The next link in the chain is created by the addition of phar-macists and other providers of medical equipment and services. In this stage the pharmacist creates value by further investigating the medical history of patients, specifically as it relates to medications, to determine any potential risks or inter-actions that may result from the addition of new, prescribed drugs. This is a very important step in customer service and patient care.

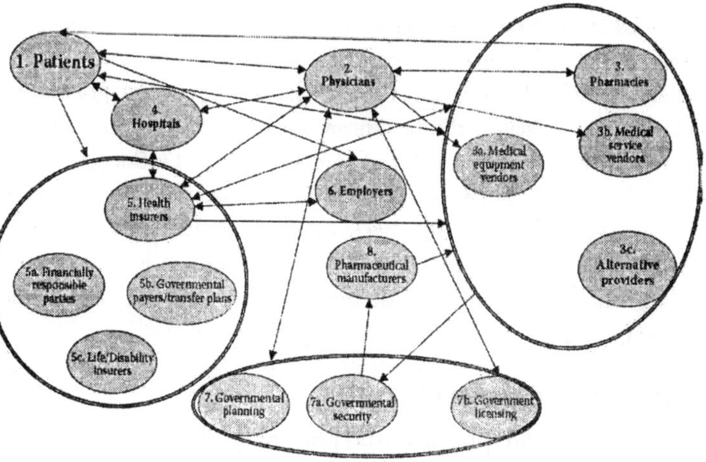

Figure: Stakeholders in the healthcare value chain (Pitta and Laric 2004).

The next addition to the value chain is that of the hospital and the related services and procedures that may be included in diagnosing patient symptoms. As explained by Pitta and Laric (2004), doctors often request that batteries of tests be performed on patients even when symptoms and other indicators suggest a course of treatment. Hospitals create and store vast amounts of medical data for patients, which can be useful going forward. The fifth member of the healthcare value chain is the health insurers, which includes both public and private entities responsible for providing financial support to those receiving care. Since many insurers require a series of diag-nostic tests and related data be completed before approving potentially costly proce-dures, patient data continues to grow. The addition of insuring groups or companies can also be a negative influence on the value chain. As one can see, with the addition of new members to the network and the creation of data at each stage, the healthcare system and participant interactions are becoming more and more complex.

Employers are the sixth group added to create another value chain. In the United States employers are the most often used source of medical insurance for employed persons and their families. Here the value is obtained by negotiating better benefits for groups of people as opposed to those offered to individuals. When the U.S. gov-ernment introduced its federal Medicare and Medicaid programs in the 1960s, it became the largest medical insurance provider in the United States. A result of this involvement is the increasing influence of government regulation and policy in the healthcare industry. As such, government becomes the seventh participant of interest here as it influences various parts of this system. The final member of the model is the pharmaceutical manufacturers. It has already been established that pharmaceu-ticals represent a significant area of cost in the healthcare industry, as well as being the primary means of preventative and curative medical treatment.

STAKEHOLDER CONFLICTS

Physicians and pharmacists/pharmacy directors clash over medications offered by the hospital. The basic conflict here revolves around the issue of product variety versus economies of scale. The doctors have professional and personal preferences that are reflected in their prescription decisions. They value their individual freedom of choice in selecting the medications that they feel best address the specific needs of the patients under their care. Drug manufacturers, sales representatives, and the appearance of new drugs in the market also influence physicians. In contrast, the pharmacy directors pay more attention to the costs associated with specific medica-tions and promote the usage of generic rather than brand drugs when available. They strive to take advantage of economies of scale whenever possible in the selection of drugs offered.

In 2005, Prosser and Walley examined the extent to which cost influenced pre-scribing behaviors of general practitioners (GPs) in the UK healthcare system. According to the authors, primary care organizations, (PCO) involvement has steadily increased as a means of providing more unified, controlled budgets for these physicians, as well as providing a monitoring mechanism of prescribing activities with this cost-containment objective in mind. The primary goal of this investiga-tion was to measure the cost-awareness of doctors and to evaluate the attitudes of these GPs towards cost-restraint policies. Another goal was to determine what effect this managerial objective might have on their professional behavior. In this case the evidence demonstrated that all of the physicians were aware of pharmaceutical costs when prescribing treatments for their patients and felt that these costs should be considered when making prescription choices. However, there appeared to be a great deal of variation in the amount of influence these costs actually had on modifying medical decisions. As expected, physicians identified patient care as their primary focus during the treatment process with cost being a secondary concern.

Prosser and Walley (2007) continued their research in this area and employed qualitative methods to examine the managerial influence of healthcare administra-tors on the prescribing autonomy of general-care practitioners. In general, physician prescribing autonomy has been challenged recently due to the greater sophistication of patients in the ability to direct medical decisions and the increased bureaucratic involvement in service delivery in healthcare. This research showed that the objec-tive of cost-containment presents a formidable obstacle for caregivers striving to offer the highest level of care and individualized service to those they serve.

This analysis showed that managerial involvement will have limited success in influencing GPs' prescribing autonomy. The conclusion was that the GPs directly resisted the attempts administrators made to modify their prescribing behaviors. The GPs maintain it is their responsibility to offer the best medications and treat-ment available to their patients, and that this autonomy is a component of provid-ing individual care. In many cases this is an area of great conflict between doctors and hospital/pharmacy administrators, since larger product formularies desired by doc-tors usually result in higher inventory costs and reduce the opportunity for cost sav-ings. When asked, doctors acknowledged the importance of controlling the costs of pharmaceuticals, but they identified the quality of patient care as being the para-mount objective. Managers placed a great deal of importance on keeping prescribing costs within established budgets.

Another divergence appears between hospitals and the group purchasing orga-nization (GPO) on the issue of product variety. Hospitals focus on negotiating the best prices for a wider selection of drugs. The attention is shown to brand-name medications in most cases. The GPO, on the other hand, strives to minimize costs in the overall system by seeking generic drugs as substitutes for medicines preferred by physicians. Again, a great deal of effort is given to the achievement of economies of scale for demanded items by considering a limited formulary (narrower selection of drugs).

The importance of product standardization for managing costs and improving clinical performance is outlined with respect to physicians' unwillingness to accept product alternatives to branded ones, even in the face of evidence regarding equiva-lence. As such, hospitals persist in the argument for wider drug selections. Both physician and nurse involvement and leadership in product analysis is necessary for successful standardization to occur, and for the provision of metrics pertaining to products and their relationship to the performance of the supply chain.

MANAGERIAL APPROACHES IN HEALTH CARE SCM

In this section of the chapter, we first explore the various strategic approaches that have been pursued in the area of SCM and inventory control. Some of the topics to be discussed are the outsourcing of distribution activities, allowing suppliers to man-age inventory levels at various distribution points, and the use of common statistical techniques to achieve organizational and system goals.

Outsourcing

Kim (2005) presents an explanation of an integrated SCM system developed to specifically address issues related to pharmaceuticals in the healthcare sector. Many industries have recognized the importance of improved information sharing through-out the supply chain, and this work considers it as the most critical success factor. Here the supply network is composed of pharmaceutical companies, a wholesaler, and hospitals. The hospital's operating procedures and policies were reviewed to determine system requirements in an effort to improve the management efficiencies of the supply chain.

Jayaraman et al. (2000) present several tools and practical ideas to improve the flow of materials in a small healthcare facility. Traditional techniques, such as Pareto diagrams and department–product–type (DPT) matrices, were employed to track item flow and identify sources of errors or difficulties. Researchers suggested sev-eral procedural and policy changes be implemented to reduce inventory manage-ment problems. Landry and Beaulieu (2000) present a descriptive study of logistics systems at hospitals from three countries—France, the Netherlands, and the United States—to identify the best practices for replenishment policies, equipment, and handling technologies.

Nicholson et al. (2004) compared the inventory costs and service levels of an internally managed three-echelon distribution network and contrasted it with an outsourced two-echelon distribution network. Their research revealed that a general trend in healthcare is the outsourcing of specific organizational activities, inven-tory management, and materials distribution to "expert" third-party providers. To this point very little attention has been given to inventory management; however, changes in pharmaceutical regulations and the formation of the DRGs prompted a shift in approach.

When outside entities can provide needed products or services more efficiently than internal departments, it can prove very rewarding. In other instances, outside providers may demonstrate the ability to provide the desired products or services at a higher level of quality than an organization may be capable of achieving (Lunn 2000). A long-term benefit of outsourcing is the ability to reduce the number of sup-pliers in the system, which will eventually lower the procurement costs for the down-stream members of the supply chain. As such, the short-term benefits of increased efficiency and higher quality, along with the long-term benefit of lower procurement costs, make outsourcing a logical approach to overall cost containment in the health-care industry and consistent with current practices in inventory management (Veral and Rosen 2001).

Outsourcing decisions in this area are motivated by three factors: the magni-tude of investment, the impact on service quality and delivery, and the availability of qualified service providers. Quality of service is arguably the paramount goal of healthcare providers (Li and Benton 1996), and it has been suggested that out-sourcing various functions allows organizations to improve the quality of its inter-nal operations. Jarrett (1998) identified several areas in which providers were able to improve internal performance. Patient care was improved, which can influence customer satisfaction and perceptions related to the quality of service provided by an organization. As the expertise develops and the capabilities of external sources grow, outsourcing becomes an increasingly attractive option. Another motivation for healthcare providers considering outsourcing the inventory management functions are the "success" stories similar to those described by Rivard-Royer et al. (2002).

Rivard-Royer et al. (2002) examined the changing role of distributors in the healthcare industry in recent years by investigating how operational processes had changed at a Quebec hospital As reported by Jarrett (1998), the ever-increasing desire to control healthcare costs have led hospitals to reevaluate many of their previous policies and operations. Inventory control is a logical area where substan-tial gains can be realized. Pharmaceuticals represent a significant cost equation related to both hospital inventory and quality patient care. As such, many hospi-tals and hospital systems have focused on this specific material management issue when restraining costs. U.S. pharmaceutical distributors were offering "stockless" replenishment where the distributors would prepackage items based on usage at individual care units (CUs), and would often provide direct delivery of drugs to these CUs (Henning 1980). By employing such a system, the distributors share in the benefits and risks associated with pharmaceutical savings or costs. The reduc-tion in pharmaceutical inventory located at the hospital central pharmacy saved hospitals valuable resources, and the shifting of duties from the pharmacies to the distributors allowed the hospitals to reduce their workforce. Another improvement was noticed in enhanced customer service. However, as one would expect, a critical success factor in achieving any benefits from such a relationship and process is the continuous exchange of information between the point of use and supplier (Bolton and Gordon 1991).

SUPPLY COORDINATION AND VENDOR MANAGED INVENTORY

According to Rivard-Royer and colleagues (2002), by the late 1990s stockless replen-ishment was a thing of the past as hospitals sought a balance between the amount of effort being spent in replenishing hospital inventories and the hospitals' inventory savings. The hospital involved with this study employed a hybrid approach since high-demand items were purchased in bulk (at the case level) for delivery directly to the patient CUs from distributors, and low-volume items were handled by the phar-macy central storage (CS). For these low-demand items, the CS was charged with breaking down the bulk purchases into smaller quantities for distribution to the vari-ous CUs as items were used. However, this hybrid approach was found to have lim-ited benefits to both the hospital and distributors. Distributors were asked to perform additional work without receiving a comparable level of additional revenue. The hos-pital was still unpacking, repacking, and preparing drugs for distribution to the CUs and failed to realize significant workload reductions as a result of this replenishment approach. Overall, the gains were very limited in this particular study.

One managerial shift has been to vendor managed inventory (VMI), which has been shown to have benefits in SCM related to enhanced material handling efficiency. Other trends in supply coordination have included online procurement sys-tems and the availability of real-time information sharing. These advances have demonstrated an ability to reduce total pharmaceutical inventory by more than 30 percent (Kim 2005). In addition, the improved information sharing throughout the supply chain allowed for more timely and accurate inventory data, which resulted in better demand forecasts and materials management.

The research of Meijboom and Obel (2007) investigated supply chain coordina-tion in a global pharmaceutical organization. The authors looked at the issues facing a pharmaceutical company with a multilocation and multistage operations structure. Simulations are used to explore various coordination activities focusing specifically on "tactical control" in the firm. Their results suggest that a functionally organized operations structure will be unsuccessful in a multilocation, multistage environment. According to the authors, firms can employ one of two methods. They can either use a centralized approach relying heavily on information systems, or maintain a decen-tralized structure that relies on transfer prices as the coordination device.

Lapierre and Ruiz (2007) developed different modeling approaches, a cost mini-mization model and a balanced schedule model, for improving healthcare inventory management by examining the impact of scheduling decisions on the coordination of supply activities while recognizing inventory capacities. Specifically, the researchers concentrated on timing issues ranging from the purchasing and delivery of inventory to the work schedules and job assignments of employees. A significant outcome of this work is the promotion of coordinated activities throughout the purchasing and procurement process such that schedules can be expanded to include more specific details for improving the resource utilization across the organization. The models were tested in a hospital in Montreal, and hospital managers believed that the sched-ules generated by the models were both efficient and well balanced.

Quantitative Modeling in Healthcare SCM and Inventory Control

One of the primary goals of our initiative is to model and improve inventory manage-ment practices being employed by hospitals. There are a number of relevant inventory models in the current body of supply chain literature that are related to this effort, and those models are examined and described herein. In this review most of the attention will focus on models addressing multi-item, single-location, and multiechelon coordination given the unique conditions germane to the industry considered. Inventory models have been collected that have been formulated to address health-care problems, have been applied, or have a high relevance to healthcare-related inventory management.

After summarizing the specifics of inventory control policies and planning frame-works in hospital pharmacies, the demand specifics are described in this section. A major portion of this section is devoted to inventory modeling; models of specific interest are multi-item–single-location and single-item–multilocation models. Literature associated with each of these modeling approaches is discussed, as well as how these models have been employed in the past.

Efficiently managing pharmaceutical inventory systems requires another approach than the continuous review reorder point model. There are at least three limitations for using the continuous replenishment model in the context of healthcare supply systems: (1) the model does not account for the limited human resources; (2) it does not account for physical storage capacities, particularly the one at the CS level, which is critical in most hospitals; and (3) the decisions are only based on costs, not accounting for inventory control activities and their restricted capacity. Each of these limitations is elaborated on next.

Continuous replenishment inventory management is usually not applicable in hospitals since visits to CUs take a lot of the employees' time. To make it more efficient, tours are made such that several CUs are visited consecutively for rounds of stock control or supply distribution. The *periodic replenishment* model seems more appropriate for healthcare organizations, as each CU is replenished according to a schedule instead of when reaching a reorder point. However, with this inventory management approach, the frequencies of the visits are determined based on the order period and the economic order quantity (EOQ). Storage capacities at CUs and the CS are important factors when deciding how frequent a CU should be replen-ished and how frequent a supplier should be called. An undersized CS and open shelves able to contain very limited quantities of the voluminous products is often the reality most hospitals have to face. This situation calls for more frequent orders to suppliers and keeping more stocks at the CU than those suggested by the EOQ model in order to satisfy requirements and respect capacities. In that context, CU's stocks are kept higher to compensate for a small CS. Thus, greater volumes of items can be stored onsite by keeping these extra quantities. Another reason for keeping more stock in the overall system is that stockouts are time expensive for the supply service that needs to make extra emergency visits, internally referred to as hot-picks, to CUs, but also for the medical staff members who waste their time making extra calls to the supply department or chasing the products at other CUs.

One of the distinct features of materials management in a hospital is the use of a periodic review par level (or order-up to level) servicing approach. A major issue in setting par levels for various items in a healthcare setting is that these levels tend to reflect the desired inventory levels of the patient caregivers rather than the actual inventory levels needed in a department over a certain period (Prashant 1991). In most cases these par levels are experience-based and politically driven, rather than data driven. This poses a problem for warehouse managers, since the inventory they hold is typically based on aggregate hospital demands, while requirements of departments when aggregated are not in line with such estimates. The literature analyzing the set-ting of optimal par levels and review periods for multiple echelons draws upon prior work in multiechelon inventory systems, which are discussed in the next sections.

On the quantitative side, among one of the first healthcare inventory models was published by Michelon et al. (1994) who developed a tabu search algorithm for scheduling the distribution operations in a hospital. In their application, the number of replenishment visits is given a priori, and the problem consists of finding the schedule that minimizes the number of carriers given several time windows and practical constraints. Another investigation concentrating on this type of inventory control situation was performed by Banerjea-Brodeur et al. (1998) who looked at an application of a routing model to match the different CUs to be visited by a laundry department in a hospital. Here the authors used a combination of quantitative tech-niques and common sense to minimize the number of routes while respecting the volume capacity constraint of a cart.

Supply chain management can be fitted into a planning framework. Vissers et al. (2001) defined a planning framework for hospitals. One of the primary objectives of this research was to balance service and efficiency throughout the organization. As identified by the investigators, there are three characteristics that ft hospital produc-tion control settings. They are as follows: (1) a demand that is, generally speaking, larger than supply; (2) restrictions on supply defined by contracting organizations; and (3) higher patient expectations on service quality (Vissers et al 2001). As with many organizations, the quandary then becomes how to maximize resources while still achieving higher levels of customer service. The developed framework consists of fve levels of planning and control: patient planning and control, patient group planning and control, resources planning and control, patient volumes planning and control, and strategic planning (Vissers et al. 2001). The researchers describe the framework, as well as explain instances where current hospital policies and practices deviate from their suggestions and where changes may benefit the organization.

Another attempt is to include SCM into an enterprise resource planning (ERP) framework. Implementation of ERP in healthcare is very challenging due to the spe-cial characteristics to consider. Van Merode et al. (2004) explain the planning func-tion of the hospital environment and identify facets of the healthcare industry that make ERP implementations and utilization more difficult. Some attention is given to explaining areas in which ERP can or cannot be used. According to the authors, hospital functions should be divided into "a part that is concerned only with deter-ministic processes and a part that is concerned with non-deterministic processes" (van Merode et al. 2004). It is their contention that the deterministic processes can be handled very well by ERP.

Demand Specifics for Hospital Pharmacy

The usage of pharmaceutical products in hospitals has specific characteristics. Typically, 40 percent to 60 percent are high-demand items that are relatively easy to handle based on usage statistics. However, much care is to be taken on the frequent changes in the medications used, and on the so-called formulary changes. New items come frequently, and an initial qualitative forecast is required. A large proportion of the items are only rarely used, and the usage times and quantities are frequently changing. Another group of items is used by patients for only a few days and finished afterward. Here the autocorrelation of the demand time series is challenging to consider.

Intermittent demand refers to the usage pattern of items that have extended time gaps separating irregular or sporadic periods of demand. If the quantities of the usage are also variable, we have the so-called lumpy demand that is a major challenge in pharmacy inventory management. The study of intermittent and lumpy demand has typically been approached from either a forecasting or inventory control perspective, with a number of studies incorporating both of these areas to examine practical issues related to inventory system performance. The body of work discussed in this section provides examples of this.

Sani and Kingsman (1997) provide a good review and compare various periodic inventory policies like the normal approximation (Roberts 1962), Naddor's heuristic (Naddor 1980), power approximation (Ehrhardt 1979), and several others. In addi-tion, a variety of forecasting methods were reviewed with the authors attempting to determine which are best for low- and intermittent-demand items. Before discuss-ing specific inventory control approaches or models, it is important to recognize two fundamental notations commonly used in this literature. The minimum inven-tory parameter, or the reorder point, is commonly denoted as s, while the maxi-mum inventory parameter, or the order-up-to value, is represented by S. In situations where item demand appears to be low or intermittent, variations of the (s, S) form of the periodic review inventory control system have been promoted as the optimal approach to inventory management. As the authors state in their review, forecasting demand for such items can also prove very challenging.

The research presented by Sani and Kingsman (1997) examines the management of spare parts for agricultural machinery, which includes many items with seasonal demand characteristics displaying vastly different demand from summer to winter months. After examining the various (*s*, *S*) inventory policies with respect to annual inventory costs and customer service levels, Ehrhardt's (1979) power approximation proved to be a good inventory system for managing items with low overall demand. This method not only scored well in evaluations of cost minimization but also offered reasonable service levels for items with low to medium demand. From the compari-sons, it seems that the Croston estimator (Croston 1972) is one simple forecasting method that performs adequately in most cases (using the exponentially smoothed interdemand interval, updated only if demand occurs). One surprising result was that a basic twelve-month moving average of demand yielded adequate forecast-ing results when examining both annual costs and service level, with exponential smoothing performing the worst on this measure; however, exponential smooth-ing performed best on the customer service level measure alone. It is important to note that both of the aforementioned techniques were utilized: updates every review period and the Croston forecast. Finally, the authors concluded that achieving cus-tomer service levels greater that 95 percent for lumpy demand items is impossible unless high materials stocks are kept as a means to satisfy this objective.

Hollier et al. (2005) developed a modified (*s*, *S*) inventory model to address cost control issues specific to lumpy demand patterns. This approach integrated a maximum issue quantity restriction and a critical inventory position as constraints influencing the inventory control policy. Here the primary objective was to minimize the system replenishment costs. These authors applied two algorithms, one being a tree search and the other a genetic-based algorithm to optimize the decision vari-ables. The numerical examples and results illustrate the benefits of employing such algorithms, as well as demonstrate the utility of the maximum issue quantity and critical inventory position constraints when managing lumpy demand items.

Syntetos and Boylan (2006) employ simulation models to provide an evalua-tion of various forecasting techniques, specifically simple moving average, single exponential smoothing, Croston's estimator, and a new technique introduced in their paper, when handling lumpy or intermittent demand items. Service level and stock volume were evaluated using a number of performance measures related to customer service and inventory costs. In this case the authors reported that the new estimator they developed outperformed other forecasting techniques as an inventory control method; however, it is important to recognize that the simple moving average technique yielded favorable results as well compared to the other two methods.

MULTI-ITEM, SINGLE-LOCATION MODELS FOR PHARMACY INVENTORIES

We found few papers that applied multi-item models to control healthcare invento-ries. Dellaert and van de Poel (1996) derived a simple inventory rule, a (*R*, *s*, *c*, *S*) model, for helping buyers at a university hospital in the Netherlands. The notations of *s* and *S* were as previously defined. Here R represents the length of the review period (time between orders) and *c* is the can-order level. Since most items have a joint sup-plier and the orders for a certain supplier are always placed on the same day of the week, they extended an EOQ model to a so-called (*R*, *s*, *c*, *S*) model, in which the values of the control parameters *s*, *c*, and *S* are determined in a simplistic manner. This approach resulted in substantial gains, which were observed in improved ser-vice levels, reductions in supplier orders, smaller total inventory levels and holding costs, and substantially lower system costs, for the participating hospital.

However, we could not find other multi-item inventory applications in healthcare. We summarize next the models that seem to have the best application potential for this specific area. The majority of results for the multi-item problem are for the deterministic demand case where the sizes and the multiproduct sequence of orders have to be determined. The problem is known to be NP-complete (nondeterministic polynomial time complete) and therefore many heuristics have been proposed. For an overview on the approaches, see Gallego et al. (1996), Hariga and Jackson (1996), and Minner and Silver (2005). The early investigations in stochastic multiproduct inventory problems were gen-erated by Veinott (1965), Ignall (1966), and Ignall and Veinott (1969). Later, in the study of Beyer et al. (2001), the researchers examined the management of multiple items with a warehousing (storage) constraint, which was based on the early model of Ignall and Veinott (1969), and generated results for finite-horizon and infinite-horizon discounted-cost problems. This work demonstrates optimal policies suitable for the various conditions that occur in healthcare.

Ohno and Ishigaki (2001) examined a continuous review inventory system for multiple items exhibiting compound Poisson demands and created a new algorithm for determining the optimal control policy. This alternative method was derived using the policy iteration method (PIM) and resulted in a substantial decrease in processing time needed to evaluate and improve the optimal policy. In addition, the new algorithm was tested using three joint ordering policies.

Minner and Silver (2005) analyzed the stochastic demand, continuous review lot-size coordination problem for Poisson demand, and negligible replenishment lead times. A formulation as a semi-Markov decision problem was presented to find the optimal replenishment policy and several heuristics were suggested and tested in a numerical study. However, the results only apply for pure Poisson demand and cycle inventories (i.e., without safety stocks). With the assumption of negligible lead times, safety stocks here serve to avoid the negative consequences of transaction sizes that exceed available inventory rather than covering against demand uncertainty over the replenishment lead time.

In a recent paper, Minner and Silver (2007) analyzed a replenishment decision problem where each replenishment has an associated setup cost and inventories are subject to holding costs. The solution of this trade-off results in order batch sizes. The warehouse space for keeping inventories is limited, which generally restricts these batch sizes. A second aspect of their analysis is that demands are random, here being modeled by a compound-Poisson demand process. This further complicates the anal-ysis because now safety stocks and cycle stocks share the limited warehouse space.

Single-item, Multilocation Models: Multiechelon Coordination in Pharmacy

The literature analyzing the setting of optimal par levels and review periods for multiple echelons draws upon prior work in multiechelon inventory systems, which are discussed next. One of the first investigations in the area of multiechelon distribution networks was performed by Allen (1958), who attempted to optimally redistribute stock among several locations. Since then, numerous works extended this model (see Simpson 1959; Krishnan and Rao 1965; Das 1975; Hoadley and Heyman 1977). Another significant effort in this area was conducted by Clark and Scarf (1963), as it was the first study that attempted to generate and depict an optimal inventory policy in a multipe-riod, multiechelon, distribution model involving uncertain demand. Other research in this area has focused on the setting of optimal lot sizes and inventory safety stocks in a multiechelon supply chain (Deuermeyer and Schwarz 1981; Eppen and Schrage 1981; Nahmias and Smith 1994).

Sinha and Matta (1991) and Rogers and Tsubakitani (1991) present modeling stud-ies in this research domain. Both studies focused on two-echelon inventory systems employing periodic review under stochastic demand with fixed lead times. Rogers and Tsubakitani concentrated on finding the optimal par values for the lower echelon such that the penalty costs were minimized. A budget value acted as a constraint of the maximum inventory investment. The optimal par level is achieved by utiliz-ing a critical ratio that is adjusted by the Lagrange multiplier subject to the budget constraint. Sinha and Matta focused on minimizing the holding costs of multiple products at both echelon levels with the presence of penalty costs at the lower ech-elon. Similarly, the results demonstrated that the optimal par values for the lower echelon items were obtained using a critical ratio; however, the holding cost function provided a method for generating the optimal values for the upper echelon.

Nicholson et al. (2004) extend the work of Rogers and Tsubakitani (1991) and Sinha and Matta (1991) by considering a three-echelon inventory system. Specifically, this research concentrated on the healthcare sector and sought to compare an inter-nally managed three-echelon system to an outsourced two-echelon distribution system. Comparisons focused on inventory costs and service levels. The results suggest that outsourcing the targeted functions yielded lower inventory costs without sacrificing customer service. As mentioned previously, the use of periodic review par level servic-ing at the departmental level (i.e., at the individual care units) is a unique characteristic to hospital material management;

however, it is important to note that the central phar-macy often operates in a similar manner utilizing another set of par values reflective of aggregate inventory requirements. Zhu et al. (2005) found similar results in their study by using numerical simulations and sensitivity analysis of two models. Like that of Nicholson et al. (2004), this work demonstrated cost savings with high service levels for the two-echelon distribution network where item demands were monitored by the distributor and delivered directly to the departments for use, as opposed to orders being routed through the CS as they would be in a three-echelon system.

Some models consider the case of lost sales. Nahmias and Smith (1994) examine a two-echelon supply chain where stockouts can penalize the retailer in cases where customers are unwilling to wait for their orders to be filled. The authors assume instantaneous deliveries from the warehouse to the retailer, which is often not the case in practice. Andersson and Melchiors (2001) executed a similar study that allowed for excess demand to be handled using back orders. The supply chain in this work was comprised of one warehouse with multiple retail outlets being serviced. Demand here is independent Poisson processes, and lead times are considered con-stant. The heuristic developed by the authors provides a mechanism to evaluate this type of supply network on elements of cost and service level.

Another research study examining the lost sales case is that of Hill et al. (2007), which looked at inventory control in a single-item, two-echelon system with a con-tinuous review policy. Again, a central warehouse services several independent retailers and then has its stock replenished by an external supplier. The system oper-ates such that any excess customer demand at the retailer can be filled from the ware-house provided the item is in stock; however, any items that are not in stock result in lost sales. Lead time for the retailer is equal to the transportation time required to move the item from the warehouse to the specific retail outlet.

The influence of order risk was examined by Seo et al. (2001) in a two-echelon distribution system. They claim that the service policies should reflect the avail-ability of real-time stock information. Their model adjusts the reorder time on the basis of an approximated order risk, which is associated with orders that are filled immediately versus those that are delayed. Results show that this order risk policy performed well when warehouse lead time was short, where item demand was low, and where there was an intermediate number of retailers in the supply chain.

Axsäter (2003) used an approximation technique to optimize inventory control in a two-echelon distribution network. Items displayed stochastic demand, and the system relied on a continuous review (*R*, *Q*) policy. In this situation, holding costs at all locations and back-order costs at the retailer were assumed to be linear. Axsäter presents a simplified method for estimating reorder points by using normal approxi-mations for demand at both the retailer and the warehouse. Lee and Wu (2006) examined a simplified two-echelon supply chain system comprised of one supplier and one retailer. Here the retailer has a choice between two restocking policies: tra-ditional methods (such as an EOQ or periodic review approach) or a statistical pro-cess control (SPC)–based method. The results show support for the SPC method in addressing inventory variation issues and in reducing order backlogs. Benefits are apparent in the areas of demand management and inventory control, which leads the authors to suggest this as an alternative method for managing supply chain and inventory costs.

Practical Solutions for Inventory Management of Pharmaceuticals in Hospitals

The following section discusses some practical solutions to issues facing managers when dealing with prescription drugs. The manner in which hospital pharmacies and drug distribution/dispensation historically occurred is examined. First we discuss the traditional method and then the current trends. We also describe the dilemmas hospital personnel face in filling prescribed medications and the alternative methods employed to satisfy drug orders. The managerial predicaments associated with man-aging skilled labor in this system are also explained in limited detail. We close the section with the summary of the main results of a project targeted to provide deci-sion support to inventory management of a hospital pharmacy.

Traditionally, hospital pharmacies operated in a centralized manner. Medications were stored in a central pharmacy and then distributed by pharmacy technicians using dose carts to make deliveries to the various hospital floors and CUs. A setup such as this requires large amounts of inventory to be stored in a single location while also allowing for quick, easy access to items. These technicians were charged with the task of moving the various medicines in the correct amounts or in individual cassettes for each patient. These dose carts contained individual cassettes of medica-tions for each patient, which the nurse or caregiver was then charged with adminis-tering to the patient. If for some reason the patient's drug order changed, a special trip would be required to retrieve the necessary medications and then return to the CU. Thus, changes in medication or dosage may have taken hours to satisfy, result-ing in time delays in care, increased labor requirements, and an overall increase in system costs associated with wasteful or excess operations.

To avoid prolonged delays in administering medications, it was common practice for nurses to borrow a medication from another patient. That resulted in additional problems in the distribution process and potentially dangerous situations where patients may have received the improper medications. Other difficulties associated with the specific pharmaceutical types existed. Specifically, federal and state regula-tions require a variety of documentation associated with the dispensation of narcotic drugs. From the time a narcotic is delivered to the hospital until it is administered to the patient, the drug must be tracked by the hospital and is surrounded by a number of tasks such as checking the ordered medication against the patient's medical record, searching for narcotic keys to the cabinet, documenting for administrative records, and reconciling narcotic records after each shift. This example demonstrates some specific challenges in controlling and monitoring items in healthcare SCM. Pharmacists are highly paid professionals being asked to spend long amounts of time handling excessive documentation and a labor-intensive drug dispensation and distribution process rather than practicing pharmaceutical care. The opportunity to reduce repetitive and tiresome tasks was very appealing to administrators and phar-macists alike. As such, the ability to automate these processes and take advantage of computer information systems was valued by stakeholders.

Hospitals have typically employed a variety of methods and policies to resolve pharma-ceutical inventory management issues. A few of the more prominent solutions are dis-cussed in this section to demonstrate the modern approaches seen in industry. Specifically, outsourcing, VMI, and information technology (IT)–based solutions are presented.

Outsourcing

As described in the previous literature review, outsourcing has been widely used in the healthcare industry. Regardless of the specific product, entering into partner-ships with suppliers and distributors for the purposes of combining services have generated benefits for the healthcare providers (see, e.g., Li and Benton 1996; Jarrett 1998; Lunn 2000; Veral and Rosen 2001; Nicholson et al. 2004). The magnitude of resources linked to pharmaceutical inventory and its management, the desire to shift or reduce pharmacy workloads, and the opportunity to refocus resources on patient care make this an appealing proposition for healthcare providers. However, as shown by Rivard-Royer et al. (2002), all parties must benefit from such arrangements to provide long-term gains.

VMI

Another trend is the growing usage of VMI strategies (Kim 2005). This a specific type of outsourcing in which pharmaceutical inventories located at various distribu-tion locations (i.e., at the CUs) around the hospital are monitored by the supplier, in this case the pharmaceutical company or distributor, and replenished as needed. Currently, several hospitals employ a continuous review (s, S) inventory control pol-icy. When demand for an item reaches a predetermined minimum level (s), an order is automatically generated and transmitted directly to the supplier. The supplier, in turn, ships the amount necessary to refill the distribution centers to the maximum quantity (S). Depending on the specific circumstances, materials can be either sent to the pharmacy for repacking and distribution or sent directly to the point of service, which bypasses the pharmacy entirely.

IT-based Inventory Management Solutions

Information systems play a significant role in all of the aforementioned suggested approaches; however, they are perhaps even more critical in the next solution. Perini and Vermeulen (1994) reviewed a number of devices (e.g., Lionville CDModule, Meditrol, Argus, MedStation™, Sure-Med, and Selectrac-Rx) focused on the dis-pensing of medicines located around the hospital in the patient care unit with the purpose of replacing the traditional dosage carts used by pharmacies, and to shift control of locally stored pharmaceutical inventories and controlled substances to caregivers at the point of use. Inventory stored in the CUs offer caregivers the opportunity to dispense medications quickly to patients; however, restocking these units can take extra time. These medication-management machines are designed to offer financial and practical advantages over traditional operating procedures where inventories are stored in a central pharmacy and then distributed by dose carts as needed. Another benefit of using these local devices is the ability to quickly create, store, and access point-of-service patient information, which can also expedite the documentation requirements associated with drugs. The technology employed by these solutions enhances operating efficiency and facilitates customer care by low-ering the risk of patients receiving incorrect medications. Regardless of the specific solution, these systems usually offer pharmaceutical administrators the ability to reduce inventory carrying and other costs, to improve billing and usage informa-tion, and to increase staff productivity by creating a highly integrated, data-driven information flow. In this section we summarize the main results of a project targeted to provide decision support to inventory management of a hospital pharmacy. The available equipment and current management system are described first; the new quantitative models developed by the authors of this chapter are summarized next; and the managerial decision support potentials close the section (see the details in Kelle et al. 2008).

Pharmaceutical Distribution Equipment and Control Case

The drugs are stored in the local depots (Pyxis© MedStations) in close to a hundred different areas of the hospital. Each area has a different selection of drugs. The Pyxis MedStation registers each transaction date, the quantity of demand (withdrawal), each delivery (refill), and the actual inventory level. It is connected to the central depot (Tallyst© system) electronically.

As the inventory level decreases to a reorder point (min par level) an automatic order is triggered by the local depot. The order quantity is determined by the order-up-to level (max par level). The par levels can be selected and fixed for each drug. Currently, the par levels are based on so-called experiences, but no modeling or optimization is involved in setting these control values. The central depot satisfies the order within a day. Shortage in the central depot is rare, and in that case the wholesaler (GPO) refills within a day or an emergency supply is provided. The demand for each drug is uncertain. The daily usage data is available for each drug for the period of one year. High service level is essential in the drug supply. In case of a shortage at a local depot (Pyxis), a very costly emergency delivery is nec-essary. The refill from the central depot is also constrained and expensive because a highly educated pharmacist must supervise it. One major goal of the pharmacy management is to minimize the number of refills per day. If the refill per day is very large, it cannot be done in two shifts, and to provide an extra shift is difficult and costly.

The capacity (the total space) of the Pyxis systems is limited. It consists of draw-ers. Each drawer is subdivided by spacers that can be relocated so different cubicles are constructed and assigned to each drug. Different drugs cannot be stored in the same cubicle. The total room for the cubicles is fixed. The inventory holding cost factor is not a major concern for the hospital because the wholesaler is financing it. However, we will include inventory holding cost later and will examine the effect of its consideration.

The main goals of the management are to:

- Provide a high service level for each drug
- Minimize the total number of expected refills (orders) per day for a Pyxis
- Use the limited space of a local depot (Pyxis) in the best way by subdivid-ing it to separate areas (cubicles) for each drug

The decision variables are the reorder point (the min par level) and the order up level (max par level) for each drug. The average daily demand and the standard deviation of the daily demand can be calculated from historical data. Also, we know the storage space requirement for a unit of each drug and the maximum storage space in a Pyxis.

Quantitative Modeling Issues

We formulated different optimization models. In the first one we minimize the total num-ber of expected refills (orders) per day for a Pyxis MedStation subject to two constraints:

- The service level for each drug is a fixed high level

- The total space needed for the maximum inventory level *(Si)* for each drug is not more than the available total space of the Pyxis MedStation

We have some challenges that are not handled in literature including the large dimensions (around 250 drugs in a Pyxis) and demand uncertainty; the service-level constraint combined with space constraint; and the fast solution and simple sensitiv-ity analysis requirement. For this reason we provided a simplified model and solution for the optimization problem. We consider the two constraints (service level and space) and the two sets of decision variables separately, and solve it iteratively using power approximation (see Ehrhardt 1979) for handling the service level.

In the first step we set the reorder point, based on required service level, for each item of a Pyxis station, using power approximation formulae. The achieved service level depends also on the reorder level, which depends on the cost factor. We can show that the optimal order quantity implicitly (by the analogy of the EOQ model) sets the optimal cost rate. We need to apply an iterative solution starting with an initial estimate. We can select the initial estimate for the reorder point without safety stock consideration as the expected lead-time demand and provide the initial estimate. In the second step we minimize the number of orders per day under the space constraint considering the reorder points set before (see the details in Kelle et al. 2008).

MANAGERIAL DECISION SUPPORT

The result shows that the optimal allocation of the space for the order quantities of the items is proportional with the square root of the demand over space rate. It is proportional to the available free space (space remaining for cycle stock, after taking out the space requirement for the reorder point stock). The reorder point stock is the sum of expected demand during the lead time plus the safety stock. The lead time is the refill time.

The trade-off between the number of orders and free storage space for a given service level can be expressed in a simple functional form depending on the remain-ing free storage space for cycle stock (above safety stock), so our function implicitly includes the service level trade-off. For a fxed service level, the trade-off curve has a hyperbola shape that is shifted to the right (higher space requirement) with increasing service level requirement. This property allows a simple trade-off analy-sis including managerial questions such as:

- Service level versus expected number of daily orders (worker capacity requirement)
- Number of drugs stored (formulary) versus service level
- Storage volume versus service level and worker capacity requirement
- Extension of formulary versus additional worker capacity requirement

SUMMARY AND RESEARCH PROSPECTIVE

This chapter was introduced with a scenario of an ER supply problem which, with variations in details, will possibly be experienced at some time by individuals who read this book. The researchers have presented a broad view of characteristics that make healthcare supply chain management a very intriguing area of study. The health-care industry operates in a unique manner in that it has a number of special constraints all being enforced at once. Specifically, the focus is on maintaining a high level of ser-vice and controlling costs, as opposed to reducing them. In traditional supply chains, these variables are manipulated to achieve the optimal economic operating setting. However, in the healthcare industry, trade-offs are not as easily achieved. Furthermore, medicines are special products as noted by Almarsdottir and Traulsen (2005).

First, the significance of the healthcare industry is demonstrated by the provided cost breakdown and by conveying the importance of affordable, quality care to the described stakeholders. Second, a review of current literature in this specific area is presented. It is important to recognize that the need for continued research in this domain is warranted. Many of the proposed inventory control models have yet to be tested in a healthcare setting or have not been evaluated under conditions of vary-ing demand types (i.e., intermittent or autocorrelated demand). Finally, traditional operations of hospital pharmacies are described and contrasted with some common managerial approaches seen in practice today. Specifically, outsourcing and VMI in some form are used extensively to alleviate strains on pharmacy resources and mate-rial management issues. Information technology plays a significant role in determin-ing the success of these solutions, but the widespread use of materials-management machinery in hospitals and throughout hospital systems makes this task even more daunting. It seems clear that investments in these resources will continue in the future as hospitals increase their reliance on the information created and controlled by these machines.

The body of work in healthcare SCM provides a good foundation for further study in this area; however, there are a number of gaps that should be addressed. The managerial literature in this area has generally focused on identifying stakeholders and relationships within the healthcare system and distribution network, with other works exploring trends in funding mechanisms and the influence of cost-containment policies on this industry. Very few best practices and benchmarks have been identified for healthcare managers to use as performance guidelines or indicators. We believe that future research targeting the changing relationships of stakeholders and supply chain partners should be pursued to offer valuable insight into the impacts of outsourcing and other supply chain coordination techniques currently in use. Both outsourcing and VMI are used extensively in modern healthcare supply chains, but little is known about the influence these business relationships have had on organiza-tions or their operations outside of cost. As many hospitals employ outsourcing and IT-based medicine distribution machines as a means of simplifying their inventory management systems, they are actually adding to the complexity of their pharma-ceutical distribution network. To this point, little is known about these arrangements or their implications.

In addition to the managerial literature, there are a number of gaps in the quanti-tative modeling research as well. Although there are a number of inventory control models that may be applicable to pharmaceutical management within hospitals, many of these models have yet to be tested in this setting. The special product characteris-tics mentioned in the earlier part of the chapter present unique challenges to manag-ing such inventories and warrant further study. In addition, the use of the medicine machines at local care units (like Pyxis machines) suggests that multiple constraints must be considered when determining the control values employed at both the local and central storage areas.

Service level, not inventory holding costs, is the primary concern in this system. Models combining space, workload, cost, and service-level constraints have yet to be developed; however, efforts in this area could prove invalu-able to pharmaceutical managers as they attempt to focus on supply chain operations that offer cost-containment benefits. It is also important to develop models showing the trade-off between the extension of the formulary (variety of drugs provided) ver-sus additional cost, workload, storage capacity requirement, and service problems.

To that end, the authors of this chapter are currently examining such problems and developing models to facilitate multicriteria decision support.

In conclusion, as we strive to comprehend and mend healthcare's woes we must remember that healthcare spending in the United States reached $2.3 trillion in 2007 and is projected to reach $3 trillion in 2011. Healthcare spending is projected to reach $4.2 trillion by 2016 (Poisal et al. 2007). The United States spends six times more per capita on the administration of the healthcare system than its peer Western European nations (McKinsey Global Institute 2007). The *McKinsey Quarterly* (2004) reported that health insurance expenses are the fastest growing cost com-ponent for employers. Our endeavor while academic in nature cannot heal all of healthcare's illnesses; however, our goal is to provide a practical model for executive decision support specifically in pharmaceutical inventory control. Our contention is that this research model will help to optimize inventory levels, maximize space usage, reduce pharmacy personnel workloads, and maintain high customer-service levels, thus decreasing cost and enhancing efficiencies in healthcare.

7

Inventory Modeling for Complex Emergencies in Humanitarian Relief Operations

INTRODUCTION

In 1998 there were 400 natural disasters reported in the International Federation of the Red Cross World Disasters Report (1999). These natural disasters affected more than 144 million people, resulting in 90,000 deaths and 5 million temporarily displaced persons. In 1998, the governmental donor community spent more than $3 billion responding to the immediate effects of natural disasters and man-made emer-gencies (International Federation of Red Cross and Red Crescent Societies 1999). In 2005, the International Federation of the Red Cross World Disasters Report stated that the number of disasters had risen dramatically to an average of 707 disasters per year from 1999 to 2003, affecting an average of 213 million people per year (International Federation of Red Cross and Red Crescent Societies 2005).

The challenge for nongovernmental organizations (NGOs) and other relief agen-cies responding to global emergencies (e.g., volcanic eruptions, earthquakes, foods, war) is how to prepare and manage relief activities in an unpredictable environment. Even with modern scientific advances, the onset of large-scale disasters can occur with little warning, and once a disaster strikes, the relief response often necessitates a variety of NGO expertise. Regardless of an NGO's operational specialty (e.g., hous-ing and shelter, water and sanitation, pharmaceuticals), and whether the response is on a national or international level, each NGO shares the common critical objective of rapidly delivering the correct amount of goods, people, and monetary resources to the needed locations. As a result, the ability of an NGO's supply chain and logistic operations directly affects the success of a relief effort.

Recent studies such as Fenton (2003) and Thomas (2003) often compare the cur-rent state of supply chain management capabilities within humanitarian organizations to that of the commercial sector in the 1970s and '80s. At that time, the commer-cial sector began to realize the strategic advantages and significant improvements supply chain management could offer in effectiveness and efficiency. This led to extensive research in the area of supply chain and logistical analysis. Even so, quan-titative methods and principles are rarely applied to humanitarian operations. Also, as global relief responses are growing in scale and magnitude, humanitarian sup-ply chain management is becoming increasingly complex. The growing logistical needs are outpacing the capabilities of current management approaches. This is partly due to the aid sector's regard for logistics as a necessary expense (rather than an important strategic component in their work), the lack of depth in operational knowledge (due to high humanitarian agency employee turnover), and the gen-eral lack of investment in technology and communication. The trends of increas-ing numbers of natural disasters and increasing emphasis on accountability have served as motivating factors to increase understanding and improve the capacity for delivering humanitarian relief. This work focuses specifically on developing an inventory management strategy for a warehouse supporting a complex emergency relief operation.

LITERATURE REVIEW

Quantitative tools for emergency relief have typically come in the form of mathe-matical and network flow models. Oh and Haghani (1996) analyze the transportation of large amounts of many different commodities, such as food, clothing, medicine, medical supplies, machinery, and personnel in the most efficient manner to mini-mize the loss of life and maximize the efficiency of the rescue operations. The result is a formulation and solution of a multicommodity, multimodal network flow model for a generic disaster relief operation. The model is constructed to have four nodes, five arcs, and three transportation modes. Two heuristics are developed with the first utilizing a Lagrangian relaxation approach and the second employing an iterative fix-and-run process. Oh and Haghani (1997) further explore their heuristic models and provide more detailed analysis.

As has been well documented in disaster relief analysis, the infrastructure for the transportation of relief supplies is often unreliable. Due to this unreliability, Barbarosoglu et al. (2002) abandon dependence on road networks and focus on the use of helicopters for aid delivery and rescue missions during natural disasters. Their research is mainly concerned with developing mathematical models that solve tactical and operational scheduling decisions regarding helicopter activities. The authors uti-lize existing research in helicopter routing to address crew assignment, routing, and transportation issues encountered during the initial response phase of disaster man-agement. Infrastructure unreliability as an obstacle to developing and maintaining supply chains was also the motivation behind Thomas (2002). The author develops a method for quantifying the reliability of supply chains for contingency logistics sys-tems based on reliability interference theory. Barbarosoglu and Arda (2004) further explore modeling the uncertainty involved in emergency response. They develop a two-stage stochastic programming framework for transportation planning in disaster response. In this work, the authors expanded on Oh and Haghani's (1996) determin-istic multicommodity, the multimodal network flow problem to include uncertainties that exist in estimating resource requirements of first-aid commodities, the vulner-ability of resource provider facilities, and the survivability of the connecting routes in the disaster area.

Ozdamar et al. (2004) examines logistics planning in emergencies involving dis-patching commodities to distribution centers of affected areas. The network flow model developed by the author addresses a dynamic time-dependent transportation problem, and repetitively derives a solution at given time intervals to represent ongo-ing aid delivery. The model regenerates plans incorporating new requests for aid mate-rials, new supplies, and transportation modes that become available during the current planning time horizon. The plan indicates the optimal mixed pick up and delivery schedules for vehicles within the considered planning time horizon as well as the optimal quantities and types of loads to be picked up and delivered on these routes.

Sakakibara et al. (2004) also examine commodity flow in a road network dur-ing disaster response, and partitions the road network into isolated components. The authors use a topological index to quantify road network accessibility, and then evaluate the isolation of districts in a disaster location. The authors present a methodology for specifying effective road links for avoiding functional isolation of districts.

Mathematical modeling of inventory management in emergency relief efforts has received little attention in the literature. Depending on the nature of the disaster, humanitarian emergency operations can continue for many years. To ensure continu-ous capacity in long-term responses, NGOs often institute arrangements for the stor-age of relief items in warehouses located near the response location. This research focuses on developing an inventory management policy to improve the effectiveness and efficiency of emergency relief during long-term humanitarian responses.

SYSTEM TO BE MODELED: SOUTH SUDAN RELIEF EFFORTS

The last decade has seen a decisive increase in the loss of life, property, and material damage due to the rising occurrence of natural disasters (United States Agency for International Development 2005). Also on the rise and equally as devastating, are man-made disasters, which are referred to within humanitarian agencies as complex humanitarian emergencies (United States Committee for Refugees and Immigrants 2004). UNICEF (2003) defines a complex humanitarian emergency as, "A humani-tarian crisis in a country, region, or society where there is significant or total break-down of authority resulting from internal or external conflict and which requires an international response that extends beyond the mandate or capacity of any single humanitarian agency."

Complex humanitarian emergencies are typically rooted in racially, ethnically, or religiously charged warfare, and are frequently characterized by horrific violations of human rights. The disturbing trend with complex humanitarian emergencies is that when conflicts erupt within the borders of a country, the dividing line between civilians and combatants is frequently blurred. Militant or rebellious groups are usu-ally the same civilians living and socializing in and around the villages they attack. This type of warfare commonly resorts to the use of insidious tactics where humani-tarian agencies are denied access to groups of people in need of assistance. Also, at the center of these shocking developments is the emergence of civilians, including women, children, and humanitarian workers, as the deliberate targets of warfare rather than its incidental victims. The vast devastation of complex humanitarian emergencies can also be attributed to the typically long length of the disaster, which imposes not only financial hurdles, but also legal, moral, and political dilemmas to those attempting to provide relief. Humanitarian efforts responding to complex emergencies often last for many years, and therefore require logistics systems that can support long-term relief activities.

The destruction resulting from long-term complex humanitarian emergencies has recently been witnessed in the Balkans tragedy, the genocide in Rwanda, and most dramatically in the civil war in south Sudan. The United States Holocaust Memorial Museum (2005) describes the warfare in Sudan, Africa's largest country, as one of the most devastating humanitarian crises ever to affect the world. Since 1983, civil war has ravaged south Sudan, leaving over 2 million dead and over 4 million displaced (United States Committee for Refugees and Immigrants 2004). For over twenty years, humanitarian agencies have been responding to the emer-gency by airlifting aid to many parts of the underdeveloped south Sudan region. The United States Committee for Refugees and Immigrants World Refugee Survey: Sudan (2004) estimates that millions of people are dependent on the relief supplies provided by humanitarian agencies. Air access is vital for agencies providing relief as the existing roads in Sudan are often in poor condition, heavily mined, prone to attack by bandits and militia, and at times impassable due to seasonal rains (United States Holocaust Memorial Museum 2005). The south Sudan civil war has been fought primarily with guerrilla warfare tactics, which are based on prin-ciples of ambush and sabotage. The result is a sporadic need for humanitarian aid in unpredictable quantities. Prepositioning of relief supplies near the affected area has proven to be an effective strategy for responding to emergencies of this nature (UNICEF 2005).

In 1989, in response to the continual need for humanitarian aid in south Sudan, Operation Lifeline Sudan (OLS) was created under the coordination of the United Nations as a consortium of UNICEF, the World Food Programme, and more than thirty-five NGOs. The purpose of OLS was for the United Nations to provide the necessary air transport and security for NGO operations, and to provide a strict code of conduct to maintain high standards and impartiality in the delivery of human-itarian assistance to Sudanese civilians. OLS operates out of a United Nations base in the northwest Kenyan town of Lockichoggio, and provides more than a dozen daily airlifts of food, relief supplies, and people (Humanitarian and War Project 2005). The air transport and security provided by the OLS have allowed many NGOs to preposition relief items in warehouses throughout Lockichoggio. As such, Lockichoggio has developed into a logistical hub for the south Sudan relief efforts.

Global prepositioning of relief supplies is an expansion of the warehousing strat-egy typically seen in complex humanitarian emergency responses. This response strategy allows NGOs to respond quickly to disasters with relief supplies from stra-tegically stocked warehouses throughout the world. Global prepositioning is a rela-tively new approach, and currently only a few NGOs can support the large expense of operating a warehouse that serves the international community. World Vision International has taken the lead in implementing a global prepositioning system. Their global prepositioning units (GPUs) are part of a strategy that allows them to respond rapidly and effectively to large-scale emergencies. The GPU system was initiated in 2000 with three warehouse locations (Denver, Colorado; Brindisi, Italy; Hanover, Germany), but the full impact of their operations has yet to be determined. The trade-off of operating a global prepositioned system is rapid response but large transportation costs. The challenge for NGOs is to integrate a GPU system into a long-term humanitarian relief response effectively and efficiently.

The objective here is to develop an efficient, quick-response warehouse inven-tory policy for a humanitarian organization responding to a complex humanitarian emergency. The analysis is based on a case study of a single humanitarian agency operating a warehouse in Lockichoggio and responding to the south Sudan crisis within the OLS framework.

HUMANITARIAN RELIEF INVENTORY MODEL

Quantitative multisupplier supply chain inventory modeling is an active area of research (see Minner and von-Guericke [2003] for a review of such models). Our research develops a multisupplier inventory model that accounts for the unique demand patterns that occur in humanitarian emergency relief operations. We will first provide the relevant model framework and then describe our model in detail. Our model develops an inventory policy for the unique characteristics of a long-term complex humanitarian emergency relief response, considering the specific charac-teristics of the ordering process and demand distribution, yielding new expressions for on-hand inventory, stockout probability, expected number of back orders, and ultimately the decision variables Q_1, r_1, Q_2, and r_2.

General multisupplier inventory models, such as Moinzadeh and Nahmias (1988), assume a continuous review inventory system with two options for resupply. These models are an extension of the standard (Q, f) inventory policy that allows for two lot sizes (Q_1 and Q_2), and two reorder levels (r_1 and r_2). An order of size Q_1 is placed when the inventory position reaches r_1 (this is a regular, or normal reorder option). An emergency reorder option is an expedited order of size Q_2 placed when the inven-tory reaches a position of r_2 (where $r_1 > r_2$). The lead times for normal and emergency reorders are assumed constant in the model and are represented as t_1 and t_2, respec-tively (where $t_1 > t_2$). In addition to requiring a shorter lead time, the items ordered through the emergency resupply channel are also assumed to incur higher fixed and per-unit ordering costs than the normal orders. The rest of the notation is given next with units in parentheses, and will be used throughout the rest of the chapter.

Summary of Modeling Notation

- K_1: Fixed cost for placing a normal order ($)
- K_2: Fixed cost for placing an emergency order ($)
- c_1: Per-unit cost for a normal order ($)
- c_2: Per-unit cost for an emergency order ($)
- h: Inventory holding cost per item per unit time ($)
- p: Back-order cost per item per unit time ($)
- p: Probability of a stockout occurring within a cycle
- OH: On-hand inventory per cycle (number of items)
- BO: Number of back-ordered items per cycle (number of units)

- 7: Expected cycle length (time units)
- *m:* Expected demand rate (quantity per unit time)
- *D:* Annual demand (number of units)
- Q_1: Quantity of relief items in a normal reorder (units)
- Q_2: Quantity of relief items in an emergency reorder (units)
- r_1: Reorder level for normal orders (units)
- r_2: Reorder level for emergency orders (units)

In this section, we present a multisupplier inventory model for the south Sudan relief operations. Data was collected on site in Lockichoggio, Kenya, from warehouse manager interviews and warehouse stock-keeping cards during September 2004. We developed the Sudan humanitarian inventory model as a continuous inventory review system with two options for resupply. The model allows for two lot sizes (Q_1 and Q_2) and two reorder levels (r_1 and r_2). An order of size Q_1 is placed when the inventory position reaches r_1 (a regular, or normal resupply option). The expedited emergency resupply option is of size Q_2 and placed when the inventory reaches a position of r_2. The normal and emergency resupply options represent placing orders with a supplier in Nairobi and an international supplier, respectively. The international supplier may be directly affiliated with the relief agency, as with the GPUs of World Vision, or may have no affiliation at all.

Our process for developing the model begins by analyzing the expected reorder level for each cycle. Next, we focus on the on-hand inventory and expected number of back orders, compute the probability of a stockout per cycle and the total cost equations, and finally derive optimality conditions.

Assumptions

These assumptions will apply to the humanitarian relief model:

- $r_1 > r_2$, in a given cycle, an emergency order will never be placed before a normal order.
- $T_1 > T_2$, an emergency order has a shorter lead time.
- The international supplier will not experience stockouts.
- Replenishment lead time for normal orders is eight days, and for simplification is assumed constant.

- Items ordered through the emergency resupply channel incur a higher fixed and per-unit ordering cost than normal orders.
- Replenishment lead time for emergency orders is two days, and due to relative low variation is assumed constant.
- $Q1 > r_1$, an order quantity will be large enough to not automatically trigger an additional reorder.
- Demand $\sim U[1, b]$ units.
- Demand occurs in discrete ten-day intervals.

Conclusions and Future Research

In this research, our objective was to develop an inventory model for a prepositioned warehouse responding to a complex humanitarian emergency, which is one of the three emergency classifications to which humanitarian and nongovernmental agen-cies respond (rapid onset and slow onset are the other two). Complex humanitarian emergencies are unique due to their unpredictable demand patterns and long dura-tions. The high (often life-threatening) stakes of humanitarian relief place a heavy emphasis on a quick logistics response. It is essential that humanitarian logistics operations (including warehousing in a complex emergency) be performed as efficiently and effectively as possible. Field research for this chapter was performed with our host organization, World Vision International. Data was collected from its warehouse operations in Lockichoggio, Kenya, as it was responding to the complex humanitarian emergency in south Sudan. Based on our recorded data, we developed a mathematical model that optimized the reorder quantity and reorder level based on reordering, holding, and back-order costs.

The research presented in this chapter is a first step in developing strategic inven-tory management systems for humanitarian relief. The model investigated a single "item" (which may be interpreted as a single type of relief kit or a single set of items), developed order quantities that were independent of vehicle or container sizes, and assumed a continuous demand approximation. Future work would investigate the effects of a (correlated) multi-item system that incorporates container sizes, which would likely prove especially important in a relief situation. Another next step would include explicit modeling of the discrete inventory removals (rather than using a con-tinuous approximation). Additionally, a more thorough study to understand the full implications of back-order costs within humanitarian logistics is needed. The back-order cost represents a penalty for unmet demand, but since there are no financial prof-its made in humanitarian logistics, the lost sales approach used in commercial logistics is not necessarily appropriate. A back-order cost in humanitarian logistics represents potential suffering (or loss of life) endured by a potential recipient from not receiving a relief item, but also for the "advertising" opportunity lost by the relief agency for not delivering an item. NGOs do not have an income stream to fund their work outside of donations and therefore must remain vigilant that their actions are being noticed within the donor community. The back-order cost used in our model is a one-time penalty applied to each unit of demand that could not be immediately met from inven-tory. Eventually, back orders are met from an expedited order, but the length of time required to fulfill back orders is not considered. In the real system, there is a window of opportunity during which relief items can be used in the field, and the longer the delay for a needed item, the more devastating the effects. Future research would ana-lyze the impact of time-dependent shortage costs and develop a more detailed quantification methodology for assessing shortages in humanitarian logistics.

Acknowledgments

This work was partly supported by the Interdisciplinary Program in Humanitarian Relief at the University of Washington. The authors would also like to thank World Vision International, and especially Randy Strash and George Fenton for their sup-port and effort during the data gathering process, and to the anonymous referees for their helpful comments and suggested improvements.

8

Seeing Inventory as a Queue

INTRODUCTION

There have to be good reasons to look at the control of inventories from a queuing perspective, as the two subjects seem to have little in common. Such a viewpoint must offer insights and measures that are otherwise unavailable. This chapter explains the ideas and illustrates the benefits that can accrue from adopting such a standpoint.

Inventory control is concerned with how to order and monitor inventory levels to provide a company's customers with a level of service that, at the very least, meets their requirements at a competitive cost. Thus the emphasis is on predictability and how best to attain it. Classical queuing theory considers random processes and is couched in probabilistic terms. Its aim is to build mathematical models of situations where queues can occur. Usually the goal is to try to minimize the amount of time lost waiting in queues. Thus the two topics occupy opposite extremes of a spectrum of uncertainty ranging from the deterministic to the wholly random.

While both employ mathematical models, basic inventory control theory is relatively straightforward and intuitive; although the fundamental ideas have been embellished over time. Queuing theory, on the other hand, requires a degree of math-ematical sophistication, even when dealing with the most basic models. It suffers from two further handicaps. The first is that many real-world situations cannot be precisely handled, in the sense that they lead to useful formulae. Often only average behavior can be described. Unfortunately, excessive stocking costs are commonly incurred when the system's behavior is anything but average. The second difficulty is that models can change quite dramatically with small changes in the structure of the system being modeled. Examples of such changes are in the number of servers employed (a generic term for the mechanism that processes the entities forming the queue), how they are linked, the pattern of arrivals, the pattern of service times (i.e., how long it takes to process each entity), and so on.

What then does a queuing standpoint bring and how can the shortcomings of the approach be surmounted? The answer to the first question is that it provides a dynamic view of inventory. More precisely it permits us to compare what was planned with what actually happened. Indeed we can go further and then examine the causes for these deviations from the plan and rank them by their severity. No counterpart of such an approach seems to be available in traditional inventory con-trol theory. The answer to the second question comes from the use of yet another theoretical tool—information theory. This reveals an entirely unexpected link into a specific form of queuing behavior. It indicates that inventory can, in some ways, be regarded as a special type of queue and is typical of the unsuspected relationships that mathematics sometimes uncovers.

This chapter, therefore, is structured in the following way. The ideas will probably be familiar to readers. Then comes a short introduction to the simplest models in queuing theory as, fortunately, these are all that we will require. The third section sets out some of the concepts that underpin information theory. More depth is provided here as the material is probably less well known.

It records the findings that were obtained on the workings of a com-plex network of supply chains. It illustrates how viewing inventories as dynamical queues can identify and prioritize problem areas in a way that is not possible simply by applying standard inventory control techniques.

Throughout, mathematics will be kept to a minimum with only key formulae pre-sented and explained. Our goal is to provide understanding and insight, not proofs. However, notes are provided at the end of the chapter. Here more formal and techni-cal explanations can be found about topics appearing in the main body of the chapter, but where such detail would be a distraction. These will be indicated by a superscript in the text. The list of references at the end is intended primarily for readers who would like relevant background. So, for example, they will provide proofs of the relevant theorems behind the standard results quoted in the chapter. The list is not meant to be exhaustive.

BASIC INVENTORY CONTROL

This section summarizes those parts of inventory control theory that will be needed in the remainder of the chapter. The focus is only on so-called independent demand inventory control (the words *inventory* and *stock* will be used interchangeably; Axsäter 2006). Here we assume the existence of some form of warehouse where inventory accumulates. It will contain a variety of different products; these are referred to as stock-keeping units (SKUs). The demand for any one product (SKU) is independent of the demand for any other. Products are ordered from a supplier—this could be an internal supplier—and are shipped to a customer. There can, of course, be several suppliers and several customers involved. Independent demand means that we need to only consult the demand history for the particular SKU in which we are interested.

The goal of inventory control is to minimize the total cost of inventory. It bal-ances the costs of holding stock with the cost of ordering, the so-called economic order quantity, and the cost of lost business through being unable to supply. One consequence of independent demand is that the total inventory costs will simply be the sum of the costs of holding individual items.

The inventory that is held is sometimes classified into two categories, active stock and buffer stock. Active stock is the inventory that is assumed to be required; buffer stock is inventory held just in case. In other words, with total knowledge of the future demand pattern and assured deliveries, a buffer stock is not required. However, uncertainty can arise in at least three ways: changes to the level of demand, suppliers not meeting delivery promises, and failing to deliver the quantity ordered.

It is worth reiterating that management chooses the key control parameters: the reor-dering mechanism (reorder point or reorder frequency), how much to reorder, when to reorder, and what level of buffer stock to hold. The principal measures of the system's performance include how well the com-pany meets customers' demands, average levels of inventory held, the money tied up in inventory, and the number of stockouts. Most systems will probably include other metrics such as the performance of the suppliers delivering to the warehouse.

Queuing Theory

The basic ideas behind queuing theory are simple and are summarized in Figure 7.2. Entities arrive to be serviced at a "server" and, when the service is complete, they leave. If the server is busy when an entity arrives, it is forced to wait and a queue is formed. The entities arrive at a certain rate, the *arrival rate,* and are serviced at a certain rate, the *service rate.* Queues are so common that it is scarcely necessary to give examples; most people have experienced queuing at checkouts in supermarkets or waiting to get through airports.

Queuing theory attempts to answer a number of important questions: When is a queuing system stable, in a statistical sense? What is the average waiting time for entities in the queue? What is the average service time? How long might a queue become? The answers help in designing facilities that will have adequate capacity.

Surprisingly, however, there are relatively few general results available. Two important ones are given here. The first derives the general condition for stability in a queuing system.

Types of Queues

The simplest form of queue comprises a single server, entities arriving one at a time, being serviced on a first come, first served basis and leaving immediately after the service has been completed. The arrival time is random and the service times are also randomly distributed.[2] This type of queue is given the following three-part descrip-tion; it is called an *M/M/1* queue. *M* stands for Markovian (named after Markov, one of the founders of the theory of random processes). The first letter describes the arrival pattern and the second the distribution of the service time; the third part gives the number of servers.

There is one other type of queue to mention. This is the *D/D/1* queue, where *D* stands for deterministic. In other words, the arrival times of entities are precisely known, as are the service times. This is the one queue where p can be equal to one. Here we are able to time the arrivals to come at exactly the point where the service on the preceding entity has been completed.

So far we gain little from taking a queuing perspective, apart from two insights. The first is that we should not try to run the system fat out, where $r = 1$, unless we were to exercise total control, which is, of course, impossible. The second is that we pay for loss of control in terms of greater inventory; hardly a surprising result. The other measures furnished by the queuing theory are nothing more than we calculate anyway in inventory control. For example, the average number in the system, *N*, is simply the average inventory level. What is more, this number can be recorded directly in a ware-house, not derived from a mathematical formula of only limited applicability.

Something is missing. We need to develop a measure that can be calculated by directly observing the inventory (queue) sitting on a shelf while providing insights not available from the existing inventory control theory. In addition we want to employ some of the ideas and structures from queuing theory but without the short-comings highlighted earlier, such as having to build a mathematical model for each type of queue we encounter. We would then have a more empirical and hence more robust approach.

INFORMATION THEORY AND ENTROPY

The missing link is provided by information theory. This section spends a little time explaining the ideas, as, in contrast to queuing theory, some of the concepts are quite subtle, but the mathematics are relatively straightforward.

Information theory is largely the creation of one man, Claude Shannon, devel-oped while he was working at Bell Laboratories at the Massachusetts Institute of Technology. His interest was in the mechanics of sending and receiving messages. He envisaged a sender linked in some way to a receiver, possibly through a wireless connection. This link is called the *channel of communication*, or *channel*. He real-ized that to send a message remotely, it had to be translated into a form that could be transmitted. For example, the earliest wireless messages were sent in Morse code. This translates letters of the alphabet into a series of dots and dashes (*characters*). He described the activity as *coding* the message. The message would then need to be decoded at the other end by the receiver. It meant that the sender and receiver had to agree in advance on a coding scheme.

Shannon (Shannon and Weaver 1999) asked himself what corresponded to an efficient code, that is, one that was flexible enough to enable any message to be encoded but was as short as possible (*data *compression*); the shorter the length of the encoded message, the more quickly it could be sent. In addition, frequently used letters of the alphabet should have shorter codes (*codewords*) than those used infrequently. For instance, although Morse code is not a particularly efficient code, the letter E is coded as a single dot.

Shannon was also interested in how quickly a message could be sent (the *trans-mission rate*). This turns out to be the capacity of the channel; the so-called channel *bandwidth* (Cover and Thomas 2006). Linked to that was the important issue of noise—roughly speaking, characters received that have nothing to do with the mes-sage. Clearly the presence of noise will reduce the effective capacity of the channel. One of Shannon's extraordinary discoveries was that it is possible to transmit nearly noiseless messages provided that the channel capacity is not exceeded.

Information (also known as self-information), as defined by Shannon, is a measure of the content of information associated with an event

The third aspect of this formula is the introduction of a logarithm. This is a little harder to explain. Basically a message is a string of characters (letters, numbers, etc.). Each character will contain a certain amount of information. Taking logarithms is a way of "counting" the number of characters in the string, that is, the information content. Taking logarithms to the base 2 reflects the fact that we are in a digital age where we deal, ultimately, with only ones and zeros. The definition of a bit only applies when we employ logarithms to the base of 2.

Entropy

The idea of counting will become clearer when the concept of entropy is explained. Entropy (or more correctly entropy rate) is the lower limit to which a message can be compressed. It is also a measure of the *average* random uncertainty in a message. Entropy.

Here *H* is the symbol for entropy, *X* is a random variable describing an event, and *p(x)* is the probability associated with the occurrence of *X* (formally of *X* taking the value *x*). *N* is the number of random variables involved.

BRINGING THE STRANDS TOGETHER: ENTROPY, QUEUES, AND COMPLEXITY

All of this is somewhat peripheral to inventory control. It still needs to be established how the ideas developed so far are linked together. The first step is to model the process of taking observations; in our case, the movement of inventory in and out of a warehouse.

The process of observation is shown in Figure 7.3. This diagram suggests that there may be parallels between taking observations and the passing of messages. We might think, rather fancifully, of the system "sending messages" to the observer, which he or she then records. There is a major difference, however: the system's goals differ from those of the observer. The former is to offer a level of customer service, the lat-ter to record accurately what is happening. One consequence is that the observation process must actively avoid impacting on the system as it might interfere with the lat-ter achieving its goals. For example, if the recording mechanism itself impacted the accuracy of the resultant record, then deliveries could be compromised, adversely affecting the level of service. Such a situation used to occur when inventory move-ments were recorded manually. Stock records sometimes might only be updated at the end of a working day, or even the end of a week. In the interim, dispatch promises were made based on incorrect data.

This noninvolvement is described as treating the system as though it were *secretive* (Frizelle and Suhov 2008). In practical terms it means that, when we come to analyze how the inventory system is performing, we have to rely solely on our record. So, for exam-ple, we cannot interrogate the system—except possibly in extreme circumstances.

However, secretiveness is also an issue even when setting up the system. Suppose we decide to create an inventory control package to sell as a commercial product. We need to specify our new offering. Two obvious fundamental parameters will be how many SKUs our product can handle and how big the stock records will need to be. Might we have customers that have millions of items in stock, for instance? Clearly what we need in each case is a number that is big enough to guarantee that we can accommodate whatever requirements our prospective customers demand of us. How do we calculate this number? The proposed system itself cannot tell us. We might try to find what existing competitive systems do, we might try to discuss the matter with potential customers, we might survey the literature, or do all of these things and more. However, the fact is that such a number can never be calculated (this is a fascinating topic in its own right; interested readers are directed to Cover and Thomas [2006] or Hofstadter [1979]). All we can do is make well- or ill-informed guesses.

The goal will be to assess how well the inven-tory control system is performing. That generates more questions: What precisely do we observe? What measure do we use? Do we need more than one measure?

Now there is a surprising relationship that allows us to address the first two ques-tions. It turns out that our inability to ever provide definitive answers to such ques-tions as "how many SKUs do we allow for?" when designing the system, holds the key. We have to conclude that, in general, we are never going to be able to determine an upper limit in the total certainty that it will never be breached—although it may be possible in specific instances. Stating this in mathematical terms, we must work on the assumption that the systems we are dealing with can have an infinite number of states.[8] We must be careful about what we are saying; it is that we are never able, in general, to determine an upper limit, so we have to treat systems as if no such limit exists.

However, as the reader will probably have guessed, we will want to use entropy as our measure. That creates a problem, as Equation 7.7 now takes the value of infinity. It raises practical difficulties if we want to use it as a measure, particularly when comparing two systems.

The question is then, is it possible to have a system with an infinite number of states but finite entropy? The answer is yes. We can find a mathematical condition that puts an upper limit on the entropy per state and ensures that the overall entropy is finite, even though the number of states is not. We can state the condition for the entropy to be maximized but remain finite; the probabilities must follow the so-called geometric distribution.

Now comes the surprising bit: This distribution has exactly the same structure as the formula for the $M/M/1$ queue. The only difference is that the probabilities are replaced by the traffic intensity. This completes the jigsaw for it suggests that when looking at input–output systems, we need to observe queuing behavior, and when we take an entropy measurement we measure queuing entropy. Moreover, when we compare two systems, we do so on the basis of the dynamics of their respective queues. It tells us, among other things, which of the two exhibits the most complex behavior.

There is more. When the queue behavior can be modeled as *M/M/*1, its entropy is at a maximum for the specific value of the traffic intensity. This is what was meant when it was stated at the start of the chapter that queues (specifically *M/M/*1 queues) sit at one end of a spectrum of uncertainty. Equally, if the system was to be wholly deterministic, the *D/D/*1 queue, then the entropy will be zero—the other end of the spectrum. It says, in effect, that we can model a real-world queue as being composed of two elements: a deterministic bit and a random bit.

The notion of active stock was introduced at the start of the chapter, as represented by the saw-tooth. As pointed out, everything is known (deterministic): the demand, the delivery time, the delivery quantity and so on. Thus active stock rep-resents variety without probability. We can go a stage further and say that achieving the stock profile represented by the active stock is the immediate goal of the stock control system

In practice, of course, we can never be wholly certain. If we look at the actual inventory profile of a SKU over time, it will be the conflation of the planned and unplanned. However, if we know what was meant to happen, then we can separate the planned from the unplanned.

The idea is shown in Figure 7.4. The light gray is the planned profile—the goal the system is trying to achieve. It has been drawn in an irregular fashion to emphasize the fact that the shape of the profile is irrelevant. This line has to be "constructed," as it is unlikely to exist in any inventory records. It is done by looking back at planned orders and deliveries. The dark gray line is the actual profile and this can be drawn directly from the inventory records. The shaded area is the variation between the two; the unexpected element giving rise to the entropy.

Analysis

Two key pieces of analysis are carried out. The first is to assign causes to the varia-tions between the planned and actual performance.

There is, of course, no definitive list of such causes. However, typical examples include customers changing their minds (e.g., canceling orders, modifying orders, rescheduling orders, replacing orders), the inability to dispatch to customers through having insufficient stock on hand, late delivery by suppliers, delivery shortages, and erroneous deliveries from suppliers. The list is determined by the specific nature of the stocking operation, what that particular management wants to know, and what data are available.

The second key piece of analysis is making comparisons. These can be between the performance of individual SKUs, between suppliers, or between customers. Other useful data include whether incomplete deliveries are more of a problem than late deliveries. We might assume that if we ordered one hundred of a particular SKU, it is preferable to have, say, thirty delivered on the day required with the balance later, than having all one hundred delivered late. However, it may not prove to be so in practice.

The table shows deliveries into and out of a warehouse for a single SKU. Under "Planned," columns A and B record the quantities planned to be delivered from the supplier and the dispatches required by the customer. The resulting planned inventory levels, at the end of each day, are given in column C along with the opening stock. Under "Actual," columns D, E, and F show the actual performance under the same three headings. The inventory variation is recorded in column G.

It will be clear from this example that poor delivery to the customer is being caused by poor delivery from the supplier. Thus, the first order that was supposed to be delivered on Monday does not come until Tuesday (see columns A and D). On Wednesday the supplier only delivers ten instead of the thirty required. Thursday's order is delivered a day late and then not in full, as twenty of the quantity delivered form part of Wednesday's order. This inability to supply causes violent fluctuations in the stock levels, with a stockout on Thursday. However, that is not the whole story. On Monday there was sufficient inventory in the warehouse to make a full delivery of eighty (column F, opening stock). However, the customer changed his mind and asked for only fifty, with fifty the following day and the balance on Wednesday (column E). This was because the customer was unable to take the whole eighty in a single delivery.

Here the supplier and the warehouse performance are separated: the former is given in columns A, B, and C; the latter in columns D, E, and F. The causes, summarized in the previ-ous paragraph, are recorded in column G. Notice that no mention has been made here about the supplier's late deliveries on Monday, Tuesday, or Wednesday. This is because a key role of a warehouse is to provide a reliable dispatch service to the customer and is one of the principal reasons for holding inventory. Thus while poor service from the supplier was a problem, it is not the major cause for the pattern of dispatches on those three days.

Estimating Probabilities

There are three practical reasons and one theoretical one. The first practical one is that entropy aggregates variation, in a way that probabilities do not; the latter always sum to unity. You can think of it as an indicator of the level of turbulence in a system—the system behaving in unexpected ways. The greater the tendency for this to happen, the more turbulent (complex) the process becomes. In terms of Figure 7.4, the two lines will progressively diverge from one another as turbulence increases.

The second reason is that it is possible to allocate levels of turbulence to their causes.[10] Thus, for example, we can differentiate between causes about which we can do something and those we cannot.

Indeed we can go further and look at how much disruption a particular event causes when it happens as against how much of a problem it causes overall.

For example, a particular supplier may deliver late and cause considerable inconvenience to a num-ber of customers—very disruptive when it happens. However, it is rare for that sup-plier not to be on time so, overall, it is not a major issue.

The theoretical reason is that Equation 7.5 can be applied wherever a random variable can be defined and probabilities assigned to the various outcomes. This has the great advantage that any type of queue can be studied. It frees us from having to build a new model for every specific queue we encounter. This is a powerful advan-tage because we can make comparisons between very different stock profiles within the same warehouse, for example. There are drawbacks in using the measure.

The first and most obvious one is the very strangeness of the measure, not to mention its mathematical structure. Managers feel uncomfortable about being asked to trust a measure that they do not fully understand. Experience has shown that trust grows when it highlights matters with which the management is already familiar and when it is used in conjunction with more traditional metrics.

A second drawback is the very versatility of entropy as a measure. As we have just seen, entropy values can be calculated irrespective of the nature of the variable under consideration. This is also a weakness when comparing systems. The mea-sure itself gives no guidance as to the validity of the comparison being made. We could just as easily compare chalk with cheese as chalk with chalk. We need some additional model to ensure that this does not happen. That is another reason why the link between entropy and queues is so important; it leads us always to compare queuing behavior.

Data Analysis

A major simplifying assumption was made. This was that each of the supply chains could be considered in isolation from the others, except where a stockout of a par-ticular SKU caused a dispatch to be delayed to an end customer. Thus, for example, the variation between what should have been delivered to stock and what was for one SKU was independent of the variation between what should have been delivered to stock and what was for a different SKU.

Making valid comparisons was a concern. It helped that queues (inventory levels) were always being observed and always at the same location. It enforced a degree of uniformity on the exercise. Nonetheless practical difficulties regularly cropped up. One such difficulty is when the same SKU exists in different package sizes, for example, pallets, boxes, cartons, and so forth. Counting had to be consistent, so the unit chosen was the smallest one encountered.

Thus if a pallet was delivered to a storage location but was then split into cartons for onward delivery, the unit of mea-sure would be cartons by the size of the "Shipment to DC" bar. The reason for this was not altogether clear but seems merely to be a refection on the haulers' performance—they delivered when they were asked to. In other words, the haulage stage from the factory to the DC has not aggravated the situation. What is clear is that by the time products come to be delivered to the end customer, turbulence is still present, although considerably attenuated from that seen further up the chains. It is concluded that holding inter-mediate inventory in a warehouse is not providing a total buffer against fluctuations generated further back in the operation.

Finally, the "Inventory" bar shows the impact of the various sources of turbulence on inventory performance, in terms of how far the actual level deviates from the planned level. Such fluctuations have to be covered by a buffer stock. Therefore one can—at least in theory—estimate the cost, in terms of excess stocking costs, of hav-ing a turbulent supply chain.

It was also possible to identify which factories were the problem suppliers, which customers created the greatest difficulties in terms of changing their minds about what to order, and which of the nine products proved the most difficult to manage through the chains. One particular factory was found to be having special problems.

The case study illustrates the benefits that can accrue when viewing inventory as a dynamic queue. It offers a way to assess the performance of a complex net-work of supply chains by providing a single measure at a key node in the network. The measure creates both an absolute performance metric (how closely the SKU achieves its goal of meeting the planned inventory profile) and a comparative mea-sure (the relative performance of suppliers, customers, and other participants in the network). Where the investigation does not provide the complete answer, it at least highlights those locations that need to be examined in depth. Such an analysis would not be possible relying solely on the data provided by traditional inventory control systems.

Conclusions

We have attempted to demonstrate the additional benefits that accrue when we view inventories as a class of queue. The principal one is that it encourages us to consider the dynamical behavior of inventories. This is revealed in the inventory profile shown in Figure 7.4, which is part planned and part random. Moreover, the figure demonstrated how the two components can be separated; in other words, the total behavior is the sum of the predicted and the random elements.

However, the viewpoint brings a second benefit. We say that a virtual server is involved. This assumes that service begins when an item goes into stock (joins the queue) and is complete when it leaves. It encourages us to think in terms of server states, that is, is the server behaving as it should or, if not, what is it doing. The important aspect of this rather odd standpoint is to highlight the link between server behavior and queue behavior. In rather more prosaic terms, we look to see what causes the queue to behave as it does and, more important, put a measure on the amount of turbulence that is created as a result.

In fact, this linkage of server to queue states allows the ideas to be applied to two forms of inventory not usually included in traditional stock control theory and, for that reason, not considered in the body of the chapter. However, they need a brief mention for completeness. The first is where a real server exists, for example, a resource in a factory (Frizelle and Suhov 2001). The queues involved are often referred to as work in process. The nature of the factory dynamics is then revealed by analyzing the server states, for example, is the resource working or in a state of breakdown.

The second form of inventory is that found in industrial processes. Here we are dealing with gases, liquids, or solids. In mathematical terms, they are described by continuous variables. Inventory control is not an issue, apart from making sure that supplies are delivered when required. As the materials are usually stored in some form of container—tanks, silos, or bins—there is a physical upper limit on how much can be held. Indeed a pro-cess plant will have been designed with these capacities in mind.

We also described the benefits that come from using entropy as a performance metric. First, entropy is a measure of turbulence and is, more generally, a measure of one form of complexity. Second, it is independent of what is being measured. This means that we can compare similar systems, which in this context means the queuing behavior of different SKUs. It also releases us from first having to specify a queuing model to enable us to carry out measurements. Third, entropy provides an absolute measure, in the sense that no uncertainty means no entropy and maximum entropy is defined relative to the traffic intensity of the queue.

However, the real benefit comes from being able to apply the ideas in practice. Observing the queue dynamics in a large distribution depot provided insight into how a complex network of supply chains was performing. The analysis revealed likely causes of the problems and indicated where unnecessary costs might accrue through having to hold excessive buffers in the system. Such insights cannot be gleaned from ordinary stock control theory.

It was commented at the start of the chapter that adopting this perspective can only be justified if it provides some fresh viewpoints. The hope is that this has been demonstrated to be the case.7

9

Fuzzy Inventory Models

INTRODUCTION

The efficient management of inventory requires managers to make decisions on two fundamental questions: (1) how large should an inventory replenishment order be, and (2) when should an inventory replenishment order be placed. These two decisions are integral in the support of an overall inventory management program that typically has the objective of providing a desired level of customer service at a minimal cost. Beginning in 1913 with Harris's economic order quantity (EOQ) model, numerous mathematical inventory models have been published in the inven-tory literature to assist managers in determining the size and timing of an inventory replenishment order in support of this objective.

Mathematical inventory models can be broadly categorized into two groups: deter-ministic models and stochastic models. Deterministic inventory models were the first class of inventory models to evolve. In the years following the introduction of the Harris EOQ model, numerous variants and extensions of the EOQ model rapidly appeared in the literature. Deterministic inventory models typically contain few parameters, and all input data for these parameters are assumed to be known with complete certainty. The total cost function includes the costs associated with ordering, holding, and purchasing inventory. The optimal order quantity that minimizes the total cost function, then, can be easily found. Deterministic models also assume that the demand and lead-time charac-teristics of the inventory system are known with complete certainty, leading to a simple and straightforward mathematical structure for modeling demand during lead time.

Stochastic inventory models first appeared in the literature in the early 1950s. These models were formulated to capture the uncertainty and variability that exist in most real-world inventory situations but were assumed away in deterministic inventory models. As a result of incorporating uncertainty in demand and lead time, stochastic models require more model parameters than deterministic inventory mod-els, and require that some input parameters be defined in probabilistic terms. The optimal solution of a stochastic inventory model generates a set of policy variables, which minimize an expected total cost function. Seminal papers by Arrow et al. (1951) and Dworetzky et al. (1952a, 1952b) established the foundation for stochastic inventory models and led to the introduction of shortage costs.

Stochastic inventory models assume that demand, lead time, or both factors can be described by random variables. The underlying mathematical structure for a sto-chastic inventory model is more complex than that of a deterministic model and requires a policy statement from management for the inventory system performance measure such as a service level or fill rate.

In practice, implementing either form of inventory model requires the acceptance of a set of assumptions that govern the model use, as well as the recognition that estimates must be made for model parameters such as demand rates, lead times, and inventory-related costs.

Obtaining realistic input values for the parameters of a mathematical inventory model is a challenging task. The analyst performing this task is often operating in a decision environment that is characterized by uncertainty, ambiguity, and the lack of perfect information on customer demand rates, manufacturing, and delivery lead times, in addition to inventory cost structures for ordering, holding, and shortages.

Fuzzy set theory is primarily concerned with how to quantitatively deal with imprecision and uncertainty, and offers the decision maker another tool in addition to the classical deterministic and probabilistic mathematical tools that are used in modeling real-world problems. Fuzzy set theory was introduced in the engineering/ computer sciences literature by Zadeh (1965) and has gained widespread promi-nence as a means to model vague data in production management applications. A comprehensive review on the application of fuzzy set theory in production manage-ment can be found in Guiffrida and Nagi (1998).

In deterministic inventory models, the analyst must assign a unique numerical value to each model cost parameter as well as to the demand and production rates that characterize the market place and production environment in which the model operates. Similarly, for stochastic inventory models, the assignment process involves using random variables to quantify these inputs under conditions of uncertainty. The advantage of using fuzzy set theory in inventory management lies with its inherent ability to quantify vagueness and imprecision. The purpose of this chapter is to pro-vide a review of the application of fuzzy set theory to inventory management. The review will highlight how fuzzy logic has been used in inventory models and will provide inventory analysts with an alternative, and perhaps complementary, method-ology for developing inventory models.

The chapter is organized into two major components. Collectively, Sections 8.2 and 8.3 provide the motivation and foundation for using fuzzy set theory in modeling inventory systems. In Section 8.2, we address the current state of the no fuzzy mod-eling efforts for obtaining estimates of the cost parameters of inventory models. The literature on formulating cost estimates for inventory model parameters is reviewed. The robust properties of inventory models to errors in parameter estimation and misspecification of optimal lot sizes are also discussed. In Section 8.3, a review of classi-cal inventory models is presented. In Section 8.4, we build upon this framework and demonstrate a review of the literature on fuzzy inventory models. A summary and conclusion for the chapter is presented in Section 8.5.

PARAMETER ESTIMATION IN CLASSICAL INVENTORY MODELS

In this section we summarize the literature on determining input values for the inventory cost parameters of order, holding, and shortage. These three parameters are present in nearly all inventory models which have been reported in the literature. The property of robustness is also introduced and material is presented that demon-strates the sensitivity of inventory models to specific errors in the optimal lot size and in the specification of individual parameters.

Mathematical inventory models, like all management science/ operations research models, require the assignment of numerical values to the input parameters of the model. There is widespread agreement among inventory analysts as to the need of assigning such numerical values; however, the process of estimating the parameters is of concern. Wagner (1980) presents a comprehensive review of the practical prob-lems associated with implementing inventory control systems. A key issue identified in this review is the need for a thoughtful and scientific investigation of the issues relating to the specification of demand forecasts and costs related to inventory modeling.

Deterministic inventory models typically require inputting at least two cost param-eters: an order cost for making replenishment and an inventory holding cost for carrying items in inventory. Stochastic inventory models generally require a cost associated with stocking out and back-ordering, in addition to ordering and invent holding costs. Zanakis et al. (1980) refer to cost estimation in inventory control as the thorn that aggravates the users of inventory control models. Gardner (1980) states that the commonly and almost universally accepted belief held by inventory analysts is that relevant cost information for determining the input values for the parameters of an inventory model can somehow be obtained from a firm's accounting system.

The major concern throughout the studies outlined in Table 8.1 is the capture of accurate and relevant cost data that can be used to describe the costs associated with ordering, holding, and shortages. Today's advancements in inventory control software, such as material requirements and enterprise planning systems, as well as the growing implementation of radio frequency identification, has made the handling and integration of inventory-related information more efficient and available to the decision maker in real-time. However, the troublesome issue of defining numeri-cal values for the input parameters of an inventory model still exists. It must be recognized that totally error-free parameterization of inventory models is not very likely. In the next section we examine the extent to which the robust properties of the inventory models themselves afford protection again parameter misspecification.

The sensitivity of the inventory cost of the EOQ to errors in the estimation of its model parameters can be found in numerous inventory management textbooks that were published between 1950 and 1975. Starr and Miller (1962, 14) introduced the concept of "sufficient accuracy" with respect to the measurement of inventory-related costs. They note that the typical EOQ-based inventory analysis is not overly sensi-tive to reasonable errors in the measurements of cost, and that the optimal course of action as suggested by the solution of the inventory model is not likely to be changed very much, even by relatively large errors in the measurements of costs. As such, inventory analysts often take comfort in the knowledge that uncertainty and error introduced when specifying the numerical value of parameters input to an inventory model may have little effect on determining the value of inventory policy variables as a result of the "robust" property inherent to some mathematical inventory models.

Analyses that highlight the robustness of EOQ-based inventory models have developed beyond the scope of inventory management textbooks and into the main-stream inventory management research literature. The research on this topic has developed in two ways. First, researchers have examined the effect of incorrect lot sizes on the total cost performance of the EOQ inventory system; second, research-ers have examined the effects of misspecifications of individual and group param-eters on the total cost performance of the EOQ inventory system.

MISSPECIFICATION OF ORDER QUANTITY PARAMETERS

Lowe and Schwarz (1983) note that the parameter inputs for the EOQ lot-sizing model are assumed to be stationary and known, when in reality these quantities are often nonstationary and more accurately defined as a function of time or a range of val-ues. They develop two measures for assessing the accuracy (or "goodness") of using parameter estimates in the EOQ model as well as two procedures (minimax and expected value criteria) for estimating the uncertain parameters. For the stationary cases, formulae based on the minimax and expected value criteria are used to develop parameter estimators based on ranges where uncertain parameters are defined by minimum and maximum values. In the nonstationary cases, formulae are developed that introduce time dependency into the range-based parameter estimates. A numeri-cal example is used to demonstrate change in inventory policy resulting from the application of the difference in accuracy measures and estimation procedures.

Dobson (1988) extends the work of Lowe and Schwarz (1983) and demonstrates through a series of propositions a more detailed quantification of the insensitivity of the EOQ inventory model under conditions of parameter uncertainty. Error bounds for the expected error ratio are defined for the joint distribution of the order cost, holding cost, and annual demand parameters of the EOQ. The error bounds are derived for the distribution independent case (e.g., estimates are only dependent on the range endpoints) and for the case when the distribution of the parameters follows the gamma and beta distributions.

Yu (1997) studied the EOQ model under two robust criteria: (1) minimizing the maximum total inventory cost, and (2) minimizing the maximum percentage devia-tion from the optimal total inventory cost. Under these criteria, the input data of the EOQ model are defined by continuous intervals. A linear time algorithm was developed to find robust decisions under each criterion. A stochastic EOQ model, in which the model parameter inputs are defined by known probability distributions, is formulated and solved, and the results of the stochastic optimization are compared to the solutions achieved under the robust decision criteria. Theorems are presented that show that the robust decision criteria outperform the stochastic optimization approach with respect to the EOQ inventory model.

The scope of robustness with respect to the parameterization of inventory input parameters may be limited for several reasons. First, the properties of robustness have only been studied in the literature for the EOQ inventory model. Second, inven-tory experts have expressed disagreement as to the assurances that robustness offers in the parameterization of inventory models, such as the EOQ. Peterson and Silver (1979) state that the robustness of the EOQ model is an important fundamental con-cept in operational inventory control. Zangwill (1987) takes the position that reliance on the robust properties of the EOQ model can lead to false or misleading results, especially when viewed from the zero inventory philosophy.

The Inventory Management Literature

A comprehensive review of all inventory models published since 1913 has never been undertaken and would be a daunting task due to the sheer number of published inventory models. For example, a search using the phrase "mathematical inventory models" in Google Scholar returns over 90,000 hits. In this section we present a summary of literature reviews on inventory models that have appeared in the litera-ture.

Bramson (1962) presents a review of inventory models with variable lead time. Models are classified according to two coding schemes. The first coding scheme consists of three variables that describe the type of inventory control policies used in the inventory model to govern order review, size, and treatment of shortages. Within this first coding scheme, the order review policies encoded are: (1) continuous review, (2) periodic review, (3) random review, and (4) other/irrelevant. Order sizes are coded as: (1) $Q = 1$, (2) optimal Q, (3) a fixed multiple of Q, and (4) other/irrelevant. Demand under a shortage is treated as: (1) completely back-ordered, (2) completely lost, (3) partially back-ordered and partially lost, and (4) other/irrelevant.

The second coding scheme consists of one to three letters and is used to classify the type of distribution used for demand and lead time. A single letter signifies the form of the distribution used in the model to define customer demand. A second let-ter identifies the accompanying lead-time distribution. Demand and lead-time distri-butions considered are: (1) normal, (2) Poisson, (3) exponential/geometric, (4) Erlang, (5) gamma, (6) negative binomial, (7) unit demand, or (8) other. When all three let-ters are used, the third letter denotes the time interval between demands.

The coding schemes are used to classify ten inventory models published in the literature from 1955 to 1961. Pursuant to the theme of this review paper, Bramson (1962) provides a step-by-step derivation of an expression for comparing the vari-ability of the demand and lead-time distributions for variable demand inventory models in an appendix to the paper.

Aggarwal (1974) provides a comprehensive classification of the literature in math-ematical inventory control models that appeared from 1964 to 1973. The classification scheme used to organize inventory models in the paper is identified using a well-designed and easy to read figure found on page 444 of the paper. Within this classification scheme, inventory systems are broadly classified as either static or dynamic models. The static model subgroup is further broken down as to whether the models represent single or multiple items. Both model forms (single or multiple items) are further partitioned based on the number of locations and echelons the models engage. Models in the dynamic subgroup are broken down as to whether the model is deterministic or stochastic. Stochastic models are further classified as to whether they possess a known or unknown demand distribution.

A list of eleven quantifiable inventory variables present in the literature is then dis-cussed, to which Aggarwal (1974) adds four additional variables that cannot be eas-ily quantified. Individual research papers from the inventory literature are grouped into six specific categories. These categories are: (1) models for determining opti-mum inventory policies (twenty-three papers), (2) lot-size optimization (five papers), (3) optimization of specific management objectives (eight papers), (4) models for opti-mizing highly specific situations (twenty papers), (5) applications of advanced math-ematical theories (nine papers), and (6) models bridging the gap between theory and practice (five papers). The author concludes the review paper with an interesting dis-cussion of the limitations set forth for the general practicability of inventory models.

Two additional inventory review papers that present detailed classification schemes for inventory models are found in Nahmias (1978) and Silver (1981). The classification schemes presented in these papers differ from those of Bramson (1962) and Aggarwal (1974), in that models for perishable products are now included as a part of the overall inventory model classification scheme.

Nahmias (1982) reviewed the literature on inventory models for perishable invento-ries. The review is restricted to the ordering policies of perishables. Ordering policies for inventory that is subject to obsolescence is excluded. Prior to being introduced as a distinct class of inventory model in the classifications schemes presented by Nahmias (1978) and Silver (1981), selected perishable inventory models published prior to 1973 were reviewed by Aggarwal (1974) under the classification of "models for optimizing highly specific situations."

The classification scheme used by Nahmias (1982) is based on two major group-ings: (1) models for single and multiple products with fixed lifetime perish ability under conditions of deterministic and stochastic demand, and (2) models with ran-dom lifetime perish ability in which the product lifetime follows either a known prob-ability distribution or experiences exponential decay. Similar in form to his prior review paper

(Nahmias 1978), a detailed and thorough explanation of each class of model addressed in the review is provided. Thirty papers from the literature are reviewed under the category of models with fixed life perish ability; nine papers are reviewed under the category of random lifetime perish ability. Noting the analogy between queuing models with customer impatience and perishable inventory models, two papers that apply analytical results from the queuing application are examined. The review concludes with the acknowledgment that interest in perishable inventory problems has been influenced by problems in blood bank management, and selected papers from the literature on blood bank management are reviewed.

Raafat (1991) presents a review of the literature on continuously deteriorating mathematical inventory models (also known as inventory models subject to expo-nential decay or age-independent perishable inventory models). Following the classification scheme defined in Silver (1981), eight groupings are defined for categorizing the literature on continuously deteriorating inventory models. Within seven of the groupings, two distinct subgroupings are introduced to further partition models found in the literature. Nine classes of continuously deteriorating inventory models are identified and each class of model is then categorized according to the classification scheme defined in the paper. Within a given model class, relevant papers from the literature are addressed. A total of sixty-three papers are reviewed across the nine model classes.

Benton and Park (1996) reviewed the literature on inventory lot sizing models with quantity discounts. The taxonomy adopted consists of three nested classifications. The first classification categorizes quantity discount models according to whether the demand profile underlying the model is time phased. Second, within each demand class the type of discount model (all-units discount or incremental discount) is established. Last, the model is classified from the point of view of the parties involved (e.g., from the lot sizing perspective of the buyer only or from the joint lot sizing perspective of both the buyer and supplier).

A total of fifty-one papers on inventory lot sizing models with quantity discounts were reviewed. The vast majority of the papers incorporated models that were not time phased with respect to demand (thirty-five papers). Forty papers had models that were based on incremental discount schedules; eleven papers had models that were based on all-units discount schedules. The vast majority of the papers did not adopt a joint buyer–supplier orientation with respect to lot sizing (thirty-six papers), and no papers addressed the buyer–supplier interaction under a time-phased demand orientation. Benton and Park (1996) acknowledge that more complex models are needed to address the buyer–seller interaction with respect to the lot sizing decision involving quantity discounts when demand is time phased.

Goyal and Giri (2001) present a review of the literature on deteriorating inventory models published since the early 1990s. Their review addresses new contributions to the literature on deteriorating inventory models that have been published since the earlier review of the field Raafat (1991). Their review is classified according to three categories: (1) models for inventory with fixed lifetimes, (2) models for inventory with a random life, and (3) models for inventory with decays corresponding to the propor-tional inventory decrease in terms of its utility or physical quantity. The detail of the review effort is impressive with consideration given to the demand structures used by researchers in modeling deteriorating inventory, as well the specialized model attributes that address pricing, scheduling of payments, the time value of money, and inventory storage. The review encompasses more than 120 new contributions to the literature on deteriorating inventory models.

Several authors have published recent reviews of specialized topics within the inventory management literature. These reviews are summarized in Table 8.2.

FUZZY INVENTORY LITERATURE

In this section we will review the literature on fuzzy inventory models. The review is organized along seven general classes of inventory models and their extensions. These classes are economic order quantity models, economic production quantity models, joint economic lot sizing models, single period newsvendor models, multiperiod inventory models, multiproduct inventory models, and systems (continu-ous and periodic review) for inventory control.

The objective of this survey is to identify how fuzzy set theory has been used in the formulation of the fuzzy inventory model. The semantics of fuzzy set theory will not be discussed as a part of this review. The interested reader is referred to Kaufmann and Gupta (1988) for the supporting details on the mathematics of fuzzy inference. An introduction on how to use fuzzy set theory in mathematical inven-tory models is found in Buckley et al. (2002) and Buckley (2005). These references expertly illustrate how to apply fuzzy set theory in the formulation and solution of inventory models.

As in the traditional inventory literature, the fuzzy economic order quantity has provided the genesis for the evolution of fuzzy inventory models. Six papers have addressed the basic EOQ model under varying schemes of fuzzy parameter assignments. An additional seven papers model the fuzzy EOQ with back orders. Ten papers provide extensions to the fuzzy EOQ model.

We introduce the following notation for use throughout this section. Let C denote a crisp (nonfuzzy) model parameter/attribute; let F denote a fuzzy model parameter/ attribute.

The economic order quantity model assumes that all units of the EOQ lot size are delivered from an outside vendor at the same time. Hence, if the EOQ was used as an internal production lot sizing model, the assumption of instantaneous replenishment would equate to an infinite (and unrealistic) production rate. By relaxing the instan-taneous replenishment to allow for a production rate that is greater than the demand rate, the EOQ model can be modified to determine the optimal production lot size as a function of setup and inventory holding costs. This modification of the traditional EOQ model is often referred to as the economic production quantity (EPQ) model. An early treatment of the formulation of the EPQ model is found in Eilon (1956).

Tables 8.5 and 8.6 overview twelve fuzzy EPQ models have been identified in the literature. Four papers are based on the traditional (crisp) EPQ model and use fuzzy numbers to model the input parameters and the optimal production lot size; eight of the papers apply fuzzy logic to extensions of the traditional EPQ model that addresses multiple items, constraints resulting from cost budgets and limited storage space, and imperfect product quality.

Inventory models that address issues of inventory coordination between a buyer and seller have been extensively studied in the literature. This class of inventory models is commonly referred to as joint economic lot sizing (JELS) models. The objective of these models is the development of a jointly coordinated buyer– seller inventory strategy that is more beneficial to each member's individual noncoordinated inventory strategy. A detailed review of the literature on crisp model formulations of the joint economic lot size model is found in Ben-Daya et al. (2008).

The newsvendor model is a single-period, probabilistic inventory model whose objec-tive is to determine the order quantity that minimizes expected underage costs (costs due to shortage) and overage costs (costs due to holding inventory). Alternatively, the model can also be formulated to maximize expected profits. The interest in the newsvendor model is high with more than fifty papers published on applications of the model in inventory control. A detailed review of the literature up to 1999 was conducted by Khouja (1999).

Fuzzy extensions to the newsvendor model are found in nine papers (see Table 8.8). Early papers (Petrovic et al., 1996; Ishii and Konno, 1998; Li et al., 2002) concen-trated on using fuzzy numbers as an alternative to modeling demand as a random variable and for defining potentially imprecise cost-input parameters. Later papers (Kao and Hsu, 2002a; Dutta et al., 2005; Shao and Ji, 2006) concentrated on dem-onstrating how specialized solution procedures from fuzzy set theory could be used to solve the fuzzy newsvendor problem. Most current papers (Yao et al., 2006; Dutta et al., 2007a; Dey and Chakraborty, 2008) investigate general extensions of the fuzzy newsvendor model into areas of cash management, multiple procurement opportuni-ties, and resalable returns.

In real-world applications, inventory and production decisions are interdependent and temporal in nature. Fuzzy logic has been useful in formulating multiperiod lot sizing models. Table 8.9 provides an overview of fuzzy multiperiod inventory models.

Multi-item models make up a large number of fuzzy inventory models found in the literature. These models typically require advanced solution methodologies such as genetic algorithms, fuzzy simulation-based optimization, and fuzzy non-linear programming.

The trade-offs associated with using continuous review versus periodic review inventory control systems are well addressed in the inventory literature (see, for example, Silver et al., 1998). The majority of inventory models reported in the fuzzy inventory literature have adopted a continuous review inventory control system.

Summary and Conclusions

This chapter has addressed an extensive literature review and survey of fuzzy set theory in inventory management. Eighty-three inventory models organized into seven general classes of inventory models have been reviewed. The emphasis in each review was to identify how fuzzy set theory was used in the formulation of the inven-tory model.

The chapter has also provided a summary of published literature reviews on traditional inventory models. Issues concerning the parameterization of traditional inventory models were also discussed. It is against this landscape that researchers in inventory management may identify the potential benefits of using fuzzy set theory. This chapter should give researchers in inventory management new tools and ideas on how to approach modeling problems in inventory management. The chapter also provides a foundation for researchers currently engaged in research of fuzzy inven-tory models, and hopefully may identify and stimulate new advancements in the application of fuzzy set theory to problems in inventory management.

10

Modeling Hidden Costs of Inventory Systems

A THERMODYNAMIC APPROACH

The earliest inventory model that is available in the literature is the economic order quantity (EOQ) model developed by Harris (1913). Since its introduction, Harris's model has been the basis for many models in inventory management, supply chain management, and reverse logistics. The popularity of the EOQ model has been rec-ognized by both academics and practitioners (e.g., Osteryoung et al. 1986). Some of the positive features attributed to the popularity of the EOQ model are its simple mathematics and the insensitivity of the total cost to changes in the order quan-tity (batch size). Despite its popularity, the EOQ model has been criticized by some researchers on the basis that its assumptions are never met (e.g., Woolsey 1988). Some of these works are reviewed next.

Adkins (1984) observed that the application of EOQ in some firms led to results that ranged from disappointing to disastrous. Selen and Wood (1987) cautioned that substantial miscalculations or misinterpretations during parameter input (most specifically the holding cost and the order cost) determination often led to poor results. Woolsey (1988) severely critiqued using the EOQ model to the extent that he wrote: "If you continue to love and use the EOQ without knowing what it is costing you, I can only suggest that you deserve each other" (p. 72). Jones (1991) cautioned that most accountants fail to identify relevant costs in a system and, consequently, most manufacturers who use the EOQ formula to minimize relevant annual costs will cal-culate a lot size higher than what it would be if the model were employed correctly.

Therefore, the common cost parameters used in the EOQ model are aggregated costs, particularly the ordering cost, holding cost, and shortage cost, and some of their components are difficult to estimate, so the results obtained may be misleading. For example, the holding cost may include all (or some) of the following: cost of money tied up that is either borrowed (on which interest is paid) or could be put to other use (in which case there are opportunity costs); storage cost (supplying a ware-house, rent rates, heat, light, etc.); loss (due to damage, pilferage, and obsolescence); handling (including all movement, special packaging, refrigeration, putting on pal-lets, etc.); administration (stock checks, computer updates, etc.); insurance; and taxes (Waters 2003). In addition to the usual reported costs, there are hidden costs associ-ated with production/inventory systems that are not usually accounted for (Ullmann 1982; Pendlebury and Platford 1988; Gooley 1995; Crusoe et al. 1999; Konar and Cohen 2001; Fisher and Siburg 2003; Callioni et al. 2005).

In recent years, there has been a call by a few researchers in the field to think outside the box of classical inventory management (e.g., Sprague 2002; Bonney et al. 2003; Chikán 2007). This may result in researchers attempting to bridge their fields with others to gain insight into their own, benefiting from the synergies of such processes. For example, some researchers in the discipline of operations research management science have applied Shannon's (1948) information theory and entropy approaches to account for disorder when modeling the behavior of production or supply systems (e.g., Karp and Ronen 1992; Ronen and Karp 1994; McCarthy et al. 2000). However, few have applied classical thermodynamics reasoning to modeling such systems. For example, Jaber et al. (2004) postulated that the behavior of produc-tion systems very much resembles that of physical systems. Such a parallel suggests that improvements to production systems may be achievable by applying the first and second laws of thermodynamics to reduce system entropy (or disorder). Jaber et al. (2004) introduced the concept of entropy cost to account for hidden and difficult-to-estimate costs associated with inventory systems. This chapter will discuss the works along this line of research, and will propose a future research direction. The remainder of this chapter is organized as follows.

Section 9.2 provides a review of the literature for those works that bridged thermodynamics and operations research/management science.

THERMODYNAMICS AND OPERATIONS RESEARCH

Operations research (OR) has always been synonymous with management science, with the names being interchangeable (e.g., Barish 1963). OR tools, such as opti-mization, queuing theory, game theory, decision analysis, and simulation, are being applied to solve real-world problems in inventory theory, supply chain and logistics management, production planning, scheduling, and so forth.

Researchers have been using OR tools to analyze and design more efficient and productive systems. However, few researchers started thinking of such systems as being analogous to physical systems (Goodeve 1953; Wilson 1970), while others attempted to bridge the two disciplines. Drechsler (1965) was the first who attempted to show how the "law of disorder" or the "second law of thermodynamics" (or entropy) influenced management thinking. The second law of thermodynamics sug-gests that every system, left unto itself, tends toward disorder (Drechsler 1968), which frequently appears in the form of queues of materials waiting to be processed, machines waiting for service, finished products waiting for customers, and so forth. Drechsler (1968) applied the law of disorder to analyze complex-decision-type sys-tems where he modeled a decision tree similar to a steam-power generation plant using a thermodynamic analogy. Samaras (1973) argued that the effects of entropy include common problems of inefficiency and related elements such as higher costs, lower outputs, greater wastes, and lower profits. Entropy effects also include a low-ered capability to adapt to changes in the world, low morale, and loss of motiva-tion and business failure. Tyler (1989) presented a model of manpower systems and suggested that entropy can be evaluated from the tenure profles of manpower systems.

This research interest, although slow, continued in recent years. Whewell (1997) argued that logistical processes for supply chains are as significant as are the laws of thermodynamics for technologists. By making parallels between a logistic system and a thermodynamic system, his analysis suggests that suppliers must give their customers increased choice, flexibility, and value from the service they provide if they want to win a larger market share from competitors. Harris (1999) argued that the second law of thermodynamics works. It helps understand the need to achieve higher availability; that is, to keep more customers coming back by having better ser-vice on less-costly items. Chen (1999) matched elements of the business process to components of thermodynamics, and compared the managerial functions of a socio-economic system to the thermodynamic behavior of the physical universe. Two laws of the business process based on those of thermodynamics were derived. The first law states the conservation of resources. Losses in the process, which consume resources and erode system productivity, have been discussed. The second law discusses the governing principle that makes the output of a system acceptable to customers. Tseng (2004) applied the first and second laws of thermodynamics to constrain the pro-cesses by which raw materials are transformed into consumable goods and these goods are distributed afterward. He suggested that the size of the sales force can be determined by introducing the concept of temperature from thermodynamics to rep-resent the flow (demand) of goods as hot (high) or cold (low).

More recently, Jaber et al. (2004) postulated that the behavior of production sys-tems very much resembles that of physical systems. Such a parallel suggests that improvements to production systems may be achievable by applying the first and second laws of thermodynamics to reduce system entropy (or disorder). The EOQ and just-in-time (JIT) models were used to demonstrate the applicability of these laws. Along the same line of research, several models have been developed by the authors in inventory management, supply chain management, and reverse logistics.

The Laws of Thermodynamics and the Concept of Entropy

Thermodynamics is a branch of physics that deals with the energy and work of a system, the transfer of energy between the system and its surrounding, and the con-version of energy from one form to another. Temperature, volume, pressure, and chemical composition are the properties that define a thermodynamic system. A thermodynamic system is said to be in equilibrium when the values for these properties remain unchanged over time. Mainly, there are two laws (the first and the second) of thermodynamics that govern the creation of energy and its flow that are of interest here. For more details, the textbook on thermodynamics by Cengel and Boles (2002) is recommended.

The first law of thermodynamics states that energy is conserved, that is, energy can-not be created or destroyed. Energy can be added to a thermodynamic system from a high-temperature reservoir or lost to a low-temperature sink by a heat (work) pro-cess. The internal energy of a thermodynamic system is the amount added by heat-ing (dQ) minus the amount lost by doing work (dW) on the system. This difference, $dU = dQ - dW$, is the internal energy of a thermodynamic system that is associated with the random, disordered motion of molecules. Analogously, if heat were money, then one could say that a change in savings (dU) is equal to the money deposited (dQ) minus the money withdrawn or spent (dW).

The second law of thermodynamics places constraints upon the direction of the flow of heat between the system and its surrounding. It suggests that it is not pos-sible for a device to operate in a cycle receiving heat and producing a net equivalent amount of work; and that it is not possible for a device to operate in a cycle and produce no effect other than the transfer of heat from a lower-temperature reservoir to a higher-temperature reservoir. The second law of thermodynamics is always asso-ciated with the concept of entropy, which is a measure of the amount of energy that is unavailable to do work (wasted energy) or a measure of the disorder of a system.

The second law of thermodynamics also suggests that the entropy tends to increase with time, that is, entropy is an arrow of time itself. The change in entropy over time, dS/dt, is represented as the heat added or removed over time, dQ/dt, divided by the temperature, that is, $dS/dt = (dQ/dt)/T$ or $dS = dQ/T$.

A thermodynamic system is defined by its properties, which are temperature, vol-ume, pressure, and chemical composition. Analogous to a thermodynamic system, a production system could be described by its characteristics too, which are price and quality of a commodity. For example, reducing (increasing) the price (tempera-ture) of a commodity (energy) below (above) the market price (surrounding tem-perature) conceptually increases customers' demand (energy flows from a high- to a low-temperature reservoir), and produces a commodity flow (sales) from the system to its surrounding (market). Part of the work done on the system to generate this flow of commodity is wasted in accordance with the second law of thermodynam-ics. Figure 9.1 shows some of the commodity flows (sales) to the market that are converted to revenue (equivalent to useful work) and wasted work (hidden cost) that result from this flow process.

Entropy and its Cost

Heat, or energy, can never pass spontaneously from a cold to a hot body. Work needs to be done on the system to allow energy to transfer. This transfer has one direction as the process is irreversible. A parallel could be drawn for a supply system. For exam-ple, a supplier that seeks to increase its share of the market will attempt to increase and sustain customer satisfaction relative to its competitors, and/or attempt to reduce costs associated with providing the same level of satisfaction (Whewell 1997, 18). Whewell (1997) advocates that changes to improve customer satisfaction can alter the established practices in at least one part of the supply process. Such changes can create disorder (entropy) and the costs associated with it are difficult to quantify.

Extensions and Applications

The model developed by Jaber et al. (2004), described in Equation 9.9, was extended to other inventory situations and its applicability was investigated in supply chain and reverse logistics contexts. The extensions to the model of Jaber et al. (2004) and its applications are briefly discussed in the following subsections.

Inventory Management

The work of Jaber et al. (2006) differs from the work of Jaber et al. (2004) by assuming a constant rather than an increasing demand rate for a finite rather than an infinite planning horizon. In Jaber et al. (2006) the price of the commodity contin-ues to decrease as a result of competition in the market, where the firm can predict with certainty that the equilibrium price would reach a target value$P_0(j)$, where $P_0(0) > P_0(T)$, and Tis some future point in time when the firm has no information on how the market price will behave. Their results suggested that for large values of the order cost, A, it might not be necessary to include the entropy cost. This may caution managers who wish to reduce the order (setup) costs to simultaneously reduce entropy costs.

Jaber (2007) extended the model of Jaber et al. (2004) to account for permissible delays in payments. Like quantity discounts (e.g., Crowther 1964; Dolan 1987), per-missible delays in payments is a business practice used by many suppliers to promote commodities and gain larger market shares by offering credit terms to their custom-ers. The EOQ model was investigated for permissible delays in payments (e.g., Haley and Higgins 1973; Kingsman 1983; Goyal 1985; Salameh et al. 2003).

Reverse Logistics

Since the 1980s, manufacturers have been moving toward shorter product life cycles, smaller lot sizes (e.g., JIT), and frequent deliveries to sustain their competitive advantage in a dynamic and global marketplace. This quickened the forward fow of products in a supply chain resulting in faster rates of product waste generation and depletion of natural resources. Consequently, manufacturing and production processes have been viewed as culprits in harming the environment (Fiksel 1996, in Beamon 1999). This concern gave rise to the concept of reverse logistics (RL) or the backward flow of products from customers to manufacturers to suppliers (e.g., Gungor and Gupta 1999). Like supply chains, reverse logistics manages the flow of products to be recovered, however, in the opposite direction (i.e., from downstream to upstream), and therefore managing inventory in reverse logistics is of importance (e.g., Fleischmann et al. 1997).

Jober and Rosen (2008) applied the first and second laws of thermodynamics and the concept of entropy cost developed by Jaber et al. (2004) in a closed-loop model (Richter 1996a, 1996b). The production environment described in Richter (1996a, 1996b) consists of two shops. The first shop is for production and recovery (e.g., repair, remanufacturing), while the second shop is for collecting used/returned items from the market at some rate.

Richter (1996a, 1996b) investigated the EOQ model where recovered items are considered as good as new. The total cost function was an aggregated cost of production, recovery, and holding costs of produced/recovered and used items. Since this model assumes both forward and backward flows of goods to and from the market, Figure 9.1 is altered to model the collection rate (commod-ity flow in the reverse direction), where $V(f)$ is the collection price the manufacturer is willing to pay for a used product, and V_0 () is the collection price a customer can obtain for his/her used product if sold individually where $P_0(f) > P(f) > V(t) > V_0(t)$.

SUMMARY AND CONCLUSIONS

This chapter presented a survey of the recent works that models commodity flow as an energy flow closing boundaries (system to market). These surveyed works pos-tulated that the behavior of production systems resembles that of physical systems. Such a parallel suggests that production systems may be improved by applying the first and second laws of thermodynamics to reduce system entropy (disorder). The rationale for this new concept is to account for the hidden, difficult-to-estimate costs that usually are not accounted for when analyzing inventory systems.

This entropy (disorder) cost (Jaber et al. 2004) was investigated in different con-texts including inventory management (Jaber et al. 2004, 2009; Jaber 2007, 2009, 2009a, 2009b,), supply chain management (Jaber et al. 2006), and reverse logistics (Jaber and Rosen 2008). These studies suggested that when accounting for entropy (disorder) costs, it is cheaper to manage large lots than the small ones. It was further suggested that it might be more relevant to account for entropy for expensive items than for inexpensive ones.

This chapter also extended the model of Jaber et al. (2004) assuming that a com-modity flows from the production/inventory system to the market as a result of price and quality differentials, rather than price alone. A basic mathematical model was developed with illustrative numerical examples. The numerical results described the conditions for three commodity flow strategies. The first strategy, an aggressive one, proposed that a firm competes in its market on both price and quality. This is possible when investing to improve quality is economically feasible and when the unit cost is relatively low compared to price. The second strategy proposed that a firm competes on price alone when it is too expensive to improve the quality of the product. The third and last strategy proposed that a firm competes on quality alone when the unit cost is relatively high compared to price. The models surveyed in this chapter could be revisited and investigated for both price and quality. This is left for future work.

11

Inventory as Money

INTRODUCTION

Why should you care about the financial aspects of inventory? Because inventory is money.

Even if you do not have a financial background, it is impor-tant to understand and appreciate that inventory information in financial statements can be useful in the operation of your busi-ness. A basic understanding of how inventory appears on the balance sheet and its impact on the income statement and cash flow statement will improve your ability to have the right item in the right quantity in the right place at the right time.

Accounting for Inventories

There are three basic types of inventory:

1. Raw Materials—raw materials inventory is made up of goods that will be used in the production of finished products, e.g., nuts, bolts, flour, sugar.
2. Work in Process —work in process inventory, or WIP, consists of materials entered into the production process but not yet completed, e.g., subassemblies.
3. Finished Goods—finished goods inventory includes completed products waiting to be sold, e.g., bar stools, bread, cookies.

Most inventory fits into one of these general buckets, yet the amount of each category varies greatly depending on the specifics of your industry and business. For example, the types of inventory found in distribution environments are fundamen-tally different from those found in manufacturing environments. Distribution businesses tend to carry mostly finished goods for resale while manufacturing companies tend to have less finished goods and more raw materials and work in progress. Given these differences, it is natural that the accounting choices vary between distribution and manufacturing settings.

How Inventory is Valued

In order to assign a cost value to inventory, you must make some assumptions about the inventory on hand. Under the federal in-come tax laws, a company can only make these assumptions once per fiscal year. Tax treatment is often an organization's chief concern regarding inventory valuation. There are five com-mon inventory valuation methods:

1. First-in, First-out (FIFO) inventory valuation assumes that the first goods purchased are the first to be used or sold re-gardless of the actual timing of their use or sale. This method is most closely tied to actual physical flow of goods in inventory.
2. Last-in, First-out (LIFO) inventory valuation assumes that the most recently purchased/acquired goods are the first to be used or sold regardless of the actual timing of their use or sale. Since items you have just bought often cost more than those purchased in the past, this method best matches current costs with current revenues.
3. Average Cost Method of inventory valuation identifies the value of inventory and cost of goods sold by calculating an average unit cost for all goods available for sale during a given period of time. This valuation method assumes that ending in-ventory consists of all goods available for sale.
4. Specific Cost Method (also Actual Cost Method) of in-ventory valuation assumes that the organization can track the actual cost of an item into, through, and out of the facility. That ability allows you to charge the actual cost of a given item to production or sales. Specific costing is generally used only by companies with sophisticated computer systems or reserved for high-value items such as artwork or custom-made items.
5. Standard Cost Method of inventory valuation is often used by manufacturing companies to give all of their depart-ments a

uniform value for an item throughout a given year. This method is a "best guess" approach based on known costs and expenses such as historical costs and any anticipated changes coming up in the foreseeable future. It is not used to calculate actual net profit or for income tax purposes. Rather, it is a work-ing tool more than a formal accounting approach.

4. Inventory on the Balance Sheet

The balance sheet shows the financial position of a company on a specific date. It provides details for the basic accounting equa-tion: Assets = Liabilities + Equity. In other words, assets are a company's resources while liabilities and equity are how those resources are paid for.

- Assets represent a company's resources. Assets can be in the form of cash or other items that have monetary value—in-cluding inventory. Assets are made up of (a) current assets (as-sets that are in the form of cash or that are easily convertible to cash within one year such as accounts receivable, securities, and inventory), (b) longer-term assets such as investments and fixed assets (property/plant/equipment), or (c) intangible assets (patents, copyrights, and goodwill).
- Liabilities represent amounts owed to creditors (debt, ac-counts payable, and lease-term obligations).
- Equity represents ownership or rights to the assets of the company (common stock, additional paid-in capital, and re-tained earnings).

Inventory is typically counted among a company's *cur-rent assets* because it can be sold within one year. This infor-mation is used to calculate financial ratios that help assess the financial health of the company. Note, how-ever, that the balance sheet is not the only place that inventory plays a role in the financial analysis of the company. In fact, in-ventory shows up on the income statement in the form of *cost of goods sold.*

INVENTORY ON THE INCOME STATEMENT

The income statement is a report that identifies a company's rev-enues (sales), expenses, and resulting profits. While the balance sheet can be described as a snapshot of a company on *a specific date* (June 30, for example), the income statement covers *a given-period of time* (June 1 through June 30). The *cost of goods* sold is the item on the income statement that reflects the cost of inventory flowing out of a business.

The old saying, "it costs money to make money," explains the cost of goods sold. You make money by using or selling in-ventory. That inventory costs you something. Cost of goods sold (on the income statement) represents the value of goods (inven-tory) sold during the accounting period. See Exhibit 2-3.

Ratio Analyses and What They Mean

Is something good or is it bad? To answer this question we often compare one thing to another. That is what a "ratio" is: It is an expression of how many of one item is contained within an-other.

Ratios can be used in the business world by selecting parts of an organization's finacial statements and comparing one set of financial conditions to another. A company's financial state-ments contain key aspects of the business. By reviewing these aspects, you can determine an organization's economic well-be-ing. One way of reviewing these financial conditions is to com-pare one to another through dividing one by the other. For example, if you had \$200 cash and \$100 worth of debts, you could divide the cash (assets) by the debt (liabilities) getting a ra-tio of 2 to 1. In other words, you have twice as many assets as you do liabilities.

Ratios are useful tools to explain trends and to summarize business results. Often third parties, such as banks, use ratios to determine a company's credit worthiness. By itself, a ratio holds little meaning. However, when compared to other industry and/or company-specific figures or standards, ratios can be powerful in helping to analyze your company's current and his-torical results. Companies in the same industry often have simi-lar liquidity ratios or benchmarks, as they often have similar cost structures. Your company's ratios can be compared to:

1. Prior period(s)
2. Company goals or budget projections
3. Companies in your industry
4. Companies in other industries
5. Companies in different geographic regions

6. In particular, here are three ratios that are useful when as-sessing inventory.

Current Ratio. The current ratio assesses the organiza-tion's overall liquidity and indicates a company's ability to meet its short-term obligations. In other words, it measures whether or not a company will be able to pay its bills. Techni-cally speaking, the current ratio indicates how many dollars of assets we have for each dollar of liabilities that we owe.

Current Assets, refers to assets that are in the form of cash or that are easily convertible to cash within one year, such as accounts receivable, securities, and inventory. *Current Liabilities* refers to liabilities that are due and payable within twelve months, such as accounts payable, notes payable, and short-term portion of long-term debt.

Standards for the current ratio vary from industry to indus-try. Companies in the service industry that carry little or no in-ventory typically have current ratios ranging from 1.1 to 1.3—that is, $1.10 to $1.30 in current assets for each dollar of cur-rent liabilities. Companies that carry inventory have higher cur-rent ratios. Manufacturing companies are included in this latter group and often have current ratios ranging from 1.6 to 2.0; not only do they have inventory in the form of finished goods ready for sale, but they also carry inventory of goods that are not yet ready for sale. Generally speaking, the longer it takes a company to manufacture the inventory and the more inventory it must keep on hand, the higher the current ratio.

What the current ratio might mean: *A* low current ratio may signal that a company has liquidity problems or has trouble meeting its short- and long-term obliga-tions. In other words, the organization might be suffering from a lack of cash flow to cover operating and other expenses. As a re-sult, accounts payable may be building at a faster rate than re-ceivables. Note, however, that this is only an indicator and must be used in conjunction with other factors to determine the over-all financial health of an organization. In fact, some companies can sustain lower-than-average current ratios because they move their inventory quickly and/or are quick to collect from their customers and therefore have good cash flow.

A high current ratio is not necessarily desirable. It might in-dicate that the company is holding high-risk inventory or may be doing a bad job of managing its assets. For example, fashion retailers may have costly inventory, but they might also have significant trouble getting rid of the inventory—if the wrong clothing line was selected for example. This makes it a high-risk company, forcing creditors to require a bigger financial cushion. Further, if a high current ratio is a result of a very large cash account, it may be an indication that the company is not rein-vesting its cash appropriately. Even if the current ratio looks fine, other factors must be taken into consideration, as liquidity prob-lems might still exist. Since ratios look at quantity, not quality, it is important to look at what the current assets consist of to deter-mine if they are made up of slow-moving inventory. In order to assess inventory's impact on liquidity, another test of liquidity should be taken into account—the Quick Ratio (or Acid Test).

Quick Ratio or Acid Test. The quick ratio compares the organization's most liquid current assets to its current liabili-ties.

Assume that an industry that sells on credit has a quick ra-tio of at least 0.8. In other words, the company has at least 80¢ in liquid assets (likely in the form of accounts receivable) for every $1 of liabilities. Industries that have significant cash sales (such as grocery stores) tend to be even lower. As with the current ra-tio, a low quick ratio is an indicator of cash flow problems, while a high ratio may indicate poor asset management as cash may be properly reinvested or accounts receivable levels are out of con-trol. An organization's ability to promptly collect its accounts re-ceivable has a significant impact on this ratio. The quicker the collection the more liquidity it has.

Inventory Turnover Ratio. The inventory turnover ratio measures, on average, how many times inventory is replaced over a period of time. In its simplest sense, an inventory turn occurs every time an item is received, is used or sold, and then is replaced. If an SKU came in twice during the year, was used/sold, and then replenished, that would be two turns per year. If this happened once per month, it would be twelve turns per year, and so forth.

Inventory turnover is an important measure since the abil-ity to move inventory quickly directly impacts the company's liquidity. Inventory turnover is calculated as follows:

Inventory Turnover Ratio = Cost of Goods Sold %* % Average Inventory

Essentially, when a product is sold, it is subtracted from in-ventory and transferred to cost of goods sold. Therefore, this ratio indicates how quickly inventory is moving for accounting pur-poses. It does not necessarily reflect how many times actual physi-cal items were handled within the facility itself. This is true because the cost of goods sold number may include items you sold but never physically handled. For example, items that we purchase and then have drop-shipped directly at our customer's site aren't ever handled within our facility.

Note that if the inventory has increased or decreased signif-icantly during the year, the average inventory for the year may be skewed and not accurately reflect your turnover ratio going forward. Also, if the company uses the LIFO method of account-ing, the ratio may be inflated because LIFO may undervalue the inventory.

Unlike the current ratio and quick ratio, the inventory turnover ratio does not adhere to a standard range. Organiza-tions with highly perishable products can have inventory turns of 30 times a year or more. Companies that retain large amounts of inventory or that require a long time to build their inventory might have turns of only two or three times a year. In general, the overall trend in business today is to reduce carrying costs by limiting the amount of inventory in stock at any given time. As a result, both individual inventory turnovers and industry aver-ages in this area have increased in recent years.

It is important to understand, however, that many factors can cause a low inventory turnover ratio. The company may be holding the wrong type of inventory, its quality may be lacking, or it may have sales/marketing issues.

Obsolete Stock

Any stockkeeper who has had to repeatedly move really slow moving or outright dead stock out of the way or finds herself hurting for space because obsolete product eats up square foot after square foot knows that these items "just gotta go."

Why You Have Been Told Not to Dispose of It

Why is the dead stock still here? The three reasons most often given as to why the product can't be disposed of are:

1. It's already paid for.

2. We might use it someday.
3. We might sell it someday.

These explanations seem logical and the idea of throwing away dead stock may be counterintuitive. Indeed, there are some very real practical problems with simply hauling it off to the dumpster.

Problems with Convincing Decision Makers That "Its Gotta Go"

Decision makers often have difficulty with disposing of dead in-ventory because it will adversely impact the balance sheet and deplete resources considered to be valuable for lending purposes.

Impact of write off Anything that appears as an asset on the balance sheet has an accounting value. This value, consisting of an item's original cost minus depreciation, is called the "book value." It is irrelevant that the item may actually be worthless to either a customer or as part of a manufacturing process. If it has a one-dollar value on the books, then disposing of dead inven-tory has an accounting consequence to our organization.

If we sell dead inventory that has a monetary value at a deep discount, throw it away, or give it away to a charity, we will have to immediately write-off the book value of those items, which will, of course, have a negative impact on the financial statements.

If your organization is sensitive to making extraordinary adjustments to the balance sheet and never or seldom writes off dead inventory, you may have a difficult time ever convincing any decision maker to dispose of these items. The decision maker will simply not be willing to "take the hit on the books."

Organization's capital structure Almost everyone has heard the expression, "cash is king." The problem for many organ-izations is that cash flow doesn't always keep up with our needs.

Often organizations raise operating capital by borrowing against (a) their accounts receivable and (b) the book value of the inventory they are carrying.

"Accounts receivable" are the amounts due from customers resulting from normal sales activities. Depending on the indus-try, banks will generally lend up to *75* percent of the value of ac-counts receivable due in ninety days or less.

Bankers will also lend against the book value of inventory. The willingness to lend against this asset is not as straightfor-ward as with accounts receivable. The more complex nature of these transactions comes from the fact that in accordance with accepted accounting practices, we should value inventory at the *lower* of cost or fair market value. Therefore, dead stock should logically be valued at a fair market value of zero dollars no mat-ter what it originally cost.

In spite of generally accepted accounting practices and even though parts of your inventory have no real market value (and should be valued at zero dollars), bankers will often loan your organization 50 to 60 percent of the value of the inventory *as that value is shown on the books.* So, companies will sometimes continue to carry dead stock so as to retain this artificial value on the books. This is an area most stockkeepers will not have any direct control over. However, the arguments below may over-come the need to keep inventory values artificially high.

ARGUMENTS IN FAVOR OF DISPOSING OF DEAD STOCK

Strong arguments can be made in favor of disposing of nonpro-ductive stock including recapture of space, better use of labor and equipment, plus a reduction in the costs associated with having inventory sitting around.

Recapture of Space

In terms of space utilization, there are some simple math-ematical facts to keep in mind: —Multiplying an item's length times its width tells you the amount of square feet the item is occupying. —Multiplying an item's length times its width times its height tells you the amount of cubic space it is occupying.

If you were to actually figure out the cubic space taken up by dead product, you would gain a powerful argument in favor of disposing of this inventory. To bolster the argument, you may want to ask your organization's financial officer how much the company is paying per square foot for rent. Multiplying the square footage being consumed by dead product times the rent per square foot often results in a truly eye-opening dollar amount. Providing actual numbers to a decision maker is far more effective than speaking in generalities like, "dead stock is taking up a lot of space." Pointing out that obsolete stock is "tak-ing up 4,000 square feet" or "represents $2,000 per month in per square foot costs" should help you convince your decision maker that "its gotta go."

Efficient Utilization of Labor and Machine Resources

Not only does obsolete inventory take up a lot of space, it can also get in the way of workers. Repeatedly moving obsolete product out of the way hurts efficient use of both labor and machine time.

Too often, in trying to argue against keeping obsolete stock, stockkeepers will state generalities like, "it takes us a lot of time to move that stuff around." How long is "a lot of time"? Is it an hour a day, four hours per week? Without specific numbers your arguments will sound hollow.

As many business writers have noted, "You cannot con-trol what you do not measure." There are two things to do to get specific time and dollar amounts you need to:

—During each week for one month, every time you or your staff move dead product out of the way, measure the amount of direct labor that goes into that effort. Remem-ber, if two workers are working together to move the items and they work for fifteen minutes, that represents fifteen minutes times two, or thirty minutes of direct labor.

—At the end of the month, divide the total amount of la-bor hours by four to determine a weekly average. To de-termine the amount of yearly labor involved in moving dead stock, multiply the weekly average times the num-ber of weeks in a year your company operates.

Once again, obtain base information from your financial of-ficer and multiply the average hourly wage you pay your work-ers, including benefits, times the annual labor number. The result will make a rather impressive argument as to how the or-ganization can save thousands of dollars per year by disposing of its dead stock.

Reduction of Carrying Costs (the K Factor)

The K Factor represents the number of pennies per in-ventory dollar per year a company is spending to house its inventory. It is generally expressed as a percent. In other words, a K Factor of 25 percent means that you are spending 25¢ per inventory dollar per year to house your inventory. A one dollar dead item that sits on your shelf for a year would cost you *25¢* that year, a total of 50¢ at the end of the second year, a total of *75¢* at the end of the third year, and so on.

There are two ways of computing the K Factor—a tradi-tional method in which you add together various expenses di-rectly related to carrying inventory and a rough rule-of-thumb method.

Since it always costs something to carry inventory, it is ob-vious that the longer dead stock remains in your facility, the more it will cost. Two approaches can be used to effectively ar-gue this point: 1. Demonstrate the impact of carrying costs on your exist-ing dead stock. This addresses the "We've already paid for it," argument in favor of retaining dead stock. 2. Demonstrate that if the product remains long enough, even selling it at a profit will not recapture your original cost. This addresses the "We might need it someday," and, "We might sell it someday," arguments in favor of retaining dead stock.

A percentage is used to indicate the amount of dead stock in the facility. Note, however, it is always more convincing to a decision maker if you use actual lists and dollar amounts to demonstrate those items that are dead rather than using a generality like a rough percentage.

Methods of Disposal

Various approaches to disposing of dead stock exist:

- Sell at net price
- Temporarily raise commissions for salespeople
- Discount the price
- Return to vendor
- Donate it
- Write it off
- Auction.

It is important to remember something about convincing decision makers of anything. Ordinarily, when reports or other information flow up a chain of command, the level of detail at each level *decreases*. Generally, each higher level of management wants to see less and less information with which to make deci-sions. You should resist providing only minimal data in making arguments regarding dead stock. This is a time to let the detail do the talking.

CARRYING COST AND PURCHASING

Although you should only have the minimum amount of inven-tory on hand required for either production or distribution, be careful not to purchase small quantities over and over again. Buying small amounts frequently will lead to an excessive cost of replenishment (the "R Factor"). A simple example of how an excessive R Factor can be cre-ated would be the following:

Assumptions: It costs a certain amount of money per line item, per pur-chase order to buy something. Assume $2.59 per line item, per purchase order for this example. Determining the R Factor.

You Purchase 1 million widgits per year.

If you bought all 1 million widgits at one time, the R Factor would be $2.59 since there was only one purchase order with one line item on it.

If you bought 250,000 widgits at a time, the R Factor would be $10.36. That is because you would have four purchase orders with one line item each at a cost of $2.59 each.

If you bought 1 million widgits one at a time at an R Factor of $2.59 each the replenishment cost would be $2,590,000!

Because of the R Factor, modern purchasing dictates that you buy larger quantities on fewer purchase orders, but with suppliers releasing items on a prearranged schedule or on de-mand.

Ultimately, the point at which your cost of carrying inven-tory matches the cost of purchasing it is the proper economic order quantity of that item. See Chapter 5, Planning and Re-plenishment Concepts, Replenishment Costs.

The objective of this chapter was to provide you ' with highlights of the most basic accounting con-cepts you, as a stockkeeper, must understand to successfully discuss and plan inventory values with your colleagues. Although you may never participate in the preparation of month- or year-end financial statements, it is in your own self-interest to review these statements and think about how the in-ventory values reflected impact your operation. And finally, whenever discussing either buying more stock or getting rid of dead stock, it is always more persuasive to use ac-tual numbers than to deal in generalities. Remember, "if you can measure it, you can control it."

12

Physical Location and Control of Inventory

INTRODUCTION

If you can't find an item you can't count it, fill an order with it, or build a widgit with it. This chapter is about setting up a sys-tem that allows you to put items where they will do the most good for your organization.

If you cannot control the location of your product or raw materials from both a physical and a recordkeeping standpoint, then your inventory accuracy will suffer.

To sustain inventory accuracy on an ongoing basis you must:

1. formalize the overall locator system used throughout the facility
2. track the storage and movement of product from
    a. receipt to storage
    b. order filling to shipping or to staging at a point-of-use
3. maintain timely records of all item storage and movement

The objective of this chapter is to provide you with a work-ing knowledge of (i) three key stock locator systems (which re-late to the overall organization of SKUs within a facility and their impact on space planning); (ii) item placement theories dealing with the specific arrangement of products within an area of the warehouse (should the box be over here or over there?); and (iii) some practical methods of attaching addresses to stock items and how to tie an item number to its location address.

Common Locator Systems

The purpose of a material locator system is to create procedures that allow you to track product movement throughout the facil-ity. Although going by many names, the most common "pure" systems are *memory, fixed,* and *random.* A type of fixed system is the *zone* system. The *combination* approach is a common mixture of the fixed and random systems.

In considering which locator system will work best, you should attempt to maximize:

- Use of space
- Use of equipment
- Use of labor
- Accessibility to all items
- Protection from damage
- Ability to locate an item
- Flexibility
- The reduction of administrative costs

Maximizing all of these considerations at the same time is difficult, if not impossible. Often each of these concerns creates

Examples of Valid Storage Considerations in Conflict

- Scenario One—*Accessibility versus Space:* Charmax, Inc. wishes to have its entire product as easy to get to as possible for order filling purposes. It therefore attempted to have a "picking face" (a front line, visible position from which the product can easily be selected) for each item. In order to actually create a picking face for each SKU, Char-max would have to assign a specific location for every product appearing on all of its pick tickets, with no two items being placed one on top of another, and no item be-ing placed behind another. Charmax quickly realized that it lacked sufficient space in its facility to have a specific posi-tion for every item it carried.
- Scenario Two—*Use of Labor Versus Protection from Damage:* Alana Banana Enterprises wishes to reduce labor hours by putting into place efficient product handling pro-cedures. Its intent is to develop standard operating proce-dures so that workers will

only handle SKUs four times: once when it is received, once when stored, once when conflicts with one or more of the others. For example, you may wish to store all cylinders together in order to utilize the same equipment to handle them or locate them together for ease of getting to and retrieving them. However, if the chemical nature of the contents of these cylinders prohibits them from being stored in the same area, safety and protection of property con-cerns overcome other considerations picked, and once when loaded. However, in order to pro-tect SKUs from bruising, items must be placed into protec-tive cartons for storage. SKUs are not picked in full carton quantities so workers have to remove various quantities at different times from the cartons. Empty cartons must then be stacked, cleaned, restacked, and taken back to the receiv-ing area for reuse. These protective measures add a number of labor intensive steps to the process.

- Scenario Three—*Ability To Locate an Item Versus Space Utilization:* Racquetballers America wants to assign a spe-cific home to each of its products for inventory control pur-poses. However, it has a small stockroom. Racquetballers realizes that if it uses a fixed storage location approach it must assign sufficient space to store the maximum amount of any one of its SKUs that will ever be on hand at one time in that location. If it uses a random location approach where items can be placed one on top of another or behind one an-other, then it will maximize its use of space. Racquetballers decides using its limited space is more important than put-ting in the extra labor and administration necessary to keep track of where everything is as it moves around the floor.

The stockkeeper should select a locator system that pro-vides the best solution given the tradeoffs between conflicting objectives. No one system is "right." What is best will depend on considerations such as:

- Space available
- Location system
- Dimensions of product or raw materials stored
- Shape of items

- Weight of items
- Product characteristics, such as stackable, toxic, liquid, crushable
- Storage methods, such as floor stacked, racks, carousels, shelving
- Labor availability
- Equipment, including special attachments available
- Information systems support

Every company has a limited amount of space available for stock storage. Some locator systems use space more effectively than do others. When choosing your locator system, you need to think carefully about how much space it will use. The following pages show several types of locator systems and evaluate the strengths and weaknesses of each type.

MEMORY SYSTEMS

Basic Concept—Memory Systems

Memory systems are solely dependent on human recall. Often they are little more than someone saying, "I think it's over there."

The foundations of this locator system are simplicity, rela-tive freedom from paperwork or data entry, and maximum uti-lization of all available space.

Conditions Under Which Memory Systems Will Work

- Storage locations are limited in number.
- Storage locations are limited in size.
- The variety of items stored in a location is limited.
- The size, shape, or unitization (e.g., palletization, strap-ping together, banding, etc.) of items allows for easy vi-sual identification and separation of one SKU from another.
- Only one or a very limited number of individuals work within the storage areas.
- Workers within the storage area do not have duties that require them to be away from those locations.
- The basic types of items making up the inventory does not radically change within short time periods.
- There is not a lot of stock movement.

Impact on Physical Space—Memory Systems

The most complete space utilization is available through this system. Why? Because no item has a dedicated location that would prevent other SKUs from occupying that same stock lo-cation position if it were empty (either side-to-side or up-and-down).

Pros—Memory Systems

- Simple to understand
- Little or no ongoing paper-based or computer-based tracking required
- Full utilization of space
- No requirement for tying a particular stocking location, identifier, bin, slot, drawer, rack, bay, spot, to a specific SKU
- Requirements of single item facilities (such as a grain silo) can be met

Cons—Memory Systems

- The organization's ability to function must strongly rely on the memory, health, availability, and attitude of a sin-gle individual (or a small group of people).
- Significant and immediate decreases in accuracy result from changes in the conditions set out in Exhibit 3-2.
- Once an item is lost to recall, it is lost to the system.

Despite its limitations, a memory system may be as efficient as any other, particularly if there are only a limited number of different SKUs within a small area.

FIXED LOCATION SYSTEMS

Basic Concept—Fixed Location Systems

In pure fixed location systems, every item has a home and noth-ing else can live there. Some (not pure) fixed systems allow two or more items to be assigned to the same location, with only those items being stored there.

Impact on Physical Space—Fixed Location Systems

If quantities of any given SKU are large, then its "home" may consist of two or more storage positions. However, collectively all of these positions are the only places where this item may exist within the facility, and no other items may reside there. Basi-cally, everything has a home and nothing else can live there.

Fixed location systems require large amounts of space. There are two reasons for this:

- Honeycombing
- Planning around the largest quantity of an item that will be in the facility at one time

Honeycombing is the warehousing situation where there is storage space available but not being fully utilized due to:

Cause	Description
• Product shape	Physical characteristics cut down on stackability and prevent use of cubic space or prevent placing one item against another.
• Product put away	Product not stacked or placed in a uniform manner causing loss of vertical or horizontal space.
• Location system rules	Situation where a location is empty but no other item may be placed there since it is not the sec-ond item's assigned home.
• Poor housekeeping	Trash, poorly placed desks, etc. force empty space around it.

Honeycombing is unavoidable given location system trade-offs, product shape, and so on. The goal of a careful layout is to minimize how often and to what extent this happens.

Honeycombing occurs both horizontally (side-to-side) and vertically (up-and-down), robbing us of both square feet and cu-bic space.

There are two simple methods of determining the level of honeycombing within your own facility. One deals with a sim-ple ratio analysis, the other with cubic space. See Exhibits 3-4 and 3-5.

The other thing that causes the fixed system to require sig-nificant space is the necessity of planning around the largest quantity of an item that will be in the facility at one time. Each SKU will have an assigned location or locations. This "home" must be large enough to contain the total cubic space the item will fill-up at the time that the largest quantity of that item will be in the facility at one time. In other words, if a thousand cases of widgits are all in the warehouse at the same time, the home of the widgits has to be large enough to hold them all. Therefore, the to-tal space required for all items in a fixed system will be the total cubic space of one hundred percent of all SKUs as though the maximum quantity of each of them was in the facility at one time.

ZONING SYSTEMS

Basic Concept—Zoning Systems

Zoning is centered around an item's characteristics. Like a fixed system, only items with certain characteristics can live in a par-ticular area. Items with different attributes can't live there.

An SKU's characteristics would cause the item to be placed within a certain area of the stockroom or at a particular level within a section of shelving or rack section. For example, irregular shaped SKUs might be placed in lower levels to ease handling, or all items requiring the use of a forklift for put away or retrieval might be located in a specific area and on pallets.

Impact on Physical Space—Zoning Systems

As with dedicated systems, the more you tightly control where a particular item will be stored, the more you will contribute to honeycombing or to the need to plan around maximum quantities.

Pros—Zoning Systems

- Allows for the isolation of SKUs according to such char-acteristics as size, variety, flammability, toxicity, weight, lot control, private labeling, and so on.
- Allows for flexibility moving items from one zone to an-other quickly or in creating different zones efficiently.
- Allows for the addition of SKUs within a zone (unlike a fixed system) without having to move significant amounts of product to create room within an assigned location or within a sequentially numbered group of items. It also does not require the collapsing of space if an item is deleted.
- Allows for flexibility in planning: Although items are as-signed to a general zone, because they do not have a spe-cific position they must reside in, there is no need to plan around one hundred percent of any given item's cubic requirements.

Cons—Zoning Systems

- Zoning is not always required for efficient product han-dling. You may be adding needless administrative com-plexity by utilizing zoning.
- Zoning may contribute to honeycombing.
- Zoning requires updating of stock movement informa-tion.

Basically zoning allows for control of item placement based on whatever characteristics the stockkeeper feels are important.

RANDOM LOCATION SYSTEMS

Basic Concept—Random Location Systems

In a random system nothing has a home, but you know where everything is. Pure random location systems allow for the maxi-mization of space since no item has a fixed home and may be placed wherever there is space. This allows SKUs to be placed above or in front of one another and for multiple items to occupy a single bin/slot/position/rack.

The primary characteristic of a random locator system that makes it different from a memory system is that each SKU identifier is tied to whatever location address it is in while it is there. In other words, memory systems tie nothing together, except in the mind of the stockkeeper. Ran-dom systems have the flexibility of a memory system coupled with the control of a fixed or zone system. Essentially an item can be placed anywhere so long as its location is accurately noted in a computer database or a manually maintained paper-based card file system. When the item moves, it is deleted from that location. Therefore, an SKU's address is the location it is in while it is there.

Impact on Physical Space—Random Location Systems

Because items may be placed wherever there is space for them, random locator systems provide us with the best use of space and maximum flexibility while still allowing control over where an item can be found.

Planning space around a random locator system is gener-ally based on the cubic space required for the average number of SKUs on-hand at any one time. Therefore, in planning space re-quirements around a random locator system, you need to dis-cern from our inventory records what our average inventory levels are and what products are generally present within that

PLANNING A STORAGE AREA AROUND A FIXED OR A RANDOM LOCATION SYSTEM

If Hammer Co was going to store product in fixed positions, it would have to plan around a minimum of 7,600 cubic feet of actual storage space. Although each of these items is required to produce Hammer Company's products, they are not all needed at the same time. On average Ham-mer only has on-hand 30 percent of any of the above items at any one time. If it used a random lo-cator system it would plan for approximately 2,280 cubic feet of actual storage area average. By multiplying the cubic footage of each of those items by the quantity of each usually onhand, you can determine our space required.

Pros—Random Location Systems

- Maximization of space.
- Control of where all items are at any given time.

Cons—Random Location Systems

- Constant updating of information is necessary to track where each item is at any given time. Updating must be accomplished through manual paper-based recording, bar code scanning, or data entry intensive updating. See pages 84-86 regarding maintenance of product location information.
- May be unnecessarily complicated if your organization has a small number of SKUs.

Basically, random location systems force a tradeoff between maximization of space and minimization of administration.

COMBINATION SYSTEMS

Basic Concept—Combination Systems

Combination systems enable you to assign specific locations to those items requiring special consideration, while the bulk of the product mix will be randomly located. Very few systems are purely fixed or purely random.

Conceptually you are trying to enjoy the best features of the fixed and random systems. You achieve this by assigning only selected items to fixed homes—but not all items. Therefore, you only have to plan around the maximum space required by the selected items instead of that required by all items. For the items not in fixed homes, you can plan around the average quantities you expect to have on a daily, ongoing basis. So, the fixed system is used for the selected items and the random system for every-thing else.

A common application of the combination system ap-proach is where certain items are an organization's primary product or raw materials line and must be placed as close as possible to a packing/shipping area or to a manufacturing work station. Those items are assigned a fixed position, while the remainder of the product line is randomly positioned else-where.

TYPICAL SCENARIOS INVOLVING COMBINATION LOCATION SYSTEMS

Scenario One: Barash Foods decided to speed up its or-der filling efforts by changing where product was located in relationship to the shipping dock. First it determined which 15 percent-20 percent of its product lines showed up on 80 percent of its orders. (See "A-B-C Categorization" on pages 66-67 for an explanation of the 80/20 Pareto's Law con-cept.) These items would be assigned to fixed positions close to the point-of-use (shipping dock), while those items found in only 20 percent of the orders would be randomly stored.

Barash had to decide if these fixed homes would be large enough to hold 100 percent of the cubic space neces-sary to house a product if the maximum quantity of it was in the facility at one time during the year.

The company de-cided it could not devote that much space per product in the limited area closest to the point-of-use. It therefore de-cided to allow for 100 percent of the space needed for one week's worth of product movement for the fixed location SKUs. In other words, while still having to follow the fixed location system rule that space must exist for 100 percent of the cubic space required for the maximum quantity of an item expected during a given time period, it controlled the space and quantity by shortening the time frame.

Random items were stored in accordance with the gen-eral rule that random space is planned around the average quantity expected in an area during a defined time period. In this case the time period was one year.

Scenario Two: Charmax Manufacturing is a "job shop" electronics manufacturer. It manufactures special order items and often will only produce one, never to be repeated run of an item. Therefore, some specific raw materials in-ventories required for any given production run may never be needed in the future. However, the company uses many common electronics components such as resisters, transis-tors, and solder in most of the final assemblies it produces. Its physical plant is very small.

Charmax carefully reviews its master production schedule to determine when various subassemblies and fi-nal assemblies will be produced. It then analyzes the bill-of-materials (the recipe of components) for the sub- or final assemblies, and orders as much specific purpose items as possible on a to be delivered just-in-time basis. This holds down the quantity of nonstandard inventory it will have in-house at any one time.

Charmax then establishes fixed positions for working stock, both special order and standard stock items, during a production cycle around the appropriate workstations. Where working stock would consume too much space around a work area, working reserve stock is placed in zone locations close to the workstations. Regular, general use product, such as resisters and transistors, is stored in ran-dom order.

This combination location system—which is com-prised of fixed, zone and random storage for working, working reserve and general stock—allows Charmax to maximize its use of space at any given time.

Common Item Placement Theories

Locator systems provide a broad overview of where SKUs will be found within a facility. Physical control of inventory is en-hanced by narrowing the focus of how product should be laid out within any particular location system. As with locator sys-tems, item placement theories (where should a particular item or category of items be physically positioned) go by many different names in textual as well as in trade literature. By whatever name, most approaches fall into one of three concepts: inventory stratification, family grouping, and special considerations.

Inventory Stratification

Inventory stratification consists of two parts:

- A-B-C categorization of SKUs.
- Utilizing an SKU's unloading/loading ratio.
- *A-B-C Categorization*

This item placement approach is based on "Pareto's Law." In 1907, an Italian sociologist and economist by the name of Vil-fredo Pareto (1848-1923) wrote his belief that 80 to 85 percent of Italy's money was held by only 15 to 20 percent of the country's population. He called the small, wealthy group the "vital few" and everyone else the "trivial many." This ultimately came to be known as the "80-20 Rule" or Pareto's Law. The concept stands for the proposition that within any given population of things, approximately 20 percent of them have 80 percent of the "value" of all of the items concentrated within them, and that the other 80 percent only have 20 percent of the value concentrated within them. "Value" can be defined in various ways. For example, if the criterion is money, then 20 percent of all items represent 80 percent of the dollar value of all items. If the criterion is usage rate, then 20 percent of all items represent the 80 percent of the items most often used/sold.

Accordingly, for efficient physical inventory control, using popularity (speed of movement into and through the facility) as the criterion, the most productive overall location for an item is a storage position closest to that item's point-of-use. SKUs are separated into A-B-C categories, with "A" representing the most popular, fastest moving items (the "vital few"), "B" representing the next most active, and "C" the slow-movers.

Providing product to outside customers is often the chief objective of a distribution environment. Therefore, the point-of-use would be the shipping dock, with SKUs being assigned in the manner. In a manufacturing environ-ment, a work station would become the point-of-use, with the most active, most often required raw materials positioned in near proximity to it.

In order to separate an inventory into A-B-C categories, it is necessary to create a sorted matrix that presents all SKUs in de-scending order of importance and allows for the calculation of those items representing the greatest concentration of value. Before attempting to understand how the matrix is mathe-matically constructed, you first have to explore what informa-tion the matrix is presenting.

What the Matrix Shows

- Column A is merely a sequential listing of the number of SKUs in the total population. In the example there are 300 items. If an organization had 2,300 SKUs, Column A of its matrix would end with row 2,300.
- Recall that there are two components within Pareto's Law. The first component refers to the percentage of all items that a certain number of items represent, and the second compo-nent represents the percentage value that the same grouping of items has when compared to the value of all other items com-bined.

Special Considerations

A product's characteristics may force us to receive/store/ pick/ship it in a particular manner. The product may be ex-tremely heavy or light, toxic or flammable, frozen, odd in shape, and so on.

Even with items requiring special handling or storage such as frozen food stored in a freezer, the inventory stratification and family grouping concepts can and should be employed to ensure efficient inventory layout.

LOCATION ADDRESSES AND SKU IDENTIFIERS

Significance

You simply cannot control what you can't find. Major contribut-ing factors to the success of inventory systems are:

- Adequate, appropriate identification markings on SKUs, including both SKU number and stockkeeping unit of measure. These markings allow a worker to quickly and easily identify an item without having to read and translate product descriptions and confusing pack size designations. This ease of recognition reduces errors and the time required for either stock selection of put-away

- Adequate, appropriate identification markings on bin/ slot/ floor/rack/drawer/shelf locations. Just like the address on a house, the address of a specific location in the stockroom lets you quickly find the "tenant" or "homeowner" SKU you are looking for.
- Procedures tying any given SKU to the location it is in at any given time. How does the post office know where to send mail to someone after they have moved? Obviously, the relo-cated person fills out a change of address form. In much the same manner, you must set up a procedure that tells your sys-tem where a product lives, and if it moves—where to.
- Procedures tying a single SKU to multiple locations in which it is stored. If you have two homes, you let your friends know the addresses. Your friends then put that information to-gether in their address books. You must do the same thing for products residing in two or more locations within the building.
- A system for tracking items, on a timely basis, as they change locations. Whatever form your "change of address" form takes, it has to be filled out and processed quickly.
- Package advertising that does not obscure SKU identifier codes.
- Use of simple marking systems that are easy to read and understand. You should avoid complicated marking systems that are difficult to read, understand, recall, or are conducive to numerical transposition. For example, markings such as "12/ 24 oz" and "24/12 oz" are quantity oriented coding employing numbers describing the quantity and size of the inner packages. However, such numbers are easily reversed or transposed, and are not intuitively understood.

If you incorporate these elements into your inventory systems, you can expect:

- Decreased labor costs related to search time for product. These search-time savings manifest themselves not only when you search for an individual item, but most definitely when product is located in multiple unspecified locations.
- Decreased labor costs associated with searching for ap-propriate storage locations.

- Elimination of the unnecessary purchase of items that are already in the facility but are undiscovered when needed.
- Correct selection of SKUs during order filling.
- Correct selection of pack size(s) during order fulfillment.

All of the above lead to more accurate inventory tracking, less wasted time to correct errors, and an increase in customer satis-faction.

Keys to Effectively Tying Together SKUs and Location Addresses

In order to keep track of where SKUs are at any given time, it is necessary to:

1. Clearly mark items with an SKU identifier.
2. Clearly mark items with a unit of measure such as pack size.
3. Clearly mark location addresses on bins/slots/shelves/ racks/ floor locations/drawers/and so on.
4. Tie SKU numbers and location addresses together either in a manual card file system or within a computerized database.
5. Update product moves on a real-time basis with bar cod-ing coupled with radio frequency scanners (see Chapter 4, The Basics of Bar Coding) or with stock movement reporting (see the section in this chapter on *updating product moves,* pages 84-86).

Clearly Mark Items with an SKU Identifier; Clearly Mark Items with a Unit of Measure

Too often managers believe that workers can read a product's markings and packaging and actually understand what they are looking at. The end result of this belief is error after error. To eliminate many of these identification miscues, you need to clearly mark out items with an identifying number and a unit of measure. Workers will make far fewer errors matching a number on a box to the same number on a piece of paper than they will trying to match words or abbreviated descriptions.

The SKU identifier is generally an organization's own inter-nal identifying code for the item rather than a manufacturer's or customer's number for that SKU. Although the SKU number itself is often adequate for identification purposes, in manufac-turing it may be necessary to also include lot and serial numbers to aid in quality control. Lot and serial numbers make it possible to track manufacturing batch, date, location, and inspector.Marking SKUs

By manufacturer

- Manufacturer prints or affixes plain, human read- able label on the item and/or a bar code label with coding on the items. Manufacturer obtains labels or you provide them.

At vendor site

- Vendor from whom you obtain the product prints or affixes your plain, human readable label on the item and/or a bar code label with coding on the items. Manu- facturer obtains labels or you provide them.

At time of receiving

- Everything comes through receiving—it is a natural node. That convergence allows you the opportunity to affix plain, human readable label on the item and/or a bar code label with coding on the items.
- You can have all product that turns even once dur-ing the year marked in this manner, with faster moving items (12 turns a year) all marked within a few weeks.

Markings related to unit of measure (such as each/pair/ dozen/ barrel/ounce/pound/cylinder/barrel/case) also serve to greatly reduce error in picking and shipping.

Clearly Mark Location Addresses On Bins/Slots/Shelves/ Racks/Floor Locations/Drawers

Just as you could not find a house in a city if its address was not clearly identified, you cannot find a storage location unless its ad-dress is clearly marked or easily discerned in some other manner. The addressing or location system you choose should have an un-derlying logic that is easy to understand. Addresses should be as short as possible, yet they should convey all needed information. You should first consider whether the system will be all nu-meric, all alphabetic (alpha), or alpha-numeric. In deciding which system to adopt, consider the following:

- All numeric systems require sufficient digit positions to allow for future growth. Because each numeric position only al-lows for 10 variations (0-9), numeric systems sometimes become too lengthy. In other words, since a single numeric position only allows 10 variations, if you required 100 different variations (for 100 different SKUs), you would need 2 digit positions, repre-senting 00 through 99 (10 x 10). One thousand variations would require three numeric positions, 000 through 999, and so on.

- Systems that are completely alphabetic allow for 26 vari-ations per position, A through Z (assuming only capital letters). Two alphas together, AA through ZZ (26 x 26), allow for 676 variations. Three alphas, AAA through ZZZ, allow for 17,576 variations. See Exhibit 3-15, Alpha-Numeric Variations. Al-though alphas provide numerous variations in a short address, systems that are completely alphabetic are visually confusing (HFZP).
- Alpha-numeric systems often provide for visual differen-tiation while allowing sufficient variations in a short address.
- *Caution:* While alpha systems require fewer characters to hold the same number of variations, they are more error prone. For example: Is that the number zero or the letter *O* ? A "one" or the letter *I* ? A two or the letter *Z*? A *P* or an *R*? A *Q* or an *O* ? If you are only dealing with a computer system, then characters are "cheap," and you could use only numerics to avoid confusion. However, if part of your system will involve human readable la-bels, placards, or markings where a long string of numbers might present a problem or where you are trying to keep a bar code label short, you might have to balance out the merits of shorter alpha-numeric systems against longer pure numeric sys-tems.

Tie SKU Numbers and Location Addresses Together

The placement of identifiers on both product and physical locations creates an infrastructure by which you can track product as it moves. The next step is marrying together an SKU number accomplished by using a simple 3 x 5 card file system (which should be computerized as soon as possible).

- In bulk storage areas, you can utilize a simple grid de-noted with placards on walls or on the building's structural sup-ports to find an address on the floor. This is done through two lines bisecting on a flat plain.

- For vertical addresses, you triangulate three lines.
- The above is applied geometry (Cartesian Coordinates) developed by René Descartes, the famous French mathematician.

Update Product Moves

A final step in managing inventory is tracking it as it is added to, deleted, or moved. This challenge exists for any organization whether or not the company uses manual tracking, computer-ized approaches, or bar coding.

The best generally available approach for real-time tracking of items as they move is using bar coding mobile scanners with radio frequency (RF) capability. See Chapter 4, The Basics of Bar Coding.

If RF capable bar coding is not available, then updating can be accomplished as follows:

- Portable bar code scanners that capture the information within the scanner mechanism or on a disk in the scanner. The information is then uploaded into the computerized database ei-ther through the communications ports on the scanner and com-puter, or by loading the scanner disk into the computer.

SIMPLE CARD FILE TRACKING SYSTEM

Cards are marked with all SKU numbers. Cards will be indexed in ascending number sequence––lowest SKU number in the front of the file box and the highest SKU number appearing last. All locations and quantities for that specific item are noted. As SKUs are added-to or moved, card file information is updated as often as possible. Up-dates should occur at least twice daily, for example, during the lunch hour and at the end of the workday.

- Manually captured, paper-based information is entered into the database through keying (data entry by a human being).
- Manually captured, paper-based information is manu-ally written onto file cards.

No matter what method is used, it is imperative that informa-tion relative to inventory additions, deletions, or movement be inputted into the system as soon as possible. To the greatest ex-tent possible, the shelf count (what is actually in the facility and where it is) should match the record count (the amount reflected in the main database records). The longer the time lag between inventory movement and information capture and updating of the record count, the greater the chance for error, lost product, and increased costs.

Organizations should carefully consider specific item placement within an overall location system in order to maximize each SKU's accessibility while being mind-ful of that item's point-of-use, unloading/ loading ratio, relation-ship to similar items, or characteristics requiring special handling.

Organizations lacking procedures that identify the location of each SKU within the facility suffer from excessive labor costs, "lost" product causing additional items to be purchased to cover for those on-site but unavailable when required, poor customer service, and general confusion. Controlling product location and movement centers around establishing an overall locator system that effectively reflects the organization's basic inventory nature such as finished goods in a retail/distribution environment or raw materials and sub-assemblies in a manufacturing facility. Often legitimate operational and storage objectives are in con-flict with one another resulting in final location system decisions made on the basis of a series of tradeoffs.

And finally, each item's present location must be identified with that SKU's identifier, with address and quantity changes being updated on an ongoing, timely basis.

13

The Basics of Bar Coding

INTRODUCTION

Errors and time increase dramatically the more often a human being is involved in identifying an object, inputting that infor-mation into a database, and then modifying the knowledge to keep track of changes in location, pack size, quantity, and so on.

The less you rely on human intervention to identify items, input information, and track data, the more timely and accurate your records will be. Bar coding is a major tool in capturing crit-ical data quickly and accurately.

The time and dollar savings that would be realized if your organization could eliminate the time and errors noted above will often pay for a bar coding system. The speed of information capture and the accuracy of bar coding are often sufficient reasons to cost justify installing bar coding within your operation.

Bar coding is an optical method of achieving automatic identification. It relies on visible or invisible light being reflected off of a printed pattern. The dark bars or dark areas within the pattern absorb light, and the intervening spaces or areas reflect light. The contrasting absorption and reflection is sensed by a device that "reads" this reflected pattern and decodes the infor-mation.

Bar coding is not the only automated method of identifying inventory. For example, there is also optical character reading, machine vision, magnetic stripe, surface acoustic wave, and ra-dio frequency tags.

This text will only deal with one dimensional, linear bar coding—probably the most commonly used method of auto-mated inventory identification and control. Bar code systems generally consist of three components: the code itself, the reading device(s), and the printer(s). The objec-tive of this chapter is to provide you with a working knowledge of (i) elements of a bar code symbol; (ii) the fundamentals of the more commonly used linear bar code languages/symbologies in the inventory control world; (iii) printing and scanning (read-ing) basics; and (iv) some practical bar code applications.

Elements of a Bar Code Symbol

Why can you easily read the sentence, "Inventory control is fun"? You can read that sentence because you recognize the al-phabet used and understand the rules of grammar and sentence construction utilized. A bar code "symbology" or language is very similar because it has a fixed alphabet made up of various patterns of dark bars and intervening light spaces coupled with rules for how it is presented.

There are many types of bar codes, not all of which are the linear symbols most commonly found in the inventory control world. For example:

Start and Stop Characters

In order for codes to be read from either direction or top to bot-tom or bottom to top in a vertically oriented symbol •/, start and stop characters tell the scanner where the message begins. It is customary for the character on the left or at the top of the sym-bol to be the start character, and the one on the right or bottom to be the stop character.

Data Characters

The data characters are the actual message within the code. These can be letters of the alphabet, numbers, symbols (+, -, /, =), or a combination of all three.

"X" Dimension

The narrowest bar or space in a bar code is called the "X" di-mension. This width can run from 5 mils to 50 mils. A mil is one-thousandth of an inch.

This is a very important width because it determines how wide each narrow and wide bar or space will be. The narrow bars/spaces are a single "X" in width, while the wide bars/ spaces can be two, three, or four "Xs" wide. Therefore, an ele-ment (a bar or space) can be a single "X" or several "Xs."

The larger the "X" dimension of a symbol the easier it is to read.

SYMBOLOGIES—BAR CODING STRUCTURAL RULES

Just as there are rules for how an English sentence is structured, for the relationship of upper case to lower case letters, and for punctuation, there are similar rules governing bar codes. These rules are set out in a "symbology." A symbology controls how in-formation will be encoded in a bar code symbol.

Just as there are different languages such as French, English, Spanish, Italian, Russian, Japanese, and Chinese, there are differ-ent symbologies. Common symbologies found in the inventory world are Code 39, Code 128, Interleaved 2 of 5, and UPC.

Symbologies are like typefaces with different character sets and separate printing characteristics. Some symbologies only present numbers. Some have numbers, uppercase alphabetics (A-Z), and limited special characters. Others have both upper and lowercase alphabetics (A-Z, a-z), numbers, and a wide range of special characters. Some symbologies only allow for a set number of characters in a pattern, while others allow for vari-able length messages.

Discrete and Continuous Symbologies

Bar codes can either be discrete or continuous. Characters in a discrete code start with a bar and end with a bar, and they have a space between each character. Characters in a continuous code start with a bar, end with a space, and have no gap between one character and another. The primary significance of the difference is that a discrete code is easier to print and read, but you can get more characters per inch with a continuous code. Which of the following is easier to read?

Symbologies

The word on the far left is the most difficult to read but has the greatest amount of information in the smallest amount of space, which is a good thing on a bar code label with limited space available. The word on the far right is the easiest to read, would allow for a more forgiving print job (for example, if the ink spread on the label surface between each letter, we would still be able to read it), but it takes up more space. Discrete sym-bologies are easier to print and read, but they take up more space.

Summary

The rules of a particular symbology control are:

- Character set—which alphabetics, numbers, and special characters are in the symbology?
- Symbology type—discrete or continuous?
- Number of element widths—how many different "Xs" are there in the wide bars/spaces?
- Fixed or variable lengths of characters in a pattern?
- Density—how many characters can appear per inch?

POPULAR SYMBOLOGIES FOUND IN THE INVENTORY WORLD

There are dozens of bar code symbologies. Many have failed in the marketplace because a large number of printer and scanner suppliers will not support them. Others are owned by individual companies that control and limit their use. Others have spe-cialized uses like Postnet used by the U.S. Postal Service. Some are widely supported and accepted in the inventory control world.

Universal Product Code/European Article Numbering System

Without question, when dealing with point-of-sale identification of product (as in a grocery or other retail store), the bar code used is the Universal Product Code (UPC). A very similar code, which will eventually be interchangeable with UPC, is the Euro-pean Article Numbering System (EAN).

The UPC symbology is highly structured and controlled, and it is only used in general merchandise retailing. It is an all numeric, fixed length (11 characters) symbology. The UPC sym-bol is physically arranged into two halves. The left half has six numbers that identify the manufacturer or packager. The right half identifies the product. You have to license the right to use the UPC from the Uniform Code Council (UCC), an organization created by the grocery industry.

The UPC is not suitable for inventory control use within a warehousing or manufacturing facility where there is a need for variable length messages, alpha-numeric coding, flexible identi-fication patterns, and so on.

Code 39

This symbology is the most widely used bar code in nonretail applications. It was first introduced in 1975.

Most stockkeepers will be able to find a Code 39 software to interface with their existing application software systems. In other words, you should be able to find a Code 39 bar code pack-age that will allow you to continue to use your existing in-house software, numbering systems, and internal procedures.

Code 39 is sometimes referred to as "3 of 9 Code" because three of the nine elements (bars or spaces) making up a Code 39 character are wide and the other six are narrow.

Code 39 was the first alphanumeric symbology developed. Among its most important features are:

- Entire alphabet in uppercase letters
- All numerics, e.g., 0 through 9
- Discrete symbology
- Allows variable length symbols
- Allows two messages to be decoded and transmitted as one ("concatenation")
- Can be printed in a wide variety of technologies
- Although there are only 43 data characters in the basic Code 39 set, by using certain characters as internal codes, it is possible to encode all 128 ASCII (American Code of Information Interchange) characters used by computers. This feature is cumbersome and is not widely used.
- Self checking, which means a single printing defect can-not cause an error where one character is mistaken for another

Code 128

This code, introduced in 1981, is the preferred symbology for most new bar code applications. It is one you should seriously consider if your business is going to enter into the world of bar coding. This symbology has many desirable features, such as:

- It uses three start codes to allow the encoding of all 128 ASCII characters without cumbersome procedures. Therefore, you can use the entire alphabet in both upper and lower case, all ten numerics, and all special charac-ters. Each printed character can one of three meanings.
- There is high data density and continuous symbology that uses the least amount of label space for messages of six or more characters
- Tests have shown this to be a highly readable code with high message integrity.
- Code 128 has become one of the two standard bar code symbologies used to identify the contents of corrugated boxes. (The other standard for corrugated shipping boxes is Interleaved 2 of 5 symbology.)
- Code 128 allows for concatenation.

Which Symbology is Right for Your Organization?

Each symbology has its strengths and weaknesses. There is no one "right" bar code language that will fit every organization's needs.

A starting point in reviewing appropriate symbologies actu-ally begins with your own industry. Has your industry selected a particular type of symbology? For example, the automotive in-dustry has been using Code 39 since 1980. You can obtain guid-ance from trade associations in your industry segment.

The reason to start with a symbology accepted by your in-dustry is that direct application software and hardware will have been written or created for the specific requirements of your business. It is the old question, "Why recreate the wheel?" If no symbology dominates your industry, then the real questions become What do you want the system to do for you? and How large is your budget?

SCANNING BASICS

Something has to read a bar code. That something is a scanner. These electro-optical devices include a means of illuminating the symbol and measuring reflected light.

A scanner projects a tiny spot of light that crosses the bar code symbol and then measures the exact width of the bars and spaces. The measurement is determined by the amount of reflectance off of the dark and light bars and spaces.

Software in ei-ther the scanner or in a separate plug-in device then translates the visual (analog) signal into a digital one a computer can un-derstand, and it decodes what symbology (language) it is read-ing and the message contained in the pattern.

Light reflected is converted from an analog voltage (visual) format to a digital waveform for decoding.

The spot of light must not be larger than the "X" dimension being used for that label or you will get misreads. Scanners must be purchased so that they match the "X" di-mension that will be used for printing labels or for printing di-rectly onto a surface.

Scanners can either be manual (where the user supplies the scanning motion) or automatic (where the device provides the scanning motion).

Printing Basics

Bar code printing can be done by the user on-site or by an off-site third party vendor.

On-site printing generally occurs close to where product is either being received or shipped—it's point-of-use.

There are five basic on-site bar code print technologies: di-rect thermal, thermal transfer, dot matrix impact, ink jet, and laser (Xerographic).

- Light pen (wand scanner)
  - — Makes contact with the label or surface on which pat-tern is printed —Inexpensive —Durable —Can be tied into various decoder types of equipment
- Charge Coupled Device (CCD)
  - — Has a depth of field of several inches so you do not have to make contact with the label or other surface. Therefore, you can read through shrink wrap, which is common in warehousing operations. —Floods symbol with light and reflectance illuminates photodetectors in the CCD scanner. Can read very high bar code densities —Moderate cost

- Lasers
  - Project a beam of energy off of a rotating prism or os-cillating mirror
  - Depth of field of several feet —Expensive but versatile

Off-site, commercial printers use a wide variety of printing techniques.

Common Bar Code Print Technologies

- Direct Thermal—Overlapping dots are formed on a heat-sensitive substrate (label or other foundation) by se-lectively heating elements in a printhead.
- Thermal Transfer—Same concept as direct thermal ex-cept the image is transferred to the substrate from a rib-bon that is heated by the elements in the printhead.
- Dot Matrix Impact—A moving printhead with rows of hammers that creates images through multiple passes over a ribbon.
- Ink Jet—A fixed printhead sprays tiny droplets of ink onto a substrate.
- Laser (Xerographic)—A controlled laser beam creates an image on an electrostatically charged, photoconductive drum. The charged areas attract toner particles that are transferred and fused onto the substrate.

Bar Code Applications

It is far more important that you understand what you want to accomplish with bar codes than for you to understand all of the technical aspects of them. Think of all of the bits and pieces of information you need to know in order to control inventory in a distribution environ-ment. For example:

- Manufacturer
- Supplier
- SKU number
- Description
- Pack size
- Ship to address
- Bill To address

- Credit terms
- Identification of receiving clerk, stock replenishment worker, order filler, shipping clerk
- Shipper
- Carrier
- Quantity
- Throughput rates, e.g., pieces per hour
- Time, date
- Location
- Purchase order identification

Think of all the information you need to control material in a manufacturing environment. For example:

- Particular bill of materials
- SKU number
- Quantity
- Work in process (WIP)
- Individual tasks
- Throughput rates
- Scrap
- Time, date
- Which machine
- Which process
- Location
- Machine instructions
- Job number

All of the above can be given a bar code identifier.

Bar code labels and markings can be printed directly on forms, boxes, the product itself, or on labels that are then affixed to forms, boxes, items themselves, individual parts of items, and so on.

A quick and easy way to begin using bar codes is through the use of scan boards or menu cards. A scan board or menu card is merely a sheet of paper or heavier card stock that contains on it information in both machine readable (bar code) and human readable (plain alphanumeric text).

Using Bar Coding as Part of a Maintenance Program

1. Bar codes are assigned to each part of the maintenance procedure and to various parts (engines, for example) of the piece of equipment in question.
2. Employee then uses a Time, Attendance, and Activity Menu to track the maintenance tasks.

Bar Coding and Physical Inventory and Cycle Counting

1. Bar code markings in both machine readable and human readable form are placed on both the storage locations (shelves, racks, drawers, bins) and on the product itself.
2. A counter equipped with a portable scanner:
   a. Scans in the iden-tity of the SKU.
   b. Enters the quantity through a keypad on the scanner. The record count and shelf count can be compared in a vari-ety of ways:
      (1) The shelf count as captured by the scanner and counter can be transmitted into the system by way of radio fre-quency at the time of information capture, or it can be uploaded from the scanner at a later time. The computer system would then generate an exception report of those items where the record and shelf counts did not match.
      (2) Scanners are small computers. Because of that they can contain software allowing them to have the record count stored within them. As the scanner reads the bar code and the counter enters the quantity information, the scanner could immediately compare the record count and shelf count. If there was a discrepancy, the scanner could alert the counter either through audible tones, flashing lights, or LED displays. The counter could then immedi-ately initiate a recount.

The objective of this chapter was to provide you with an overview of bar coding, various popular symbologies, and basic bar code applications. The set of rules for how the bars and spaces of a bar code language, its symbology, are arranged dictates how much and what type of data can be displayed within a particular symbol. The language that is most appropriate to your industry will be determined by how much data and in what form that informa-tion must be displayed on your goods, inventory, or other mate-rials.

Many industry segments such as automotive and retail sales have selected the symbology felt to be most appropriate for their respective needs. Often it is more economical and efficient to adopt the symbology commonly found within your own in-dustry segment.

In applying bar coding to your system, you are only limited by your imagination—and your wallet. Applications can be sim-ple ones involving scan boards or can be complex, utilizing laser scanners, radio frequency, and sophisticated sharing of informa-tion throughout the system at the time of information capture.

14

Planning and Replenishment Concepts

INTRODUCTION

The objective of this chapter is to provide basic approaches to forecasting inventory levels and to undertaking stock replenish-ment. With the proper techniques, you will have the right item, in the right quantity, at the right time, and in the right place.

Replenishment Costs

As discussed in Chapter 2, Inventory as Money, every day that an item remains in your stockroom it costs you money in the form of a carrying cost (K Factor). If you take that concept to its ultimate extreme, it would make sense to only buy items exactly when you need them. Multiple smaller quantity purchases of the same item certainly hold down your carrying costs. How-ever, it hurts your cost of replenishment—the expenses associ-ated with buying things.

It costs money to buy things. That sounds absurdly simple when you first read it. However, the cost of purchasing product exceeds the actual price paid for it. Expenses related to purchas-ing include the salaries of the purchasing staff, rent, and other overhead expenses attributable to the purchasing department. See Exhibit 5-1.

In fact, the more often you buy, the greater your internal costs. For example, if you purchased one million widgets all at the same time, your purchasing or replenishment cost (R Factor) would be the cost per line item, per purchase order (PO).

- If the per line, per PO cost is $5.00, then your cost to buy all one million widgets at one time would be $5.00.
- If you were to buy the same one million widgets 250,000 at a time, then your R Factor would be $5.00 times four (four POs with one line item each) or $20.00.
- If you purchased the widgets one at a time, the cost would be one million times $5.00 or five million dollars.

Order size versus frequency of purchase shifts the cost burden from the K Factor to the R Factor and vice versa. In other words:

- If you buy smaller quantities more often, your purchas-ing costs go up—or your R Factor increases.
- If you buy larger quantities less often, you have a higher inventory level for a longer period of time, so your car-rying costs go up—or your K Factor increases.

In a perfect world the K Factor and the R Factor would be equal. Although this is difficult to achieve, an organization at-tempting to have the correct amount of product at the overall lowest cost will strive for that balance.

Inventory Types

In the worlds of distribution, retailing, and replacement parts, an organization deals with finished goods. In the manufacturing world an organization deals with raw materials and subassemblies. Considerations of what to buy, when to buy it, in what quantities, and so on are dramatically different in these two worlds.

In distribution you are concerned with having the right item, in the right quantity. Issues relating to having the item at the right time and place are often dealt with by simply increas-ing safety stock on-hand. That is not a good solution because it leads to wasted money and space. However, traditional formu-lae used in computing inventory requirements in a distribution environment focus on item and quantity rather than place and time. In manufacturing, you are concerned with having the right item, in the right quantity, at the right time, in the right place.

Demand for finished goods and spare parts for replace-ments are said to be "independent," while demand for items in the manufacturing world are said to be "dependent." Under-standing these distinctions will assist you in forecasting your procurement needs.

Independent demand is influenced by market conditions out-side the control of your organization's operations. The demand for the widgets your organization sells will be independent of the demand for your gadgets, doodads, and whatchamacallits. Your products are independent of one another. In this environ-ment you must have the right item in the right quantity.

Dependent demand is related to another item. The demand for products built up or created from raw materials, parts, and assemblies is dependent on the demand for the final product. You would not need one item if you did not also require another, both of which would go into an assembly or finished product. In this environment you must have the right items in the right quantities at the time in order to complete a finished product. A chair can be used as an example of the above. The de-mand for the number of chairs you need is independent from the number of tables that you need because quantity required is influenced by the demand in the market for each item. The demand for chair legs, or seats, or rails is mathematically de-pendent on the demand for *finished* chairs. Four legs and one seat are required for each chair.

Dependent and independent demands demonstrate very different usage and demand patterns. Independent demand calls for a *replenishment* approach to inventory management. This approach assumes that market forces will exhibit a somewhat fixed pattern. Therefore, stock is replenished as it is used in order to have items on hand for cus-tomers.

Dependent demand calls for a *requirements* approach. When an assembly or finished item is needed, then the materials needed to create it are ordered. There is no fixed pattern because an assembly created in the past may never be produced again.

The nature of demand, therefore, leads to different con-cepts, formulae, and methods of inventory management.

INDEPENDENT DEMAND INVENTORY

Order-Point Formulae

Order point formulae are used to determine how much of a given item needs to be ordered where there is independent de-mand. In these formulae a reorder point (ROP) is set for each item. The ROP is the lowest amount of an item you will have on hand and on order before you reorder.

A Simple Min-Max Inventory System-Order point formulae are based on some relatively simple concepts.

Imagine that all of a particular SKU are kept in a single bin. If no reorder point was set, then the entire batch would be used up without any order being placed. The organization would then be unable to sell or use that item during whatever time frame was required to order and bring the SKU in—the lead time. It would therefore make sense to adopt a two-bin system with Bin 1 containing working stock and Bin 2 containing work-ing reserve. The amount of product in Bin 2 would be equal to your usage rate during that item's lead time.

In a two-bin system, if all goes as it should, then immedi-ately upon using the first item from Bin 2, you would reorder a quantity equal to both Bins 1 and 2. As you use the last item in Bin 2, the order arrives and you refill both bins. This assumes that lead time is exact, there are no vendor stockouts or back-orders, and that there are never any defects. That assumption is, of course, often false. Therefore, a true order-point system is a three-bin system, with the Bin 3 containing safety stock.

Bin 3, safety stock, relates to Bin 2 since Bin 3 is to make up for uncertainties in lead time and defects. Mathematically safety stock is 50 percent of working reserve. (The average between having nothing in Bin 2 and having it at 100 percent full is 50 percent.) However, companies adjust safety stock levels to co-incide with their actual experience.

Bins can be mathematically created or can reflect actual physical separation of items in the stockroom.

DEPENDENT DEMAND INVENTORY

Materials Requirements Planning

Controlling not only what item is purchased and in what quan-tities, but also the timing of its arrival through computerized systems is called *materials requirements planning* (MRP). This con-cept of the right item, in the right quantity, and at the right time was first introduced by Joseph Orlicky in 1975.

Independent demand inventory management is customer oriented. The objective of ROP rules and formulae is high cus-tomer service levels and low operating costs. Dependent de-mand systems, however, are manufacturing oriented. The objective of dependent demand inventory control is to support the master production schedule. Even if you have a low stock level of an item, it won't be ordered unless and until it is needed to produce something for the master schedule—a true require-ments philosophy of inventory control. MRP dependent de-mand inventory control is directed inward rather than outward like ROP inventory control.

MRP Elements

Key concepts in understanding MRP are the *master production-schedule* and the *bill of materials.*

The *master production schedule* sets out what will be built, when, and in what quantities. It can either cover short or long time horizons.

- Short horizon—planning of initial requirements sets out:
  —final product requirements
  —schedule for production of components
  —purchase order priorities
  —short term capacity requirements
- Long horizon—estimating long term requirements sets out:
  —long term production capacity required —long term warehouse capacity required —long term staffing required —long term money required

The *bill of materials* (BOM) is the recipe of raw materials, parts, subassemblies, and so on required to build or make some-thing.

There are levels to each BOM. See Exhibit 5–4 and Exhibit 6-1 on page 165 for a discussion of how inventory is relieved from stock after each level of the BOM is completed. This is a technique called "backflushing."

An example of MRP would be a decision to build one bar stool in your garage on Saturday.

The decision to build a single unit of something on a given day is the master schedule. Included in your thinking was the fact that if you had all of the pieces, parts, and tools necessary, you could actually accom-plish the task. That is rough-cut capacity planning.

You then draw-up and define what parts are required for the task. This is your bill of materials.

The next step is a parts explosion where you review your on-hand inventory levels to initially determine if any POs must be prepared and released.

You then engage in detailed capacity planning to decide if you can proceed or if the master schedule, capacity, or the planned release of POs must be changed.

Ultimately, all parts, equipment, and so on come together and the stool is built.

MRP works well because it is a forward-looking system. The predictability of events allows for careful planning and a re-duction in unnecessary inventory.

A major drawback of MRP and JIT systems is that they are highly data dependent. Not only do you have to have *all* of the data easily available on an ongoing basis, but in addition, the in-formation must be accurate and timely. Organizations lacking a strong software/hardware infrastructure will have difficulty in fully implementing an MRP system.

Just-In-Time (JIT) Inventory Systems

JIT was first developed within Toyota's manufacturing opera-tions by Taiichi Ohno in the 1970s as a means of meeting cus-tomer demands with minimum delay. In its original form, it referred to the production of goods, assemblies, and subassem-blies to meet exactly the customer's demand in terms of time, quality, and quantity. With a JIT system, the "buyer" can be the actual end user or another process along the production line.

JIT goes further than MRP, because you control not only the right item, in the right quantity, at the right time, but you also bring that SKU to the right place. Under this time-based concept, an item appears exactly when it is needed—not before, not after.

The American Production and Inventory Control Society (APICS) has the following definition of JIT:

... a philosophy of manufacturing based on planned elimination of all waste and continuous improvement of productivity. It encompasses the successful execu-tion of all manufacturing activities required to produce a final product, from design engineering to delivery and including all stages of conversion from raw mate-rial onward. The primary elements include having only the required inventory when needed; to improve quality to zero defects; to reduce lead time by reducing setup times, queue lengths and lot sizes; to incremen-tally revise the operations themselves; and to accom-plish these things at minimum cost.

There are many benefits to a JIT system, including:

- Reduction of stockouts
- Reduction of inventory levels
- Reduction of need for material handling equipment
- Reduction of time frames between delivery and produc-tion
- Significant quality improvement
- Employee inclusion in continuous quality improvement

JIT is a management philosophy rather than a technique.

The fact that certain words and acronyms have come to be used somewhat interchangeably can be confusing to anyone not in the manufacturing world. Do those terms/acronyms have in-dividual, stand alone characteristics differentiating one from an-other? Most certainly they do, however, grappling with the details of what separates one particular type of manufacturing philosophy from another closely related theory won't further your understanding of the basic concepts of inventory manage-ment and control. The terms/acronyms *MRP III, Computer Integrated Manufac-turing, Lean Manufacturing, Short Cycle Manufacturing, Just-in-Time, JIT, Enterprise Resource Planning, ERP,* and so on all relate to the fundamental notions that:

- manufacturing activities should be integrated.
- the actions and decisions of each department should complement all other departments.
- information should flow both internally throughout the organization and externally to/from suppliers/cus-tomers electronically rather than through:
  - — the movement of hard paper copies, or
  - — through individual software (accounting) modules whose data do not flow into one another both automati-cally and in real time.

- suppliers are reliable and raw materials are without de-fect.
- all employees follow the philosophy of continuous qual-ity improvement in all aspects of the operation.

Let's concentrate on how these concepts—by whatever name—relate to inventory. They all regard inventory as *waste.*

Today JIT has come to mean producing with a minimum of waste. "Waste" is used in the broadest sense and includes any nonvalue adding activities. For example, storing, inspecting, and counting materials doesn't change the items; therefore, those actions add no value. There are seven types of waste JIT systems strive to eliminate:

- Overproduction—producing more than needed. Wasted money, effort, space, etc.
- Waiting time—decreases productivity and efficiency.
- Transportation—double and even triple handling of an item from one storage position to another.
- Processing— what are the interfaces between parties, departments, you, and your suppliers? The fewer and faster the better.
- Inventory—stock simply sitting around does no one any good.
- Motion—reduce motions such as those involved in look-ing for materials.
- Defects—defective goods not only cost money directly, but they also cause stops and delays.

Implementing JIT

Take the following steps to introduce a JIT type system into your manufacturing facility:

1. Stabilize and level the production schedule.
    - All work centers should have a uniform load through constant daily production.
    - Prevent changes in the production plan for some period of time.
    - Produce roughly the same mix of products each day, us-ing a repeating sequence if several products are pro-duced on the same line. This is often called "mixed model assembly."

- Change the quantity of end-item inventory to meet de-mand fluctuations rather than through fluctuations in production levels.

2. Reduce or eliminate setup times.
   - Strive to create single digit setup times (less than 10 minutes).
3. Reduce lot sizes (manufacturing and purchase).
   - Reducing setup times allows economical production of smaller lots.
   - Close cooperation with suppliers is necessary to achieve reductions in order lot sizes since more frequent deliver-ies will be called for. In JIT systems, the old, adversarial methods of purchasing will not work. In traditional ap-proaches buyers buy an item here and another item there through a series of disconnected negotiations over price, delivery quality, and terms. In JIT systems, larger quanti-ties and types of items are purchased from fewer ven-dors. The larger purchases give the buyer more economic leverage while providing the supplier with enough financial incentive to become the buyer's busi-ness partner. Both parties recognize the critical needs, costing, pricing, quality concerns, and so on of the other.
4. Reduce lead times (production and delivery)
   - Production lead times can be reduced by:
   - — moving work stations closer together.
   - — applying group technology and cellular manufactur-ing concepts.
   - — reducing the number of jobs waiting to be processed at a given machine ("queue" length).
   - — improving the coordination and cooperation between successive processes, such as, reducing delivery times by inducing suppliers to have distribution centers/ ware-houses closer to your operation.
5. Engage in strong preventive maintenance
   - Machine and worker idle time should be used to maintain equipment and prevent breakdowns.

6. Cross-train to create a flexible work force
    - Workers should be trained to:
    — operate several machines.
    — perform maintenance tasks.
    — perform quality inspections.
7. Require supplier quality assurance and implement a zero-defects quality program.
    - Since there are no buffers of safety stock, errors leading to defective items must be eliminated.
8. Use a control system such as a kanban (card) system to convey parts between work stations in small quantities (ideally, one unit at a time).

Inventory Objectives

Inventory in and of itself is not waste. *Unnecessary* inventory is waste. A key question is: What is unnecessary in the context of your organization?

In manufacturing operations, inventory in excess of that needed to support current operations or research and develop-ment efforts would certainly be waste. However, is the inven-tory of a distributor that uses immediate availability of a large cross-section of items as an effective, profitable marketing tool, "unnecessary?"

Your company should have a "zero-tolerance" inventory policy. That is, it will not accept any inventory over a stated tar-get. But what is the target?

Is it zero-tolerance from a days sup-ply of inventory on-hand? Is it a zero-tolerance from a dollars invested standpoint (turns per year)? Is it zero-tolerance from an order fill rate of 97 percent?

For an organization to actually have useful inventory, it must understand its own objectives for the product it will have on-hand, on-order, or in-transit at any one time. What inventory level is required for your organization to profitably and effec-tively operate?

Until the answers to these questions are determined, it will be difficult to get everyone within the organization to work to-ward the common, shared goal of eliminating inventory waste.

Organizations establish techniques for forecast-ing their product level needs based on the nature of the demand characteristics of those items.

Formulae for ensuring that you have the right item, in the right quantity, in the right place, at the right time can range from relatively simple min-max models to highly sophisticated com-puter-dependent systems.

For individuals not directly involved in purchasing, suc-cessful inventory control doesn't so much flow from actually us-ing the various formulae, but rather from understanding what outcomes are supposed to result from their use.

15

Why Inventory Systems Fail and How to Fix Them

INTRODUCTION

The objective of this chapter is to provide you with an under-standing of the nature of inventory accuracy and the working tools to "fix" your inventory system. If all items are moving through a properly operating system, then it doesn't matter what the characteristics of an SKU are—expensive item, inex-pensive item, fast mover, slow mover, long lead time, critical— the *shelf count* of the item (actual balance on-hand stock levels) and *record count* (how many your records say are supposed to be here) will match.

The traditional method of determining if actual balance on-hand stock levels match book/record levels is to take an annual physical inventory. As a method of correcting inventory accu-racy problems, this costly and time consuming effort is riddled with deficiencies. Why? Consider the following:

- Accuracy is often defined in dollars rather than in actual physical units. As discussed in Chapter 1, the dollar value of product does not reflect exactly what items are in house. For ex-ample, imagine you sent out a thousand cases of peaches to a cus-tomer rather than the thousand cases of pears actually requested. An annual inventory would reflect an overall dollar value roughly equal to whatever it would have been even if the correct item had been shipped. Therefore, our shelf count is off a thou-sand over for one SKU and a thousand under for another with no discrepancy in accuracy—if accuracy is measured in dollars.

- Misidentification of product. As discussed in Chapter 3, product within a facility is misidentified for a variety of reasons. During annual inventories, misidentification often occurs be-cause inexperienced counters assisting with the effort do not rec-ognize items, misunderstand package descriptions, and so on.
- Misidentification of units of measure. Incorrect quantities are often written down during annual inventories because coun-ters simply do not understand an SKU's pack size, pack size de-scriptions, or abbreviations on packaging.
- Discrepancies "adjusted away." Perhaps the greatest problem with using the annual inventory as a method for estab-lishing accuracy is that it provides no method for backtracking through physical and paper transactions to determine why an item's shelf count and its record count do not agree—a twelve month time period is simply too long of an audit trail. Conse-quently, if the reason for a discrepancy cannot be immediately found during the inventory, an adjustment is made with the un-derlying cause of the error never being corrected.

At the end of an annual inventory, after all of the adjust-ments have been made and after the lights have been turned off, you have an inventory shelf and record count that agree. At least they agree until the next morning when the same system that spawned the discrepancies found during the effort reasserts it-self and a new group of errors is born.

Albert Einstein, the famous physicist, once said, "A prob-lem stated is a problem half-solved." Modern business writers like Peter Drucker have expressed a similar view, "A problem analyzed is a problem half-solved." The sentiment expressed in these sayings, that reviewing the nature of inventory problems is a key step in solving them, provides you with a good starting point in resolving your own inventory-related issues. Consider the following:

INVENTORY SYSTEM FAILURES—EXAMPLE CASE

The following paragraph events have been numbered for ease of reference.

1. Big Hammer, Inc. manufactures and distributes widg-ets. Manufacturing occurs at its Los Angeles, CA, plant. It dis-tributes

from two separate locations. One of these locations is in Kansas City, MO, and has been part of Big Hammer for many years. The other location is in New York, NY, and is the surviv-ing portion of Paulex Co., a distribution company just pur-chased by Big Hammer.

2. Marc, Big Hammer's president, has just reviewed oper-ating reports from all three locations and is upset. It seems that the inventory accuracy level at all three locations is off. The end result is delayed production, too much inventory, and poor customer service. In addition, various department heads in all three loca-tions clash with one another. In order to get everything straight-ened out, he hires the consulting firm of Alana, Eric, and Shawn.
3. Alana goes to KC. Eric goes to NY. Shawn goes to LA.
4. The trio immediately discovers that NY is using a dif-ferent software system than LA and KC. In addition, the LA/KC software was designed for distribution, not manufacturing. However, some modifications have been made to the LA/KC software to help with manufacturing applications.
5. The NY system allocates inventory on a real-time basis. In other words, as a pick ticket is generated for an item, the quantity in question is allocated to a specific order and is not available for any other customer—its paper life ceases.
6. The LA/KC system is a batch system. Items are relieved from stock at the time the system is updated. This usually occurs once per day when billing is done. A modification to the system backflushes[1] some items out of stock during the manufacturing cycle.
7. Eric wanders around the NY location and observes the following:
8. Sales people, customer service personnel, clerical staff, and others freely roam through all stockrooms. Eric notices that some nonstockroom personnel fill their own orders, grab sam-ples for customers, and put things back into the facility that they have previously removed.
9. Eric observes that some of these individuals document their actions immediately, while others document nothing, and others turn in necessary paperwork—later.

10. Eric observes Sally, a sales person, peering intently into her computer screen. He hears her utter an oath and declare out loud, "I just saw a whole bunch of SKU #1234 out there a little while ago." She then creates a manual invoice within the soft-ware system, prints it, walks out into the stockroom, fills the or-der she has just created, delivers it to customer Acme Widgets of the World, and later drops the signed delivery copy on the desk of her accounts receivables clerk.
11. Eric observes an angry exchange between the ware-house manager and the accounting manager of the NY location. They were arguing over a negative stock balance for SKU #1234.
12. Eric also observes Sally angrily telling the warehouse manager that one of her customers, Widgets, Gidgets, Gadgets and Such, was shorted 10 widgets on an order it received "just a little while ago."
13. Alana has also observed some interesting things in KC.
14. Alana has observed two different order fillers attempt-ing to fill orders for the same item—from the same empty shelf.
15. At 5 P.M. one evening, Alana was standing behind Car-men, the company's billing clerk. Carmen's inbox contained sev-eral inches of delivery slips ready for processing. Carmen got up and began to make preparations to go home. Alana asked her what she was doing. Carmen replied, "It's 5 P.M. I'm going home."

    Alana said, "But you still have a lot of work in your inbox."

    "So what? I'll work on it tomorrow," Carmen indignantly responded.

    "But you'll mess up the warehouse if you don't get those slips processed tonight," Alana stated.

    Angrily, Carmen stated, "I work in accounting. I don't work in the warehouse."

    Alana asked, "How long would it take you to do those?"

    Carmen glanced at her inbox and replied, "About 30 min-utes."

    "Please stay and get them done," Alana cajoled.

    "I can't even if I wanted to," Carmen said. "I'm not allowed any overtime."

Bill, one of Carmen's co-workers chimes in and says, "Why can't you get your work done during the day?"

Furious, Carmen turns on Bill and says, "Hey, you sort and distribute the mail every morning, run photocopies of all incom-ing checks while fighting with people over our one copy ma-chine, and prepare and go out to make the daily deposit like I do; and, then let's see if you can get your stuff done."

16. Hanging around the warehouse, Alana observed that receiving was done on a manual basis; and there wasn't always a copy of a PO in the warehouse to support incoming loads.

    Alana noticed on several occasions that when the receiving staff did not have all appropriate paperwork for an item, they would simply put it away or move it off to the side. Then later, or the next day, they would hunt down all of the appropriate documentation and turn everything in to the data entry people for entry into the system.

    Like Eric, Alana also observed nonstockroom individuals filling their own orders.

17. Alana also observed a curious exchange between Franklin, the accounting manager, and Carmen, the billing clerk.

    While attempting to create an invoice for an item, Carmen's computer screen flashed an error message indicating that she was trying to bill for something that had a zero stock balance in the system. The software would not let her bill for an item it did not reflect as being available for the subject sale.

    Carmen called Franklin over. She showed him the signed delivery slip indicating that the item had, in fact, been delivered.

    Franklin stated, "Those people in the warehouse can't get anything right." He then proceeded to manually override the system and entered the SKU (SKU #4567) and quantity in ques-tion (10). Franklin then directed Carmen to try again. The in-voice was created without any further problems.

    Mid-morning of the next day the stock records began to show that there were 10 of SKU #4567 in the facility. A telemar-keting sales person sold 10 SKU #4567s that afternoon. A pick ticket was generated for the order. The order filler could not find any of SKU #4567 in the warehouse. A stock adjustment form is processed to take these ten items out of stock.

18. Alana overhears a telephone conversation between Carmen and a customer. The customer wants to return five SKU #9876s and wants to ensure that it is not charged for them. Carmen notes the information, prepares a pickup slip, and issues a credit to the customer's account.

    Later that day, a salesperson sells five SKU #9876's. A pick ticket was generated for the order. The order filler could not find any of SKU #9876s in the warehouse. A stock adjustment form is processed to take these five items out of stock.

19. Meanwhile, Shawn has been talking to Ichiro, the in-ventory control clerk in LA. Ichiro is frustrated. He works hard at his job but can't seem to track work in process. Consequently, he is never sure how much of any particular item the company has available for production purposes.

20. Shawn observes a worker disassembling a sub-assem-bly He asks the worker what he is doing. The worker replies that there is a rush order they lack all of the raw materials for, so they are disassembling some less important assemblies to cannibalize the required parts.

    Shawn asks if the products being disassembled are from other orders. The worker replies that they are. Shawn asks about any paperwork that was generated to support whatever it is the worker is doing. The worker replies that he doesn't know.

DISCUSSION OF EXAMPLE CASE

After events, note problem identification and discussion.

Event #1. Big Hammer, Inc. manufactures and distributes widgets. Manufacturing occurs at its Los Angeles, CA, plant. It dis-tributes from two separate locations. One of these locations is in Kansas City, MO, and has been part of Big Hammer for many years. The other location is in New York, NY, and is the surviving portion of Paulex Co., a distribution company just purchased by Big Hammer.

Any organization that has several locations must clearly identify the answers to the "who, what, when, where, why, and how" questions:

Who is doing what? When are they doing it? Where are they doing it? Why are they doing it? and How are they doing it? If these questions are not answered materials and information will not flow smoothly between and among the or-ganization's separate departments.

Event #2. Marc, Big Hammer's president, has just reviewed oper-ating reports from all three locations and is upset. It seems that the in-ventory accuracy level at all three locations is off. The end result is delayed production, too much inventory, and poor customer service. In addition, various department heads in all three locations clash with one another. In order to get everything straightened out, he hires the consult-ing firm of Alana, Eric, and Shawn.

Although consultants are helpful in most instances, by ap-plying the concepts contained within this chapter, you should be able to resolve many system problems your organization may be currently experiencing.

Event #3. Alana goes to KC. Eric goes to NY. Shawn goes to LA.

Event #4. The trio immediately discovers that NY is using a dif-ferent software system than LA and KC. In addition, the LA/KC soft-ware was designed for distribution, not manufacturing. However, some modifications have been made to the LA/KC software to help with manufacturing applications.

Trying to integrate different software systems is always dif-ficult. Once again, any organization hoping to achieve that result must clearly lay out the timing and sequencing of the informa-tion flow within the system.

In addition, the demand patterns for items in a distribution world and those in a manufacturing environment are radically different. Purchasing patterns for finished goods and spare parts in a dis-tribution are based on past usage patterns. See the discussion of independent demand inventory on pages 120-24. Purchasing patterns for the raw materials and sub-assemblies used in man-ufacturing are based on the master production schedule. See the discussion of dependent demand inventory on pages 128-40. Different concepts and formulae are used for each type of inven-tory and, therefore, software designed for one or the other or specifically written for a combination environment should be used whenever possible.

Event #5. The NY system relieves inventory on a real-time ba-sis. In other words, as a pick ticket is generated for an item, the quan-tity in question is allocated to a specific order and is not available for any other customer—its paper life ceases.

The central problem often encountered in real time sys-tems is that there is often a time lapse between the creation of a pick ticket and the actual removal of the product from the shelves.

Since the items on the pick ticket were immediately allo-cated[3] to that order, with their paper life ceasing (see pages 9-15), those SKUs will actually be sitting on the shelves but won't appear in the then current record count.

Somewhere in the software files is the information: total items on hand, items allocated, and items actually available for sale or use. The problem is that *not everyone in the organization has access to this information!* If (a) staff members are allowed to fill their own orders, and (b) do not understand how it is possible to check the then current stock records and see a lower number of items than are actually sitting in plain view, then (c) they will stop believing in the record count, will only believe their eyes, and will raid product allocated for other orders.

Event #6. The LA/KC system is a batch system. Items are re-lieved from stock at the time the system is updated. This usually occurs once per day when billing is done. A modification to the system back-flushes some items out of stock during the manufacturing cycle.

The most significant issue created by batch software sys-tems is that items are physically gone from the shelves/building but still appear in the record count until the system is updated. The longer the length of time between updates, the more out of balance the shelf count and the record count are. Backflushing works well *if the* backflush occurs at each level of the bill of materials.

Event #7. Eric wanders around the NY location and observes the following:

Event #8. Sales people, customer service personnel, clerical staff, and others freely roam through all stockrooms. Eric notices that some non-stockroom personnel fill their own orders, grab samples for customers, and put things back into the facility that they have previously removed.

Any organization hoping to continuously have its shelf count match its record count simply must stop all unauthorized personnel from touching anything in a stockroom or warehouse. And, authorized personnel must have a paper- or computer-based document before placing anything into or removing any-thing from storage areas. These points cannot be overstated. They are imperative to inventory accuracy.

Event #9. Eric observes that some of these individuals document their actions immediately, while others document nothing, and others turn in necessary paperwork—later.

Documentation created after something has been placed into or removed from a facility creates all sorts of problems. For example:

a. If an item is physically removed without a document deleting it from inventory, then sales people, production sched-ulers, and others will believe that the item is still available for sale or use. They will then generate pick tickets for its selection. Order fillers will then waste their time looking for items that do not ex-ist. The order fillers will generate adjustment forms leading to the items being deleted from inventory. Eventually, when the origi-nal documentation goes through the system, it causes these same items to be deleted from inventory—again. Your shelf count and record count are now almost hopelessly out of balance.

b. If an item is placed into the stockroom without accom-panying paperwork, then the subject SKU is unavailable for sale or use—since no one knows its there.

Event #10. Eric observes Sally, a sales person, peering intently into her computer screen. He hears her utter an oath and declare out loud, "I just saw a whole bunch of SKU #1234 out there a little while ago." She then creates a manual invoice within the software system, prints it, walks out into the stockroom, fills the order she has just cre-ated, delivers it to customer Acme Widgets of the World, and later drops the signed delivery copy on the desk of her accounts receivables clerk.

Event #10 is an example of someone in a real time software scenario that does not understand how it is possible to have a stock record (in the computer or hard paper copy) that reflects a stock balance lower than the actual number of items on the shelves. Recall that the discrepancy is due to the time period be-tween the creation of a pick ticket with its allocation of product to an order and the physical removal of the SKUs from the stock-room.

Event #11. Eric observes an angry exchange between the ware-house manager and the accounting manager of the NY location. They were arguing over a negative stock balance for SKU #1234.

Since this is a real time system, when Sally created a manual pick ticket she caused the system to allocate and delete the sub-ject SKU. If the stock balance was zero when Sally did this, her actions have caused the balance to go into a negative.

As discussed in Event #17 of this section, Sally's actions have also created the potential for a much different problem in an entirely different department of the organization. By forcing a manual invoice through the system and dropping off a deliv-ery slip for billing, Sally has created the potential for a billing clerk to try to create an invoice for product that the system has never received into itself. Many accounting programs will not let an invoice be created for product that has never been received.

Event #12. Eric also observes Sally angrily telling the ware-house manager that one of her customers, Widgets, Gidgets, Gadgets and Such, was shorted 10 widgets on an order it received "just a little while ago."

In Event #10 it should be obvious that the product Sally took had already been allocated to a different customer (Cus-tomer #1) than the one she was taking care of at that time (Cus-tomer #2). Sally's actions caused her to raid Customer 1's order, causing a stockout for one of her own customers— Customer 1.

Event #13. Alana has also observed some interesting things in KC.

Event #14. Alana has observed two different order fillers at-tempting to fill orders for the same item—from the same empty shelf.

It is common in batch systems that are only updated once per day and in which there is no way to easily check (without go-ing to look) the availability of an item, for multiple orders to be written against the same "phantom" items. This also creates the danger of multiple adjustments adding to the overall confusion.

Event #15. At 5 P.M. one evening, Alana was standing behind Carmen, the company's billing clerk. Carmen's inbox contained several inches of delivery slips ready for processing. Carmen got up and began to make preparations to go home. Alana asked her what she was doing. Carmen replied, "It's 5 P.M., I'm going home."

Alana said, "But you still have a lot of work in your inbox."

"So what? I'll work on it tomorrow," Carmen indignantly re-sponded.

"But you'll mess up the warehouse if you don't get those slips processed tonight," Alana stated.

Angrily, Carmen stated, "I work in accounting. I don't work in the warehouse."

Alana asked, "How long would it take you to do those?"

Carmen glanced at her inbox and replied, "About 30 minutes."

"Please stay and get them done," Alana cajoled.

"I can't even if I wanted to," Carmen said. "I'm not allowed any overtime."

Bill, one of Carmen's co-workers chimes in and says, "Why can't you get your work done during the day?"

Furious, Carmen turns on Bill and says, "Hey, you sort and dis-tribute the mail every morning, run photocopies of all incoming checks while fighting with people over our one copy machine, and prepare and go out to make the daily deposit like I do; and, then let's see if you can get your stuff done."

A number of issues are raised by the Event #15 scenario, such as:

a. The morning following an incident like the one described will find everyone who deals with inventory—sales, accounting, production scheduling, customer service, and purchasing—making decisions on information they believe is as current as the night before when the system was updated. The reality is that the information is no more current than the last time Carmen made it to the bottom of the in-basket. If she hasn't made it to the bottom of her basket in several days, then the records and operations are really suffering. The problem is made worse by the fact that roughly 20 per-cent of our inventory will represent 80 percent of our most im-portant items. Therefore, not only does our shelf count not match our record count, but they don't match regarding some of our most important items.

b. Another problem revealed by the incident is that the or-ganization does not recognize the importance of getting all re-ceiving and shipping into and out of the building on both a real life and paper life basis every day. This is indicated by those duties assigned to Carmen that cause her not to complete her in-ventory related tasks on a daily basis. Although these duties are important, they should be performed by someone whose actions do not have the ripple effect that Carmen's actions have throughout the entire organization

Event #16. Hanging around the warehouse, Alana observed that receiving was done on a manual basis; and there wasn't always a copy of a PO in the warehouse to support incoming loads.

Alana noticed on several occasions that when the receiving staff did not have all appropriate paperwork for an item, they would simply put it away or move it off to the side. Then later, or the next day, they would hunt down all of the appropriate documentation and turn every-thing in to the data entry people for entry into the system.

Like Eric, Alana also observed nonstockroom individuals filling their own orders.

Virtually every organization has a purchase order system. And, in virtually every organization anyone with the authority to buy something is repeatedly told to have a PO for every-thing. In spite of those facts, in many organizations product comes in daily without any supporting documentation. This causes confusion, inefficient receiving operations, and sepa-rates an item's real life from its paper life. There should be either a hard copy or a record of the PO in the computer system available to receiving for all items that arrive at the stockroom.

When an item's real life becomes separated from its paper life, people begin to ship or use product that has not been re-ceived; to put away product that has not been received so that no one knows it is available for sale or use, creates an environment where inventory clerks and accounting personnel are making adjustment after adjustment to the record count.

Event #17. Alana also observed a curious exchange between Franklin, the accounting manager, and Carmen, the billing clerk.

While attempting to create an invoice for an item, Carmen's com-puter screen flashed an error message indicating that she was trying to bill for something that had a zero stock balance in the system. The soft-ware would not let her bill for an item it did not reflect as being avail-able for the subject sale.

Carmen called Franklin over. She showed him the signed delivery slip indicating that the item had, in fact, been delivered.

Franklin stated, "Those people in the warehouse can't get any-thing right." He then proceeded to manually override the system and entered the SKU (SKU #4567) and quantity in question (10). Franklin then directed Carmen to try again. The invoice was created without any further problems.

Mid-morning of the next day the stock records began to show that there were 10 of SKU #4567 in the facility. A telemarketing sales per-son sold 10 SKU #4567s that afternoon. A pick ticket was generated for the order. The order filler could not find any of SKU #4567 in the ware-house. A stock adjustment form is processed to take these ten items out of stock.

From Event #16, it appears here that someone delivered an item that had not yet gone through the paperwork receiving cy-cle. Then when Carmen tried to bill for it, the software would not let her.

Instead of researching what had actually happened, Franklin overrode the system and put in a quantity of 10. Car-men's billing then deleted the 10 items.

When the receiving paperwork finally made it through the system it created a quantity of 10 items that were no longer in the building. These 10 phantom items were then sold—maybe more than once.

When the 10 items could not be found, additional paper-work had to be initiated to delete the SKUs from the system.

All of the above issues are caused, in part, by a lack of un-derstanding on the part of various staff members of how the tim-ing and sequencing of the system works.

Event #18. Alana overhears a telephone conversation between Carmen and a customer. The customer wants to return five SKU #9876s and wants to ensure that it is not charged for them. Carmen notes the information, prepares a pickup slip, and issues a credit to the customer's account.

Later that day, a salesperson sells five SKU #9876's. A pick ticket was generated for the order. The order filler could not find any of SKU #9876s in the warehouse. A stock adjustment form is processed to take these five items out of stock.

Although application software systems vary widely in how items are accounted for, many systems place an item back into stock (in the data base) when a credit is issued against that item. By issuing a credit, Carmen caused the software system to place the five SKUs back into stock—even though they had not yet been returned to the building.

Again, a lack of understanding regarding timing and se-quencing of software and events causes terrible dysfunctions to stockroom operations.

Event #19. Meanwhile, Shawn has been talking to Ichiro, the in-ventory control clerk in L.A. Ichiro is frustrated. He works hard at his job but can't seem to track work in process. Consequently, he is never sure how much of any particular item the company has available for production purposes.

As indicated in Event #4, a key problem Ichiro faces is that the company is using two separate methods of relieving items from stock. One method is batch, while the other is a backflush of some items. Recall that *backflushing* refers to a software tech-nique where raw materials and other components going into a particular sub-assembly or final product are relieved from stock when that sub-assembly/product is completed.

As indicated in the discussion of Event #6, if a batch system is not updated with some degree of frequency, it is difficult to understand what is available without actually looking. This problem can be overcome through software modules that advise the stockkeeper of those SKUs that have gone into completed or-ders. This report shows a running total for each SKU that has been drawn down that day. Once the system is updated, then a new report begins.

The key issue regarding backflushing is, does the backflush occur at every level of the bill of materials? See Exhibit 6-1. (A similar example is also used in Exhibit 5-4.) If the backflush only goes down one level, but no backflush occurred at that next lower level, then all materials below that level will still appear to be in stock. In reality they have been used up.

Event #20. Shawn observes a worker disassembling a sub-assem-bly. He asks the worker what he is doing. The worker replies that there is a rush order they lack all of the raw materials for, so they are disas-sembling some less important assemblies to cannibalize the required parts.

Shawn asks if the products being disassembled are from other or-ders. The worker replies that they are. Shawn asks about any paperwork that was generated to support whatever it is the worker is doing. The worker replies that he doesn't know.

"You can't control what you don't measure." Peter Drucker

Before doing *anything* toward establishing methods to discover, an-alyze, and fix any discrepancies between actual on-hand stock levels and database record levels, you should take a snapshot of where you are *now.* There are two sets of numbers you should develop that relate to (a) inventory record accuracy (IRA) and (b) fill rate. IRA is a reflection of how well your shelf count and record count match. In other words, do your stock records accurately reflect what is actually in the stockroom? Fill rate is a reflection of how effective your inventory is. Did you have what you needed when you needed it?

INVENTORY RECORD ACCURACY

Test Counting

A quick, accurate method of establishing your current IRA is to perform a test count:

- Select 100 SKUs that represent a cross-section of all items. In other words, select all sorts of items—fast movers, slow movers, expensive items, inexpensive items, and those with both long and short lead times to acquire.
- Count all 100 in all locations where they are located. Measure accuracy by considering actual units on the floor—not dollar value.
- Divide the number of accurate counts by the total num-ber of counts. Accurate counts mean where the record count and the shelf count exactly match.
- Quotient is your inventory record accuracy. See Exhibit 6-2.

Probably not. Do you really care?

Probably not. Why? Because of the nature of the SKU in question, in this case nails, is low cost, easy to acquire, and hard to count individually (if there is a large quantity of them). Therefore, you would probably be willing to accept some percentage of tolerance in your numbers. If you were within ±5 percent of a perfect match between the record count and the shelf count, would you be satisfied?

Probably so. Would you be equally satisfied applying the same approach to a large container of diamonds? Of course not.

Many organizations allow a variance or tolerance in consid-ering IRA. That is, they allow a plus-minus percentage of accu-racy they find acceptable. These tolerances can be set using dollars, actual units, or some combination of the two. Most ac-countants use dollars. Stockkeepers should use actual units: It's either here or it isn't. Few organizations accept a tolerance of greater than ±5 per-cent on any item. In other words, a 95 percent tolerance should be the lowest variance from a 100 percent accuracy level you will accept for any item no matter what its characteristics.

If you will accept tolerances, they must be set for each item or category of item with great care. Consider the following fac-tors:

- Dollar value: The higher the dollar value, the more accu-racy you will demand.
- Usage rate: Usage rate can actually be argued in two ways:
  - The Higher-the-Usage-Rate-the-Lower-the-Tolerance-Level Argument: If you are using a large quantity of an item you will want to always know how much is avail-able so there is never a stockout.
  - The Lower-the-Usage-Rate-Lower-the-Tolerance-Level Argument: If an item is not moving very quickly, then why should there be any discrepancy between shelf and record count? A low variance percentage for a slow mov-ing item will alert everyone to a problem quickly as op-posed to waiting for a crisis. This argument assumes that if there are stockouts on higher moving products, then the situation will alert everyone anyway.
- Lead time: The longer the lead time, the lower the toler-ance level. A long lead time requires more working re-serve and safety stock.
- Level on bill of materials: The higher something is on the bill of materials, the more overall value it has. Therefore, the higher on the bill of materials an SKU is, the lower the tolerance.
- Criticality: Some items are critical for reasons other than dollar value, usage rate, or lead time. A safety equipment company may only sell a few biohazard cleanup suits per year, but when they are needed they are needed im-mediately.
- Combination of the above

Example: Considering Tolerances

Read the following scenario:

Melvin, President of Megawatts, Inc., doesn't believe in al-lowing any tolerances in his inventory levels. His friend, Sarah, President of Bright Lights Co., does.

A cross-section of 100 items was counted in each of these companies' facilities.

The actual stock count on 87 SKUs in each facility matched the respective companies' stock records.

Impact of Tolerances on Adjustments

Once you have set tolerances, you should not make adjustments to your records when a discrepancy between shelf and record counts falls within the variance allowed. If an item does fall out-side of the tolerance range, you would hunt down the reason for the discrepancy and adjust the record if necessary. See Exhibit 6-3.

Tools with Which to Uncover System Dysfunctions

To solve problems you need to engage in:

- Fact finding—what is happening now?
- Problem finding—what is wrong with what is going on?
- Solution finding—how can we fix what is wrong?

So far this chapter has focused on (a) beginning to analyze inventory problems in an intellectual, intuitive, "gut feel" man-ner, and (b) developing some measurements with which to understand your current level of inventory accuracy and avail-ability. This is part of fact finding.

Another way of determining what is actually happening at your facility is to create a number of charts.

Charts, by their very nature, allow you to analyze things. However, you need to guard against "paralysis by analysis." If everything is equally important, then nothing is important. In other words, you should only chart things that are really impor-tant to controlling inventory items, trends, operational under-takings, and so on.

Run Charts

Run charts allow you to measure a variable that changes over time.

A run chart is an x-y axis chart with the unit of measure ap-pearing on the vertical y-axis, and the timeframe running along the horizontal x-axis. The unit of measure can be anything you wish to track such as stockouts, errors, labor hours, pieces, pounds, or gallons. The timeframe can also be whatever you de-sire it to be such as seconds, minutes, hours, days, weeks, months, or years.

Flow Charts

Flow charts allow you to analyze the sequence of a set of events. A flow chart does not necessarily show the interdependence of events or which events are going on at the same time as others. Flow charts are easier to understand than written proce-dures.

Caution:

- You do not have to use traditional flow chart symbols. Be consistent however, with the symbols you do use or you will confuse yourself and others. Provide a key to symbols.
- Have version control. If flow charts are not revised as procedures change, they are worthless.

Cycle Counting

After becoming familiar with your system through utilization of the techniques described in this chapter, you should be ready to systematically approach "fixing" whatever might be causing discrepancies between your shelf and record counts.

The most systematic method of solving inventory problems and enjoying a consistently high IRA is cycle counting. Cycle counting is simply counting a statistically significant cross-sec-tion of your inventory frequently

This continuous counting leads to the discovery of discrep-ancies soon after they arise. By catching an error quickly, you can backtrack through both the paperwork and the stock movement of the item(s) to determine why that SKU's paper life became separated from its real life. Once the cause of the error is identi-fied, it can be eliminated.

Since this is a continuous process, as one cause of error after another is eliminated the system begins to operate more and more smoothly. Eventually all items move through a series of procedures that work.

Cycle counting is different than an annual inventory in sev-eral ways:

Annual Inventories

- Objectives
  - — The objective of the annual physical inventory is to pro-duce a financial valuation of the inventory on a given day.

— Every item must be counted as part of the annual in-ventory.

— The 12-month long audit trail of the annual physical is too long for any serious effort made at uncovering why an error occurred or even when—did it happen yester-day, last month, ten months ago?

Cycle Counting

- Objectives:
  - — Discover discrepancies soon after they occur
  - — Identify causes of errors
  - — Correct conditions causing errors
  - — Continuous process improvement
  - — Minimum of 95 percent accuracy on ALL items
  - — Correct statement of inventory assets
  - — Eliminate annual inventory. Most accounting firms will allow an organization to stop taking annual physical inventories once the company has established a mature cycle counting program. Generally, a company will cycle count for at least twelve months. Then, an annual physi-cal inventory is taken and the numbers from the annual are compared with the cycle count figures. If they match, then in the future the accounting firm will merely test count once per year for valuation purposes.
- Not every item in the building has to be counted as part of a cycle count, only a statistically significant cross-sec-tion of all items.

Cycle Count Methodologies

There are a number of cycle count methodologies.

- Control Group
- Location Audit
- Random Selection
- Diminishing Population
- Product Categories
- A-B-C Categorization

A key point to remember is that no matter what cycle count

methodology you eventually choose to follow, when you first begin and your inventory record accuracy is low, you *will not* count a large number of items per day. This is because it will take time to recount, review paperwork, talk to people, and do all of the other things necessary to determine why an item's record count and shelf count do not match. Why count fifty items a day if you can only count and reconcile ten of them? As your record accuracy increases, and more and more items match their record counts, you can comfortably count more items each day.

Any cycle count methodology will assist you in achieving high levels of IRA. However, not every method works in every company setting. For example:

Assumptions:

- You wish to cycle count each item 4 times per year
- Cycle count 200 days per year (4 days/wk x 50 wks = 200 count days)
- 10,000 SKUs
- 3 cycle counters working 7 hours per day
- Company A has 10,000 items that are unitized and in sin-gle locations within the stockroom
- It takes Company A an average of 2 minutes to count an item
- Company B has 10,000 items that are not unitized, would have to be counted in "onesy-twosy," and each item is found in multiple locations throughout the facility
- It takes Company B an average of 5 minutes to count an item

Treating all items equally and counting them four times per year may work for Company A; however, it seems like an un-reasonable burden for Company B.

You should select a method that fits your own organiza-tion's resources and inventory types.

Control Group Cycle Counting Method

No matter which method you eventually decide to use, always start with a small scale counting test run. By using a control group approach you will be able to:

1. Immediately identify significant system problems such as unrestricted access to the stockroom, major timing problems related to when product is moved, and when records of the move are updated.
2. Develop an understanding of the who, what, when, where, why, and how of the way your system actually works.
3. When you first begin cycle counting you will probably make adjustments only to find that you made a mistake. It is much simpler to correct errors related to only a few SKUs rather than hundreds of them.

Control Group Procedure

- Select 100 items as a control group.
- IMPORTANT: The SKUs selected must be a true cross-section of the entire population of items they represent such as some expen-sive items, some inexpensive, some fast movers, some slow, or some with a long lead time, etc.
- Count only ten items per day. Use a Control Group Count Tracking Sheet. See Exhibit 6-5.
- Count for 100 days.
- Stats: 10 x 100 = 1,000 counts
- "Cycle" is 10 days
- Each item counted 10 times during test

Because you have tracked the same items over and over again, at the conclusion of your control group cycle count you should be able to eliminate major systems problems and have a good understanding of how your overall inventory system is working.

The control group approach should only be used as a start-ing point and not as an ongoing cycle count method. The reason for this is that the control group is not statistically large enough to actually represent your entire inventory. Now you are ready to select a cycle count method that bests suits your own organization's needs.

Location Audit Cycle Counting Method

In this approach you divide the stockroom(s) up in some logical method—rooms, racks, bins, and so on. Then on each counting day you count the SKUs found in those areas.

All items are treated equally. In other words, selection of those items included on that day's count is based solely on the item being located in the area counted. No other characteristics such as cost, usage rate, and so on are considered. The length of the cycle depends on how many areas are to be counted. For example, if you were counting by rack, one rack per day, and there were 45 racks, then the entire cycle would be 45 days. You would then start over again.

The location audit approach has two significant benefits:

1. This approach does not require detailed recordkeeping of whether or not you have counted a specific item or the exact number of times you have counted it. It is administratively sim-ple to follow.
2. This approach serves as a double audit because you are checking the quantity of an item at the same time that you are checking to make sure it is in the right location in your facility. Product that has been misplaced can be "discovered" sooner than the annual inventory through the use of this method.

Two separate approaches are possible regarding how much of any selected SKU gets counted:

1. Only count the SKU in the location being cycle counted that day.

Example: Count only the quantity of SKU xyz in Rack 1. Item xyz located in Rack 10 and in both bulk storage areas ignored.

This first approach requires a higher level of sophistication within your own inventory control system. Your system must al-low you to identify not only how much of an item you have, but also each location it is located in and how much of it is in each lo-cation.

This first approach forces you to keep your shelf count and record count accurate on an ongoing basis.

2. Count the selected SKU in all locations where it may be located throughout the facility.

Example: Quantities of SKU xyz counted in Racks 1 and 10 and in both bulk areas.

With either locational audit approach, the warehouse will be counted wall-to-wall during the cycle. However, this does not mean that *all* items in the stockroom during that cycle will actu-ally be counted.

Not all items in the stockroom during the cycle will be counted because items will arrive into and leave from areas al-ready counted or to be counted during the cycle. In other words, SKUs will be coming in behind you and moving away from in front of you as you go through the count.

Does it matter if every item in the stockroom is counted during a location audit cycle? It does not matter that all items are not counted during any particular cycle because of the large number of items that are counted during that cycle.

Remember that in cycle counting you are interested in looking at the *system* not individual SKUs within the system. Whether or not a SKU's shelf and record counts match is merely a way of determining if the system is actually working. Therefore, as long as you count a statistically significant number of the total items in the stock-room, you will accomplish the cycle count objective.

Random Selection Cycle Counting Method

This is probably the easiest form of cycle counting. The items se-lected for counting are totally random. However, the SKUs se-lected must be a true cross-section of the entire population of items they represent: some expensive items, some inexpensive, some fast movers, some slow movers, some with a long lead time. The cycle is generally one year with a statistically signifi-cant number of SKUs being counted during that time frame. For example,

- 10,000 total SKUs
- 200 counting days
- Therefore, 50 items/day counted (10,000 -=- 200 = 50)
- 10,000 total counts during the year—a statistically signif-icant number!

All items are treated equally. Product characteristics like dollar value and usage rate are ignored.

A-B-C Analysis Cycle Counting Method

The most sophisticated method of cycle counting, and the one preferred by most accountants, is to break your inventory up into A-B-C classifications. Items are not treated equally. Based on classification, the A items will be counted more frequently than the B items, and the

B items will be counted more fre-quently than the C. The classifications are based on "Pareto's Law"—the 80-20 Rule. See Chapter 3, pages 66-75 for a discussion of Pareto's Law and of how to determine which SKUs go into which categories.

For cycle counting purposes, classifications are determined by "value." Value could be based on money, usage rate, or a combination of the two.

Step-By-Step Implementation of the A-B-C Cycle Count Method

- Perform Pareto analysis of SKUs utilizing desired crite-ria. See Chapter 3.
- Assign SKUs into A-B-C categories
- Decide count frequency of each category. See Determin-ing A-B-C Count Frequency below.
- Multiply respective number of SKUs per category by de-sired frequency to establish total counts. Cycle is as-sumed to be one year. See Exhibit 6-8.
- Divide total counts by the number of count days, (for ex-ample, 200 days per year,) to determine number of items to be counted each day. See Exhibit 6-8.
- Ask yourself, Is this a reasonable number of daily items? If "Yes," proceed. If "No," then change the frequencies and recalculate until a reasonable daily total is estab-lished.
- Determine how many items from each category will be counted each day:
    - Divide the number of annual counts within each cate-gory by the total (annual) number of counts. This estab-lishes the percentage of counts represented by the respective categories when compared to the total counts.
    - Multiply the A, B, and C percent of total by the num-ber of items to be counted daily. This establishes the quantity of each category to be counted each day.
- Count each category the desired number of times using the diminishing population technique.

Determining A-B-C Count Frequency Determine count frequency by:

- Decide count frequency of each category. You can count the respective categories the number of times you desire.

When To Count

The ideal time during the day to cycle count would be when there is no movement of paper or product. You may, therefore, want to count:

- at end of business day
- prior to start of day
- over the weekend
- during slowest shift

Another alternative is to creating a cycle counting cut-off during a regular business day by using time-of-day To use this approach you would:

1. Create a list of items to be cycle counted the next day.
2. Distribute the list to Shipping, Receiving, the stock put-away workers, order fillers, and data entry clerks.
3. Have Receiving, Shipping, the stock put-away workers, order fillers, and data entry clerks all note the time of day they interacted and actually dealt with any of the items on your list.
4. You now have the ability to audit back into any time frame during the day. For example:
    - You cycle count widgets at 1:00 P.M. using a stock status report generated by data entry at 11:30 A.M.
    - You find that there are 10 less widgets on the shelves than the stock status shows.
    - You review all of the paper work from these different de-partments.
    - The receiving paperwork shows that 10 widgets were re-ceived at 10:30 A.M.
    - There is no paperwork from the stock put-away workers indicating that the widgets were ever moved into stock.
    - The missing widgets are sitting out in the dock area. Your record count matches what you have in house.

Who Should Count

If there are 4 hours of counting involved in cycle counting all items on any given day, should you have a single person count for four hours and then begin any necessary reconciliations— or—does it make more sense to have 4 people count for one hour each and then let the inventory control clerk have the rest of the day to correct any problems? It makes sense to spread the raw counting portion of the cycle count among a group of people. This will allow the inventory control clerk to devote more hours of each day to actually fixing the system as opposed to spending each day counting boxes.

The objective of this chapter was to provide you with insights as to why many inventory control systems fail.

Often failure is due to individuals in different departments simply not understanding the unintended consequences of their own actions.

A review of who is supposed to write something down, what they are supposed to write down, who they are to give the information to, what that person is supposed to do with the in-formation, and the sequencing and overall timing of these events often reveals that respective departments are using dif-ferent units of measure to define inventory. Some use dollars, while others use actual physical units. In addition, seemingly simple issues like the timing of when an item is entered into the computer system or who is allowed to actually see various items of information can cause severe misunderstandings and inven-tory inaccuracies.

In analyzing "what is going on," metrics should be used, with the old management phrase, "you can't control what you don't measure," being a constant guiding principle.

By documenting the who, what, when, where, why, and how of how the system is actually working you can demonstrate to yourself and others where changes might be necessary.

Bibliography

Ashworth, G.J.: *Marketing Tourism Places*, London, Routledge, 1990.

Baum, T.: *Managing the Development and Implementation of National Human Resource Policies for Tourism*, England, Wiley, 1994.

Clough, Richard: *Construction Project Management*, New York, John Wiley & Son, 2000.

Dimson, Elroy: *Stock Market Anomalies*, Cambridge University Press, 1988.

Gregory, J.: *Marketing Tourism Places*, London, Routledge, 1990.

Ireland, Lewis: *Quality Management for Projects and Programs*, Upper Darby, PMI, 1991.

Knapp, C. L.: *Commercial Damages, A Guide to Remedies in Business Litigation*, Matthew Bender, 1993.

Lock, Dennis: *Project Management*, New York, Wiley, 1996.

Meyer, M. W.: *Theory of Organizational Structure*, Indianapolis, 1977.

Nelson, Bob and Economy, Peter: *Managing for Dummies*, Foster City, IDG Books, 1996.

Pringle, Peter: *Electronic Media Management*, Boston, Focal Press, 1999.

Robert, C.: *Understanding and Changing Your Management Style*, San Francisco, Jossey-Bass, 1999.

Robert, T.: *Practical Public Management*, New York, Marcel Dekker, 1995.

Sherman, Barry: *Telecommunications Management*, New York, McGraw Hill, 1995.

Taylor, F. W.: *The Principles of Scientific Management*, New York, 1917.

Warner, Charles: *Media Management Review*, Mahwah, Lawrence Erlbaum Associates, 1997.

William, G.: *Creativity in TV & Cable Managing & Producing*, Lanham, University Press of America, 1999.

Index